Prophesy Again!
Duplicating Daniel
Repeating Revelation

A Study of Prophetic Repetition
at the End of Time

Michael Conley
Gary Hullquist

**PRINTED IN
THE UNITED STATES OF AMERICA**

World rights reserved. This book or any portion thereof may not be copied or reproduced in any form or manner whatever, except as provided by law, without the written permission of the publisher, except by a reviewer who may quote brief passages in a review.

The author assumes full responsibility for the accuracy
of all facts and quotations as cited in this book.

2006 07 08 09 10 11 12 · 5 4 3 2 1

Not copyrighted.
Any portion of this book may be freely copied and distributed.
ISBN-13: 978-1-57258-442-6
ISBN-10: 1-57258-442-4
Library of Congress Control Number: 2006905399

Published by

TEACH Services, Inc.
www.TEACHServices.com

Prophesy Again!

Time of the Gentiles
How Readest Thou? Methods of Prophetic Interpretation

Daniel   The Outline of World History

Daniel 1	Revelation 14	Passing the Test
Daniel 3	Revelation 8	When you Hear the Trumpets
Daniel 2,7	Revelation 13	Seven Heads Rise Again
Daniel 4	Revelation 13	Wounded Heads
Daniel 8		Cleansing the Sanctuary and the Time of the End
		Double Talk
		The Dating Game
		2300 Days End Again
		The Ram Returns
		That Which Has Been Shall Be: The Esther Story
		Polluting the Santuray, Taking Away the Daily
Daniel 9		The 70 Week Prophecy Rides Again
Daniel 10	Revelation 17	Two Rivers, Two Women, Two Cities
Daniel 11	Revelation 18	He Shall Come to His End
		Of Prophets and Profits
Daniel 12	Revelation 12	Blessed is He that Waits
		Signs in the Heavens

Time of the Gentiles

Perhaps no other land in the world has been fought over more than the biblical city of Jerusalem. The birthplace of the world's three prominent religions, it is still in the spotlight of news cameras and religious spokesmen alike. What is it that makes this land of mountains and deserts so intriguing? The answer depends on who you ask. For example, if you question Christian evangelicals they will tell you that Israel and Jerusalem must, as they did originally, once again hold a "most favored nation" status. Military strategists insist that Israel and Jerusalem are critically important determinants of Middle East stability. But the purpose of the following pages is not to discuss either of these opinions. Rather, we will take a historic look at the Time of the Gentiles as it applies to Jerusalem, but with a prophetic twist.

Therefore, perhaps the best possible place to begin this journey can be found in the Gospel according to Luke. In chapter 21 verses 1-23, Jesus has been giving signs of the second coming, intermingled with the destruction of the temple. He ends by providing specific instruction to His listeners as to how and when they should leave the city. Notice what Luke writes in verse 24:

> "And they shall fall by the edge of the sword, and shall be led away captive into all nations: and Jerusalem shall be trodden down of the Gentiles, untill the times of the Gentiles be fulfilled."

According to historians, this time was known as the great "Diaspora" or dispersal. This was the time in the history of the Hebrew people when they were forcibly scattered around the globe. Early in the first century, shortly after the Christian church was formed by the original apostles, the dispersal involved the Christian Jews, who under persecution by the Jewish authorities, fled around the world to preach the gospel. Then, with the destruction of Jerusalem and the temple in 70 AD by the army of Rome, the Jewish nation ceased to exist, and the people of Israel were truly scattered for nearly two thousand years.

Saga of a City

But before we discuss the end of this time period, it is important to examine the very beginning of Jerusalem's history. As Moses led the children of Israel on their trek through the wilderness and into the Promised Land (some 1400 years before Christ) you will remember that the people who originally lived in the land were called Philistines. God had told Abraham that these people had filled their cup of iniquity, and through a series of supernatural events, God gave the land to His people as He called them out of Egypt and their life of bondage. This land of the Philistines eventually became known as the land of Palestine.

Abraham	Exodus	Davidic Kingdom	Babylonian Exile	Roman Destruction
2000 BC	1450 BC	1000 BC	586 BC	70 AD

About every 500 years Jerusalem has been visited

The Hebrews of Modern Israel still speak of how God had given this land to them. Yet, for many hundreds of years the Jews of old turned their backs on Jehovah. God sent many judges and prophets to steer the people back to Him. Even the prophet Daniel warned Israel that they had a 490 year period of probation to make things right with God. The sad story is, however, that ancient Israel failed in her commission and rejected her Messiah.

Determined to secure their freedom from Rome by force, the Jews revolted in AD 66 with a great deal of bloodshed. Under the last procurator of Judea, Gessius Florrus, the Jews and gentiles began murdering each other until all semblance of civil authority was gone. Cestius Gallus, the legate of Syria, took command of the Judean Province and in the fall of 66 marched on Jerusalem with the intent of punishing and subduing the riotous city. His troops made it as far as the northern wall before being repelled. For some unknown reason Cestius retreated entirely.

Vespasian arived in Judea the following year, but left Jerusalem alone, strategizing that the zealots inside the city could more effectively decimate themselves while he concentrated on pummeling the rest of the country into submission. By AD 69, Vespasian had turned the once lush countrysise into a wilderness. With the death of Nero, he was proclaimed Emperor and hurried back to Rome to secure his position. In his place he sent his son, Titus, who arrived in the spring of 70 AD to take command of the army and continue the seige of Jerusalem.

Titus began his attack with over 80,000 soldiers. He was aided, however, by the infighting between the different factions inside the city. Most notable among these were the followers of Simon bar Giora, John of Gischala, and Eleazar bar Simon. More than 100,000 Jews lost their lives between late May and early July. Josephus claimed that eventually more than a million perished and nearly 100,000 were taken prisoners. The ferocity of the Roman army against the rebellious Jews left the entire city and even the Temple completely destroyed. The only thing let standing was part of Herod's palace and a small section of wall from the temple foundation.

Slowly, over the next 60 years, Jerusalem began to recover from its devastating desolation. When the emperor Hadrian rebuilt over the ruins a new gentile city with a Roman name of Colonia Aelia Capitolina, another revolt in 132 AD led by Bar Cocheba, resulted in the permanent forced expulsion of all Hebrews from Israel. The Arab Palestinian Philistines were then able to re-gain possession of what they believed was their homeland.

6 Prophesy Again! **Times of the Gentiles**

With the "conversion" of Constantine in the fourth century, Jerusalem nearly became a Christian city. If one travels there today many remnants from this period abound. In fact, Constantine's mother, Helena, built a church on the Mount of Olives. Constantine himself built one of the largest churches (the Church of the Holy Sepulcher) on the supposed site of Christ's resurrection.

Roman Destruction	**Mohammed**	**Crusades**	**Reformation**	**Israel**
70 AD	614 AD	1000 AD	1500	1948-1967

With the rise of Mohammedism, the city soon fell into Persian hands. Chosroes II, who was a vicious warrior, massacred thousands of the city's inhabitants in 614. After destroying the Church of the Holy Sepulcher, he took thousands into captivity. The city was recaptured 14 years later by the Roman emperor Heraclius. But Roman control was brief, surrendering it back to the Arabs only a few years later. Jerusalem has been since that time essentially under continuous Arab control. Except for a few years during the Medieval Crusades, the City of Peace has remained Moslem. The Temple site has become home for one of the most sacred places in Islam, The Dome of the Rock.

Turkey was the last Arab power to control the region until the World War I when Lawrence of Arabia and Great Britain's General Allenby took control of Jerusalem and much of the surrounding countryside. The young League of Nations declared the region a "mandated territory" and placed it under the auspices of the British government. The population at the time was predominantly Arab with very few Jews, but the British began a policy of allowing Jews to return to the land in small communities known as kibbuzes. One to make the move to Israel was Mrs. Meirson, a former school teacher living in the United States. Golda Meirson became one of the greatest diplomats and ultimately the first Prime Minister of Israel, Golda Meir.

In 1948 the United Nations re-established a homeland for the Jews, drawing a line in the sand, by splitting Jerusalem in half. Immediately the Arab nations surrounding the fledgling nation began a campaign to destroy what they called the "Zionist state." The Jews valiantly fought off their enemies. But the most interesting event for this author during Israel's emerging years was the concerted attempt by the Arab world to destroy Israel in 1967.

The Six Day War

Most historians simply call this episode "the six day war." An Arab coalition of nations attacked Israel from all sides. The Syrians and the Lebanese struck from the north. Egypt came from the south. Jordanians and Iraqis positioned themselves on the east. The combined forces amassed against Israel presented a formidable threat.

But Israel, bolstered by support from the United States, stunningly defeated all her Arab enemies and for all practical purposes regained nearly all the land held originally by King David. Moshe Dyan, the eye-patched Israeli general, drove the Jordanians back to the Allenby Bridge and re-secured all of Jerusalem under the flag of Israel. On that day in June of 1967 the world as we know it changed forever.

It changed for several reasons. First, it changed the political landscape of the world. For the first time since 70 AD Jerusalem and Israel were fully connected. Once again Israel had taken possession of her crown jewels. In effect it was the fulfillment of what Jesus said in Luke 21:24. The "time of the gentiles" had been fulfilled.

Why is this so important? Because this date acts as an anchor point in dramatically highlighting the nearness of Christ's second coming.

Previous to this time, the anchor point was 1755, the first in a string of signs that announced the opening of the 6th seal. It also provides another anchor point after the end of the 2300 day prophecy which terminated in 1844. Christ mentioned the "time of the gentiles" as one of the many "signs" of His coming which the disciples had requested. The event becomes another sign of "present truth" to prepare His people for the Second Coming. Remember, the prophet Amos assures us that "surely the Lord God does nothing except he revealeth his secrets unto his servants the prophets" chapter 3:7. The greatest prophet who ever lived, of course, was Christ Himself. What was God revealing to Him? And what was the Lord God about to do? Let's begin in the area of war. Jesus told us that "nation would rise against nation." Just look at what has been happening in our world since 1967. Though it is true that every generation has had its wars, and the two World Wars exploded into history before this, nothing in the history of this earth has been as continuous. Humanity vowed that never again would another monster like Adolph Hitler be allowed to gain despotic power. Yet we have endured an endless string of Idi Ammins, Saddam Husseins, Ayatollah Khomeinis, etc, etc, all willing to do anything to promote their personal agenda to secure and extend their own power.

And then there are the religious wars. Yes, there have always been the clash of religions throughout history. But never has there been such a sustained global festering of "holy wars." In the late 1960's Northern Ireland erupted in a bitter conflict between Catholics and Protestants that still smolders; Vietnam was significantly precipitated by Catholic president Ngo Dinh Diem's brutal inforcement of "Ordinance #10" targeted against the majority Buddhists; Cyprus split between Greek Christians and Turkish Muslims ; the Rwanda genocide pitted Hutu against Tutsi across a Christian-nonChristian divide; Bosnia-Herzegovnia was a triangular affair between Catholic, Muslim and Serbian Orthodox; civil war in Sudan is a horrendous blood bath between Muslim and Christians; Indonesia is consumed with Christian versus Muslim outbreaks; 60,000 have died in Kashmir from hostilities between Hindus and Muslims; Iraqi Sunnis and Iranian Shi'ites slaughtered each other for eight years during the 1980's; Chechnya threatens the stability of Russia in its murderous revolt between Muslims and Christians; 65,000 lost since 1983 in Sri Lanka in the struggle between Hindu and Buddhists; Tibet has been devastated by the Buddhist-Communist conflict; Christians and Muslims battle it out in Northern Uganda...

Northern Ireland
Vietnam
Cyprus
Rwanda
Bosnia-Herzegovnia
Sudan
Indonesia
Kashmir
Iraq-Iran
Chechnya
Sri Lanka
Tibet
Northern Uganda

Who of us can forget where we were on September 11, 2001 as the twin towers of the World Trade Center fell. Osama Bin Laden, who in the name of religion, orchestrated the attack which is now indelibly seared into the collective consciousness of the world. No longer is it safe to travel the world or live in a major city. And not only America, but Europe has come into the cross-hairs of Al Qaeda. Train bombings in Madrid, Subways in London, and fires in France have all fallen prey to Arab émigrés. But lately the focus has shifted from Bin Laden to a new voice of vitriol coming out of Iran. The new president, Muhomed Ahmadinejad, is spouting the same political diatribe that fueled the Islamic Revolution during the heady days of the American Hostage Crisis in 1979 when as a student he stormed the US Embassy shouting death to the "Great Satan." Today he challenges not only the United States, but the United Nations, and the world.

The spirit of confrontation, intimidation, threatening postures and aggressive rhetoric are not limited to the upstart Persian. Our own country is not immune from such behavior. Under the pretext of "imminent danger" to the "vital American interests" we have seen a number of invasions in recent years by the premier

8 Prophesy Again! **Times of the Gentiles**

advocate of democracy. Besides Vietnam, we stormed Granada, Iraq—twice, and Afghanistan. Whether you argue for or against these military interventions is not the purpose here. Simply put, even America has been caught up in "nations rising against nations." It is, however, the opinion of these authors that a larger war, one which involves religion, trade, resources, and good versus evil, is just on the horizon.

Is it mere coincidence that a surge in echumenical fervor appeared in 1967? It was in that year that serious dialog between the Catholic church and Lutheran theologians was initiated. The issue at stake was the historical stance of both churches on the doctrine of justification. Luther, you recall, left the Mother Church over his conviction that sinners are justified through faith without any assistance or merit from human behavior or performance. But in 1967 Harry J. McSorely began to author position papers claiming that Catholic teaching had always embraced Luther's position! This all occurred in the wake of Vatican II which concluded in 1965 to embark on the road to reconcilliation with the churches of the Reformation "promoting the restoration of unity among all Christians." *The Documents of Vatican II* (New York: Guild Press, 1966), p. 341.

Another area of change is the increase in natural disasters. Famines, floods, earthquates, tornadoes, hurricanes, tsunamis…you get the point. In January 2006, the N.O.A.A. issued a report that demonstrated no definitive increase in the frequency of hurricanes from previous decades, but a decided increase in severity and power to wreak devastation. In the summer of 2005 the highest number of category 5 hurricanes formed and then slammed into the coastlines of the United States. So many struck during the season that the names exhausted the Roman alphabet of A to Z and extended four letters into the Greek alphabet! The U.S. insurance industry has been hammered by billions of dollars in damage claims leaving a chill on the entire financial world.

Melting polar ice sheets, destruction of the ozone layer, mass extinctions, global warming, hazardous ecological disasters are all sounding the alarms that have intensified since 1967. Though many nations have pledged cooperation in reversing the threats, signing the Kyoto accord and adopting Green policies is a losing proposition. This is no surprise. The apostle Paul was right when he said "the whole creation groans and travails in pain." Romans 8.

Let's look at scientific changes. The first human heart transplant was performed by Dr. Christian Bernard in Cape Town on December 3, 1967. Today, heart, lung, liver, kidney, corneal, bone marrow and now even face transplants are being performed in medical centers around the world. We now have medical technology that in 1967 was only science fiction. Many forms of cancer are being eradicated, if diagnosed and treated early through a combination of nutritional, lifestyle and advanced treatment modalities. Physicians routinely use magnetic resonance imagery, CT scans, ultrasound, nuclear isotopic diagnostics, perform microinvasive surgery through ever smaller incisions, even remotely, using devices inspired by the likes of Star Trek. Cars purchased since 1985 have more computational power than the Apollo-Saturn spacecraft that went to the moon.

Microprocessors have permeated every aspect of life, from monitoring a diabetic's blood sugars to changing TV channels to controlling traffic lights to tellling time on your digital wristwatch. The computers that filled rooms at mission control nearly forty years ago are now dwarfed by the capabilities of today's pocket PDA. Gone forever are mechanical inventions like typewriters and stencil machines. Now a few clicks on your desktop PC can balance your books, order anything from anywhere, or compose a sonnet. Super computers made it possible to accellerate completion of the Human Genome project five years ahead of schedule. The prospect of correcting and preventing a myriad of genetic diseases, DNA testing, has exploded so fast that medical ethicists are struggling to keep up.

Still another area of our life that has changed drastically is the world's financial makeup. In 1967 there were only a handful of billionaires on the planet. Today, there are many hundreds in that club, while the middle class is disappearing and personal and national debt is at an all time high. The present generation of young people can no longer expect to make more than their parents. Small businesses, let alone individuals, are withering under the change in banking and tax laws that now especially favor huge multinational corporations.

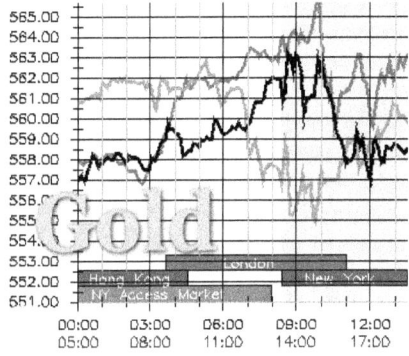

2005 saw a record number of bankruptcies while the United States international trade deficit has hit an all time high. The debt in 1967, when LBJ introduced Medicare, was peanuts compared to today's spiralling trillions. Today, almost fifty percent of every tax dollar goes to pay just the interest on America's growing debt. The average American child now inherits a $30,000 bill the day they are born.

Something else began to happen in 1967 which has changed the social complexion of our world. A protest demonstration was organized in New York city by a former Playboy bunny who burned her bra in Central Park to launch the women's liberation movement. Women were now liberated from moral tyranny and the prudish restrictions of society. Their freedom opened the floodgates of immorality in the United States that still echoes throughout our nation. Millions now freely live together with "partners" rather than commit themselves to the institution of Holy matrimony. Infidelity is epidemic. Pornography is rampant. Homosexuality is accepted and defended by main stream America. Sexually transmitted diseases like herpes and AIDS raise the cry for more government research dollars while drug abuse, meth labs, porn outlets, and tunnels under our nation's borders add even more to the ranks of the Billionare Club.

Such is the world we live in today. Since 1967, America and the world have been changing at an unbelievable pace. Not all of it has been for the good. Yet, as bad as things are today—equal to or worse than Sodom and Gomorrah—there is still a way of escape from the fate of those ancient cities. It is only through placing our complete trust in Jesus, the Author and Finisher of our faith, the One who saw the scope of history and the tremendous events that would occur when "the times of the Gentiles be fulfilled."

How Readest Thou?

When a lawyer asked Jesus about the prerequisites for inheriting eternal life in Luke 10:26, Christ questioned him back. How do you read the law? In the following pages we make a similar inquiry: How are we to read the apocalyptic prophecies of Scripture in the context of our world today?

This is, in fact, a treatise on Biblical prophecy. The Old and New Testament scriptures have much to say about the times in which we now live. Today's headlines have a ring of prophetic fulfillment. Many are acutely aware that the Word of God is now speaking to the events we are witnessing in the world around us. But before we examine individual prophecies, our frame of reference and interpretive methodology must first be established.

The apocalyptic prophecies of Daniel and Revelation are typically interpreted in one of four ways:

1. **the spiritual view.** Biblical prophecies are figurative not literal. They merely teach spiritual truths for the benefit of the church throughout history: to overcome, to remain faithful to Christ in the midst of persecution, etc. The Little Horn and the Beast simply represent the forces of evil in general and Satan in particular.

2. **the preterist view.** Biblical prophecy is literally fulfilled in past centuries culminating with the destruction of the temple in AD 70. Time intervals are literal days. There is, therefore, no future application. The Little Horn was Antiochus Epiphanes and the Beast was Nero. Liberal Protestants and Roman Catholics support this school of thought. But its limited scope ignores current world conditions and impending events.

3. **the futurist view.** This method views all prophetic fulfillment to take place in the near future of the end times. The temple will be rebuilt in Jerusalem, a global dictator Beast will secure world peace and then stop the sacrifices in the midst of the final seven years of tribulation. Catholics and conservative protestants like Lahaye, Larkin, Walvoord and Lindsey have popularized this view. The limited scope once again ignores the realities of significant past events.

4. **the historicist view.** This method sees fulfillment of prophecy within the history of the church, from ancient to modern times and to beyond the millennium. The Little Horn was the Medieval Roman Church and the Beast is its modern reincarnation in a global church-state alliance. Seventh-day Adventists and evangelical Christians prefer this position because its comprehensive scope considers all events in the full spectrum of history.

Preterist School	Historicist School	Futurist School
Antiochus, Caeser, etc.	Papacy	UN, EU, etc.
Present Progressive School		
Nimrod, Pharaoh, Nebuchadnezzar, Antiochus, Nero, Dioclitian, Papacy, Napoleon, Kaiser, Lenin, Hitler, UN, etc.		

Notice the supporters of the last three schools of interpretation. As the historicist camp, from the days of the earliest reformers, have prominently identified the Papacy as the Little Horn of Daniel 7 and 8, the king of the North in Daniel 11, the Beast of Revelation 13, and the Great Harlot of Revelation 17, it is not surprising to find Roman Catholic expositors embracing anything but the historicist point of view. So, which is the correct interpretive method? Could all three have elements of truth for those living at different time periods?

Only One Original Option
Conventional hermeneutical wisdom dictates that for any given prophecy only one fulfillment can be allowed. You must, therefore, choose between Antiochus, a pope or the UN's Rebel. Which will it be? Were the seals fulfilled in the early centuries AD or during the Dark Ages, the Reformation, the past century or are they yet future? The wisdom and genius of God's Word, however, is that it contains applicable principles, valuable lessons, and identifiable symbols for believers in every period of earth's history.

Consider the book of Joel. This minor prophet, contemporaneous with Isaiah, responds to a natural disaster in his day—a plague of locusts—to draw parallels with the coming Day of the Lord, a time of great judgment and sweeping devastation. His immediate application is to the invasion of Babylonian forces into Palestine. But there are additional applications to future assaults on the Holy Land in different ages: Roman invasions, the Crusades, world wars, and finally Armageddon itself.

Joel foretells a time when God will "pour out" His spirit upon all flesh. "And your sons and your daughters shall prophesy, your old men shall dream dreams, your young men shall see visions." He goes on to describe certain signs:

> "wonders in the heavens and in the earth, blood, and fire, and pillars of smoke. The sun shall be turned into darkness, and the moon into blood, before the great and the terrible day of the Lord." Joel 2:28-31.

Peter applied this prophecy to the events that were transpiring on the day of Pentecost. The sun *had* been darkened during those dramatic hours on Calvary. The blood *did* flow freely that awesome day. Tongues of fire did appear 50 days later. Though not on "all flesh," it *did* descend on 120 in the upper room. He even used verse 32 as his altar call: "Whoever shall call on the name of the Lord shall be saved." Acts 2:16-21. It was extremely effective! The outpouring of God's Spirit was undeniable. The church identified clearly with Joel 2 and interpreted the event as the "Latter Rain," which it was for *their* time. Peter's message was truly *present truth*.

Next, the prophetic gift witnessed by the early Advent believers was also cited as evidence of a current fulfillment of Joel 2 in *their* day. "Your sons and your daughters shall prophesy," pointed clearly to the child preachers of Scandinavia and the very young Ellen Harmon and Hiram Edson in America. The Dark Day of May 19, 1780 was seen as a present day fulfillment of Joel 2 even though it was only a regional phenomenon.

But there is yet another future application. The final outpouring of the Holy Spirit at the time of the final latter rain will be the ultimate fulfillment of Joel's prophecy when, indeed, the Spirit falls "upon *all* flesh." The "wonders in the heavens and in the earth" described in Revelation 6:12-14 and chapter 16 will be its final global-cosmic fulfillment.

Joel's prophecy is a progressive enlargement and expansion of the types and symbols of Passover and Pentecost. These two major feasts are separated by seven Sabbaths. While there is a single wave loaf at Passover symbolizing the resurrection of Christ and "many of the saints" (possibly the 24 elders), there are two wave loaves at Pentecost suggesting another type of resurrection event (a harvest of souls dead in sin who are raised "to newness of life"). While there were 120 gathered "in one accord" on the first Pentecost, there will be 144,000 unified at the final Pentecost. While 3000 were baptized on the first Pentecost, a great multitude will join the ranks of the remnant at the final Pentecost. As the destruction of Jerusalem is a model for the final destruction of the world, so the first Pentecost is a model for the final outpouring of God's Spirit on "all flesh."

12 Prophesy Again! **How Readest Thou?**

Passover	Pentecost, the 50th day	Final Pentecost	Great White Throne
Wave Loaf	two Wave Loaves	Christ + Holy Spirit	Father, Son, Spirit
one tenth deal	two tenth deals	sin offerings	sacrifice of praise
24 elders raised	120 disciples in one accord	144,000 unified	Great unnumbered
Multitude			
liberation of captives	tongues of fire from heaven rushing wind	fire comes from heaven 4 winds of heaven	fire falls from heaven
Christ is Prophet	Christ becomes High Priest	Christ is King of kings	
	High Priest inauguration day	receives the kingdom	Coronation Day
	Jubilee in Heaven	Jubilee begins 1000 yrs	Jubilee begins eternity
	sits on the throne of Grace	the throne of Judgment	the throne of Glory
	former rain of the Spirit	latter rain of the Spirit	final rain of God's fire
	3000 baptized	Great Multitude baptized	stand on the sea of glass
	gift of tongues: all hear in their own language	gift of tongues: to every kindred, tongue, nation	every tongue confesses

The Joel's locusts have been different scurges at various times; his darkness and blood have been witnessed by each era; the Spirit has been manifested in every age; spiritual and physical applications can be made in each period as can be seen below.

Roman Era	Middle Ages	Advent Awakening	Time of the End
Roman Occupation	Crusades	French Revolution 1789	War on Terrorism, WW's
Darkness & Blood at cross	"Dark Ages", bloody wars	Reign of Terror, Guillotine	Dark Day, Disasters
Day of Pentecost Tongues	Reformation 1517	Spirit of Prophecy 1844	Latter Rain of Holy Spirit
Vesuvius & Pompeii 79 AD	proto-Krakatau 536	Krakatau 1883	Mt St. Helens 1980
Leprosy	Black Plague	Tuberculosis	AIDS, SARS, bird flu

We should not be surprised, then, to discover that prophetic applications may be seen at multiple times throughout history as God, speaking through His prophets, appeals to those living in every age. Thus the prophecies serve to identify "present truth" for every generation. Daniel, for those living centuries before the cross, and Revelation, for those living in the centuries after it, demonstrate this principle of prophetic repetition.

Prophecy: History Repeated
Notice the recurring theme of these Spirit of Prophecy quotations:

Past Experiences Repeated for God's People

Abel
"From the time when the first innocent blood was shed, when righteous Abel fell by the hand of Cain, **the same history had been repeated**, with increasing guilt. **In every age** prophets had lifted up their voices against the sins of kings, rulers, and people, speaking the words which God gave them, and obeying His will at the peril of their lives. **From generation to generation** there had been heaping up a terrible punishment for the rejecters of light and truth." *Desire of Ages* p. 618.

Jacob's Sons
"The same **experience is repeated in the history** of Jacob's sons—sin working retribution, and repentance bearing fruit of righteousness unto life." *Education* p. 148.

Job's Friends
"The same error for which God had reproved the friends of Job was **repeated by the Jews** in their rejection of Christ." *Desire of Ages* p. 470; *Welfare Ministry* p. 21.

Dathan-Abiram Rebellion
"**The history of the rebellion of Dathan and Abiram is being repeated,** and **will be repeated** till the close of time. Who will be on the Lord's side? Who will be deceived, and in their turn become deceivers?—Letter 15, 1892." *Last Day Events* p. 171.

Elijah, Ahab and Jezebel
"Through the long centuries that have passed since **Elijah's time**, the record of his lifework has brought inspiration and courage to those who have been called to stand for the right in the midst of apostasy. And for us, 'upon whom the ends of the world are come' (1 Corinthians 10:11), it has special significance. **History is being repeated.** The world today has its **Ahabs and its Jezebels.** The present age is one of idolatry, as verily as was that in which Elijah lived." *Patriarchs and Prophets* p. 177.

Nehemiah
"**The experience of Nehemiah is repeated in the history of God's people in this time**. Those who labor in the cause of truth will find that they cannot do this without exciting the anger of its enemies. Though they have been called of God to the work in which they are engaged, and their course is approved of Him, they cannot escape reproach and derision. They will be denounced as visionary, unreliable, scheming hypocritical..." *Christian Service* p. 174.

Jewish Nation's Misinterpretation of Prophecy
"Satan is working that **the history of the Jewish nation** may be **repeated in the experience** of those who claim to believe present truth. The Jews had the Old Testament Scriptures, and supposed themselves conversant with them. But they made a woeful mistake. The prophecies that refer to the glorious second appearing of Christ in the clouds of heaven they regarded as referring to His first coming. Because He did not come according to their expectations, they turned away from Him. Satan knew just how to take these men in his net, and deceive and destroy them..." 2 *Selected Messages* p. 111.

Christ
"'Truth faileth; and he that departeth from evil maketh himself a prey.' Isa. 59:14, 15. This was fulfilled in the life of Christ on earth. **He was loyal to God's commandments**, setting aside the human traditions and requirements which had been exalted in their place. Because of this **He was hated and persecuted.** This **history is repeated.** The laws and traditions of men are exalted above the law of God, and **those who are true to God's commandments suffer reproach and persecution**. Christ, because of His faithfulness to God, was **accused as a Sabbathbreaker and blasphemer.** He was declared to be possessed of a devil, and was denounced as Beelzebub. In like manner **His followers are accused and misrepresented**." *COL* p. 171.

"How did men treat Christ when He came?... 'He came unto his own, and his own received him not' (John 1:11). Thus it is today. **This history is being repeated, and will be repeated again and again** before the Lord shall come in the clouds of heaven." *The Upward Look* chapter p. 48.

"The scenes of the betrayal, rejection, and crucifixion of Christ have been reenacted, and **will again be reenacted on an immense scale**" 3 *Selected Messages* p. 415, 416.

Prophesy Again! **How Readest Thou?**

"As the light and life of men was rejected by the ecclesiastical authorities in the days of Christ, so it has been rejected in every succeeding generation. **Again and again the history** of Christ's withdrawal from Judea **has been repeated.** When the Reformers preached the word of God, they had no thought of separating themselves from the established church; but the religious leaders would not tolerate the light, and those that bore it were forced to seek another class, who were longing for the truth." *Desire of Ages* p. 232.

"In quoting the prophecy of the rejected stone, Christ referred to an actual occurrence in the history of Israel. The incident was connected with the building of the first temple. While it had a **special application at the time of Christ's first advent**, and should have appealed with special force to the Jews, it has **also a lesson for us.**" *Desire of Ages* p. 597.

Apostolic Heresies
"In the days of **the apostles** the most foolish heresies were presented as truth. **History has been and will be repeated.** There will always be those who, though apparently conscientious, will grasp at the shadow, preferring it to the substance. They take error in the place of truth, because error is clothed with a new garment, which they think covers something wonderful. But let the covering be removed, and nothingness appears.--*The Review and Herald*, Feb. 5, 1901." 1 *Selected Messages* p. 162, 163

Past History Repeated

"The Lord has set before me matters which are of urgent importance **for the present time, and which reach into the future**. The words have been spoken in a charge to me, "Write in a book the things which thou hast seen and heard, and let it go to all the people; for the time is at hand when **past history will be repeated.**" *Colporter Ministry* p. 128
"Many of the prophecies are about to be fulfilled in quick succession. Every element of power is about to be set to work. **Past history will be repeated;** old controversies will arouse to new life, and peril will beset God's people on every side." *Maranatha* chapter 22.

"**All the great events** and solemn transactions **of Old Testament history** have been, and **are, repeating** themselves in the church **in these last days.**" *Selected Messages,* book 3, 339.

"We are standing on the threshold of great and solemn events. Many of the prophecies are about to be fulfilled in quick succession...**Past history will be repeated**...Study Revelation in connection with Daniel, for **history will be repeated.**" *Testimonies to Ministers* pp. 116, 117.

"The prophecy **in the eleventh of Daniel** has nearly reached its complete fulfillment. **Much of the history** that has taken place in fulfillment of this prophecy **will be repeated.**" verses 30-36 are then quoted. "Scenes similar to those described in these words **will take place.**" [future!] "We are **now entering upon the time of trouble** spoken of: And at that time shall Michael stand up...and there shall be a time of trouble, such as never was." *Manuscript Releases*, vol. 13, p. 394.

Three Angel's Messages Repeated
"The first and second messages were given in 1843 and 1844, and we are now under the proclamation of the third; but **all three of the messages** are **still to be proclaimed**. It is just as essential now as ever before that **they shall be repeated** to those who are seeking for the truth....showing in the line of prophetic history the **things that have been, and the things that will be.**--*Manuscript* 32, 1896." *Counsels to Writers and Editors* p. 26, 27

World Empires
"Prophecy has traced **the rise and fall of the world's great empires**--Babylon, Medo-Persia, Greece, and Rome. With each of these, as with nations of less power, **history repeated itself. Each had its period of test, each failed, its glory faded,** its power departed, and its place was occupied by another." *Education* p. 177, *Patriarchs and Prophets* p. 535.

San Francisco Calamity
"As we near the close of this earth's history, we shall have the **scenes** of the San Francisco calamity **repeated in other places**. . . . These things make me feel very solemn because I know that the judgment day is right upon us. The **judgments that have already come** are a warning, but not the finishing, of the punishment that **will come on wicked cities**... [Hab. 2:1-20; Zeph. 1:1-3:20; Zech. 1:1-4:14; Mal. 1:1-4, quoted.] These scenes will soon be witnessed, just as they are clearly described. I present these wonderful statements from the Scriptures for the consideration of everyone. **The prophecies recorded** in the Old Testament are the word of the Lord **for the last days**, and **will be fulfilled** as surely as we have seen the desolation of San Francisco.—Letter 154, May 26, 1906." *Last Day Events* p. 115.

Worship Decree
"**History will be repeated.** False religion will be exalted. **The first day of the week**, a common working day, possessing no sanctity whatever, **will be set up as was the image** of Babylon. All nations and tongues and peoples will be **commanded to worship** this spurious sabbath... The **decree enforcing the worship** of this day is to go forth to all the world.--7BC 976 (1897)." *Last Day Events* p. 134, 135.

Theories and Methods
"...last January the Lord showed me that erroneous theories and methods would be brought into our camp meetings, and that **the history of the past would be repeated.**" 2 *Selected Messages* p. 37.

Truth-Error Conflict
"In history and prophecy the Word of God portrays the long continued conflict between truth and error. That conflict is yet in progress. **Those things which have been, will be repeated.** Old controversies will be revived, and new theories will be continually arising." 2 *Selected Messages* p. 109.

Racial Slavery
"Church members and priests and rulers will combine to organize secret societies to work in their land to whip, imprison, and destroy the lives of the colored race. **History will be repeated.**" *The Sourthern Work* p. 75

Babylon's Fiery Furnace
"... it is said of the king of Babylon, that his visage changed toward the three faithful Hebrews. **Past history will be repeated.** Men will reject the Holy Spirit's working, and open the door of the mind to Satanic attributes that separate them from God. They will turn against the very messengers through whom God sends the messages of warning." *Spirit of Prophecy* Vol 1 p. 212.

Apparitions of the Dead
"**History is to be repeated.** I could specify what will be in the near future, but the time is not yet. The forms of the dead will appear, through the cunning device of Satan, and many will link up with the one who loveth and maketh a lie." Letter 311, Oct. 30, 1905, to 'Brethren Daniells and Prescott and Their Associates.' (*The Upward Look* chapter 303).

16   Prophesy Again!   **How Readest Thou?**

Prophecies with Special Application for the Present Time

"The parable of the ten virgins...This parable has been and will be fulfilled to the very letter, for it has **a special application to this time**...and will continue to be **present truth till the close of time**." *Review and Herald,* August 19, 1890.

"Prominent among the prophets of Israel were Samuel, Elijah, Elisha, Isaiah, Jeremiah, Ezekiel, and Daniel. in stirring words they called upon the people to turn from their evil ways, giving assurance that the lord would graciously receive and bless them, and would heal their backslidings. Some of the writings of these prophets have a **special application to the time in which we live**. They wrote of things which should 'come to pass in the last days,' or in the 'time of the end.' Isaiah 2:2; Daniel 12:4." *Christian Experience and Teachings of Ellen G. White,* p. 239.

"And I will rebuke the devourer for your sakes, and he shall not destroy the fruits of your ground, neither shall your vine cast her fruit before the time in the field, saith the Lord of hosts." I saw that this scripture has been misapplied to speaking and praying in meeting. The prophecy has a **special application to the last days**..." *Spiritual Gifts* Volume 4b p. 54.

"**In every age** there is a new development of truth, **a message** of God to the people **of that generation**. The old truths are all essential; new truth is not independent of the old, but an unfolding of it. It is only as the old truths are understood that we can comprehend the new." *Christ's Object Lessons* p. 127

Scripture Uses Multiple Applications

The principle of multiple fulfillment is also plainly taught in scripture.

Ecc 1:9   "The thing that has been, it is that which shall be;
          and that which is done is that which shall be done;
          and there is no new thing under the sun."
Matt 24:37 "But as the days of Noah were, so shall also the coming of the Son of man be."
2 Peter 2:6 "Turning the cities of Sodom and Gomorrah into ashes...making them an example" of the final judgment of the wicked.
John 15:20 "If they have persecuted me, they will also persecute you."
           Christ's experience of mistreatment will be repeated in the experience of His followers.
1 Cor 10:11 "Now all these things happened unto them for ensample: and they are written for our admonition, upon whom the ends of the world are come."

Isn't this just the Apotelesmatic Principle of Desmond Ford?

Ford deployed this term in order to maintain harmony with Adventism's traditional fulfillment of the 2300-day prophecy of Daniel 8 in 1844 while rejecting the year-day principle and the pre-advent investigative judgment which, in his opinion, destroyed the joy and peace provided by a completely finished judgment at the cross. He quotes the same Spirit of Prophecy references listed above to support his version of multiple applications, but then denies the same source where it endorses the year-day identified investigative judgment interpretation of the 2300-day prophecy, which he rejects. The serious inconsistencies imposed by this preterist position in particular, however, should not invalidate its application to multiple prophetic fulfillment in general. Ford's concise maxim is, despite its misapplication, of some value nonetheless: "All are right in what they affirm and wrong in what they deny." (Glacier View manuscript, p. 505)

It is unfortunate that multiple prophetic application has been associated with Desmond Ford's apotelesmatic principle. The validity of the former has been discredited by the later and, in our opinion, unnecessarily so. In retrospect, its diabolic timing served well the strategies of darkness. While the concept of apotelesmaticism has been criticized as having no scriptural basis, this is not the case with multiple prophetic application. The very nature of type and antitype, so prevalent in Biblical symbolism, and the basis of a wide range of soterological and escatological parallels, is but one aspect of the multiple application paradigm.

Examples
There is much yet to be learned from the dynamic, living pages of God's Word. Many beautiful multiple application examples exist with type-antitype symbolism that speak to ancient historical events, current conditions, and future developments.

Lucifer aspired to be "like the Most High,"
    the future man of sin wants to "sit as God in the temple of God."

The world begins "without form and void;"
    at the second coming it is reduced to the same condition again.

A first Adam falls to sin in the garden of Eden;
    the Last Adam overcomes sin in the garden of Gethsemane.

The serpent deceives Eve in the garden
    while the Serpent of Revelation 12 "deceives the whole world."

Abel is slain because of how he worshiped God;
    the remnant will face death over the same issue of worship.

Enoch walks with God and is translated;
    the last generation who are translated "follow the Lamb" everywhere.

Noah's world is destroyed by a flood of water;
    at the end it will be destroyed by a flood of fire.

Abraham is called out of Babylonian Ur;
    at the end the remnant are called out of Babylon the Great.

Sarah is barren but gives birth to a miracle boy;
    Hannah, Mrs. Manoah, Elisabeth and Mary all do the same.

Abraham prepares to sacrifice his only son;
    Christ, like Isaac, is a willing sacrifice and only begotten Son.

Joseph is sold for the price of a slave;
    Christ is betrayed for the price of a slave.

Joseph goes down into Egypt to save the world from famine;
    Christ goes down into Egypt to be saved.

Israel is delivered from Egypt after devastating plagues;
    the final Israel experiences Exodus after the plagues.

The Passover lamb is slain on the 14 Nisan in Egypt;
    Christ, the Lamb of God, dies on Passover (14 Nisan) in Jerusalem.

David would have died for Absolom;
    the self-sacrificing love of God for even Lucifer is here displayed.

18 Prophesy Again! **How Readest Thou?**

The New Testament apostles made frequent reference to previous events and experiences from the Old Testament with fresh application to the experiences of the new church. Paul, in the book of Hebrews, showed how the Exodus for Israel of old was being repeated in his generation. Christ was the second Moses, the second Joshua, leading His people out of spiritual Egypt into the true rest of the Promised Land. Paul looked forward to "crossing Jordan" and entering the "sabbatical" rest of the millennium (Hebrews 3, 4). He identified with Israel as it was "baptized in the sea" even as Christians were then being baptized (1 Corinthians 10:2). The temptations facing Israel in the wilderness were being repeated within the young Christian church.

Peter also appealed to the repetitive nature of prophetic experience. "There were false prophets also among the people, even as there shall be false teachers among you." 2 Peter 2:1.

The number of parallels and type-antitype pairs is amazingly vast. Each type portends a future antitype. These accounts are not couched in obvious prophetic language, but the corresponding antitypes are applications of the fulfillment just the same. Each example contains a redemptive nugget of truth, a pearl, a gem, a different facet of God and His unspeakable character of love.

Not every prophecy can have multiple fulfillments.
We can and should be alert to the possible repetition of divine themes in multiple situations. However, there are limitations to what can be legitimately duplicated. Some events of redemptive history are unique, singular, and never to be repeated.

For example, the Messianic prophecies of Micah 5, Daniel 9, Isaiah 53 and Psalm 22 can only point to the singular event of Christ's first advent, ministry and death. Jesus died "once in the end of the world" Hebrews 9:26. There will never be another Messiah at the end of time to suffer and die a sacrificial death. And yet, the remnant will also, like Christ, be condemned to death; as Christ witnessed to the Jewish nation for three and a half years, so also the two witnesses of Revelation 11 deliver God's message for the same period of time. Thus, the principle of prophetic parallels can most clearly be seen in apocalyptic prophecies involving the menacing actions of our Adversary and the deliverance of our Saviour in the framework of global historical events.

Risk of the Single Application Paradigm
The Jewish nation at the time of the first advent had narrowed their prophetic interpretations of the coming Messiah to a single geopolitical scenario. Their vision of liberation from Roman occupation, the establishment of Israel as dominant world power, Jerusalem as the world's capitol, and the elimination of all their gentile enemies, severely restricted their chances of accepting Christ when He came. Had they considered the multi-faceted nature of the Messianic types and the repetitive nature of apocalyptic prophecy they would have seen the contrasting features that distinguish the first and second coming.

They would have been sensitive to the sacrificial nature of the Lamb who would be wounded for their transgressions at His first advent, but would come as the Lion of the tribe of Judah to deal with transgressors at His second advent; He would open not His mouth as He went to the slaughter at the first advent, but come with a shout and slay the wicked with the sword of His mouth at His second appearing; He would have the meekness of the Prophet who was to come like Moses at His first coming, but would rule with a rod of iron at His second; He would be as a Root out of the dry ground with no comeliness that we should behold Him at the first advent, but comes with the glory of His Father and all the holy angels at the second advent; He would come as the Servant of servants at His first coming; He would come as the King of kings at His second.

But His people eagerly embraced the qualities applying to the Second Advent while either ignoring or rejecting the aspects of the first advent and were totally unprepared to recognize and accept their Messiah when He came. They actually feared the kingdom of grace that Christ came to establish. It threatened their expectations of the kingdom of glory which they so much desired. In reality, God was offering them both.

A similar risk exists today when the issue of multiple application is dismissed. If a prophecy is fulfilled more than once, which one is the "primary" fulfillment? Fear that "the" traditional interpretation will be weakened or displaced by additional interpretations is overwhelming. Threatened by competition, the orthodox view disavows any intruders. Holding on to cherished views, however, may in itself be a dangerous repetition of the past. Jesus said, Watch! For the Son of man may very well come in such an hour (and might we add, in such a manner and in such a set of circumstances) as you think not.

DANIEL: The Outline of History

A brief inspection of the dates for each chapter of the book of Daniel will demonstrate that they are not in chronological order. Notably, chapter 5 depicting Belshazzar's last year and chapter 8 transpiring in his third year should be positioned after chapter 7 which is identified as occurring in his first year. When the chapters are sequenced in their true chronological order, however, important eschatological significance can be recognized.

Chapter	Chronology	Daniel	Jesus, Second Adam	Adam
1	1st year of Nebuchadnezzar 605 BC	King's food	Stones to bread	Appetite
2	2nd year of Nebuchadnezzar	Can you interpret?	Jump or dash your feet	Self-will
3	between the 18th – 28th year	Fiery Furnace	Bow down to me	Worship
4	last half of his 42 year reign	King insane 7 yrs	Satan insane 7000 yrs	
7	1st year of Belshazzar	Winged Lion	Jesus the Lion	
8	3rd year of Belshazzar	Ram Little horn	Jesus the Ram	
5	Final year of Belshazzar	Fall of Babylon	Satan fall like lightning	
6	1st year of Darius the Mede	Lion's den	Jesus in the tomb	
9	1st year of Darius, son of Ahasuerus	Messiah cut off	Jesus the Messiah	
10	3rd year of Cyrus	Michael helps	Jesus the Bridge	
11	3rd year of Cyrus	North & South	Prince of the covenant	
12	3rd year of Cyrus 538 BC	Michael stands	Michael stands up	

The life of Jesus is recapitulated throughout the book of Daniel. Just look at the first three chapters as they parallel the three temptations of Christ in the wilderness. Jesus, had clearly studied this book ("let the reader understand" he said in referencing it during His Matthew 24 discourse on the signs of the Second Coming). He understood the sequence of events that would mark His life on earth. He knew exactly what His path would be and could with assurance say "My hour is not yet come" right up to the evening when He announced "Mine hour is come."

Daniel 1   What to Eat
Jesus faces His first temptation, to satisfy His physical hunger. But, like Daniel, He "purposed in his heart not to defile himself." "Let them give us pulse to eat and water to drink," Daniel said. in verse 11. "Man shall not live by bread alone," Jesus said. Matthew 4:4.

Daniel 2   What to Prove
Jesus is next tempted to demonstrate His independence, to use His own power. "If you be the Son of God, cast yourself down: for it is written, He shall give his angels charge concerning thee: and in their hands they shall bear you up, lest at any time you dash your foot against a stone," Matthew 4:5, 6. But, like Daniel, when asked "are you able?" He answered, "You shall not tempt the Lord your God," verse 7. "There is a God in heaven," Daniel 2:26.

Daniel 3   What to Worship
Jesus is finally tempted to worship the devil himself. "Fall down and worship me," Satan said, Matthew 4:9. Shadrach, Meshach, and Abednego, when tempted to save themselves from the burning fiery furnace, refused to "fall down and worship the golden image which Nebuchadnezzar had set up."

There are many other parallels between the experience of ancient Israel and that of Christ who is not only the Second Adam, but the Second Moses. Israel was led through the wilderness for 40 years by a pillar of light; Jesus was led by the Spirit into the wilderness for 40 days and said, "I am the light of the world."

The children of Israel were baptized in the Red Sea after their Exodus from Egypt (1 Corinthians 10:2); the Church was baptized on Pentecost after Christ died as its Passover Lamb, delivering them from spiritual Egypt. It was Joshua who ultimately led Israel into Canaan; it will be Jesus (Greek form of the Hebrew Joshua) who will lead the redeemed into the heavenly Promised Land (Hebrews 4). "Now all these things happened for examples, and they are written for our admonition upon whom the ends of the world are come." 1 Corinthians 10:11.

The book of Daniel continues the parallel between history and eschatology as history repeats itself:

Daniel 4   Pride before Destruction
Nebuchadnezzar, king of Babylon, is driven from the kingdom where he behaves as a wild beast for seven years. Satan is banished from heaven in Revelation 12 to this earth where he creates havoc for seven millennia (6000 years on an inhabited planet and 1000 years in solitary confinement).

Daniel 7   The Two Lions
The first beast from the sea is a lion with eagle wings. Jesus is "the Lion of the tribe of Judah" Revelation 5:5. But the devil is also a "lion seeking whom we may devour."

Daniel 8   Goat Attacks the Ram
The Greek goat defeated the Persian ram even as Satan, the ultimate goat symbol, attacked Christ, the Ram caught in the thicket (Genesis 22:13). He is "the Lamb of God which taketh away the sins of the world," John 1:29. Finally, Satan, the scapegoat Azazel, will be led into the millennial wilderness.

Daniel 5   Jesus Conquers Babylon
Babylon falls to the Medes and the Persians after being weighed in the balances and found wanting. Satan "falls as lightning" as Jesus "having spoiled principalities and powers, he made a show of them openly, triumphing over them," Colossians 2:15. Babylon will also finally fall at the end of time.

Daniel 6   Sealed in the Lion's Den
Daniel emerges victorious over his enemies. The angel came and shut the lion's mouth. So, too, Jesus was sealed in the tomb. But the angel came and set him free from the bonds of death. Moreover, Jesus was sealed with seven seals. "For Him hath the Father sealed" John 6:27.

Daniel 9   The Messiah Comes
The time comes for the Messiah the Prince, who confirms the covenant with many for one-week causing sacrifices and oblations to cease.

Daniel 10   Daniel sees Jesus
"A certain man clothed in linen, whose loins were girded with fine gold of Uphaz: His body also was like the beryl, and his face as the appearance of lightning, and his eyes as lamps of fire, and his arms and his feet like in color to polished brass, and the voice of his words like the voice of a multitude." John has the same vision in Revelation 1:14, 15.

Daniel 11   The Saints Prevail
A raiser of taxes (verses 20-22) is destined to fulfill Micah's prophecy that the Messiah should come from Bethlehem. The Roman power then works to break the Prince of the covenant by crucifying Christ.

Daniel 12   Michael stands up
Stephen looks heavenward and sees Jesus standing at the right hand of the throne of God as he is dying. Christ stands to signal that the judgment is over, the time of probation has closed.

Three Years to the Test

The book of Daniel begins by establishing a time frame. Daniel's saga as a captive in Babylon began in the third year of king Jehoiakim, king of Judah (Dan 1:1). Just as Daniel was to be "nourished" for three years before coming before king Nebuchadnezzar, and Jehoiakim was "set up" as king of Judah for three years before facing Nebuchadnezzar, so also Adam was "given dominion" in Eden where he was nourished, eating "from every tree in the garden" except Tree of Test.

Notice the parallels between Jehoiakim and Adam.

2 Ki 23:34   Pharaoh-necho made Eliakim [Raised up by God] the son of Josiah king of Judah
and turned his name to **Jehoiakim** [Whom Jehovah set up], and took Jehoahaz
[Whom the Lord sustains, as Satan is] away: and he came to Egypt [earth], and died there.

Jehoiakim, the son of Josiah mirrors Adam, the son of God (Luke 3:38)
Good king Josiah was an exceptional king and a type of Jesus, the Son of God..
- Both were named before birth (1 Ki 13:1,2; Matt 1:21)
- Both read the law (1 Ki 23:1,2; Luke 4)
- Both cleansed the temple (2 Ki 22:3-9)
- Both make a covenant (2 Ki 23:3)

Gen 1:26   And God said, Let us make man in our image after our likeness; and let them have dominion.
Adam was also "raised up by God" and given rule over the earth.
"Adam was crowned king in Eden. [co-regency] To him was given dominion over every living thing that God had created. (RH 2-24-1874) *IBC* 1082

Gen 1:29   And God said, Behold, I have given you every herb bearing seed which is upon the face of all the
the earth, and every tree in the which is the fruit of a tree yielding seed; to you it shall be for food.
Daniel 1:5   And the king appointed them a daily provision of the king's food and of the wine which he drank:

Gen 2:15   And the Lord God took the man, and put him into the garden of Eden to dress it and to keep it.
2 Ki 24:1   Jehoiakim [Adam] became his [Nebuchadnezzar/God] servant three years;
Daniel 1:5   ...so nourishing them three years, that at the end thereof they might stand before the king.
Jehoiakim repeated the experience of Adam; Daniel repeated it yet again.

Gen 3:1   Now the serpent was more subtle than any beast of the field...and he said to the woman.
Dan 1:1   And in the third year of the reign of Jehoiakim king of Judah came Nebuchadnezzar king of Babylon unto Jerusalem, and besieged it. Similarly, Satan came to earth and besieged it.
Rev 12:12   Woe to the inhabitants of the earth and of the sea for the devil is come down unto you.
verse 9   That old serpent called the Devil and Satan ... was cast out into the earth...to deceive.

Gen 3:17   Adam...hearkened unto the voice of [his] wife
2 Ki 24:1   ...and then he [Jehoiakim] turned and rebelled against him [Nebuchadnezzar].
So, too, did Adam rebel against God.
Rom 5:12   Wherefore...by one man sin entered into the world

Jehoiakim repeats the experience of Adam's failure in Eden. But Jesus is the Second Adam, retracing the path of victory.

> "As soon as there was sin, there was a Saviour…The instant man accepted the temptations of Satan, and did the very things God had said he should not do, Christ, the Son of God, stood between the living and the dead, saying, 'Let the punishment fall on Me. I will stand in man's place…'. What love! What amazing condescension! The King of glory proposed to humble Himself to fallen humanity! He would place His feet in Adam's steps."
> 1 BC 1084, 1085.

> "As representative of the fallen race, Christ passed over the same ground on which Adam stumbled and fell."
> 6BC 1092

> Luke 3:23,38   And Jesus himself…which was the son of Adam."

Into the Land of Shinar

"And the LORD gave Jehoiakim king of Judah into his hand, with part of the vessels of the house of God which he carried into the land of Shinar." Daniel 1:2

The Land of Shinar can be traced back to the tower of Babel, the very origins of Babylon.

> "And Cush begat Nimrod: he began to be a mighty one in the earth. He was a mighty hunter before the LORD; wherefore it is said, Even as Nimrod the mighty hunter before [against] the LORD. And the beginning of his kingdom was Babel [confusion], and Erech, and Accad, and Calneh, in the land of Shinar." Genesis 10:8-10.

"The whole earth was of one language" (Genesis 11:1) when Nimrod lead the rebellion against God, defying the flood judgment by constructing a tower to heaven. Their efforts were spoiled by the "confusion of tongues," turning their speech into meaningless babble. At the end of time, Babylon the Great will appear when once again the world is united in a common language, the language of the internet: English, and a common currency: the Dollar.

The Shinar Shrine

Zechariah 5 depicts the construction of a house "in the land of Shinar" where a woman [church] would be carried and installed. The angel tells Zechariah, "This is wickedness."

Isaiah 59:2 *But your iniquities have separated between you and your God, and your sins have hid his face from you, that He will not hear you.*

Ephesians 3:12 *"without Christ, being aliens from the covenant of promise, having no hope, and without God in the world.*

Genesis 3:8 *Adam and his wife hid themselves from the presence of the LORD God amongst the trees of the garden.*

So, too, Daniel is separated from his homeland to become an alien in the land of Shinar, where he would face the same temptations to which Adam fell.

Jesus would later meet the same temptations, which are demonstrated in the first three chapters of Daniel.

Daniel 1-Revelation 14: Passing the Test

Daniel, whose name means "God is my judge," was inducted into the University of Babylon and scheduled for final oral exams before the king himself after three years of accelerated study.

Jehoiakim reigned three years and then Nebuchadnezzar came to Jerusalem and besieged it. So, too, Adam faced the devil's siege of Eden. Was this also after three years?

The Remnant of Revelation 12 find themselves standing before the King of the Universe after 3½ prophetic years of "the patience of the saints" as they come under review when "the hour of His judgment is come" Revelation 14:7.

Belshazzar, the last king of Babylon, was "weighed in the balances and found wanting" in Daniel 6. Despite all the opportunities to repent and change, to worship the God of heaven, to recognize their dependence on Him, Babylon defiled itself with a final fling of wine, women and song, defying the God of Israel by dishonoring the sacred temple vessels.

Babylon the Great, the final collusion of state and ecclesiastical powers, will also fall after it fails the scrutiny of Divine judgment. The intoxicating wine of false doctrine will pollute earthly temples, and defy the God of heaven by rejecting His precepts and ignoring His law.

The last of the seven churches of Revelation 2-3, Laodicea, whose name means "A people judged," are assessed by Christ to be lukewarm and their judgment is pronounced: "I will spew you out of My mouth" if you don't change. The remedy for their state of apathetic indifference is prescribed:

> Buy of Me gold tried in the fire
> Eye salve
> White raiment

The first three chapters of Daniel describe a sequence of tests that were
> failed by Adam in Eden,
> endured in ancient Babylon by Daniel and his colleagues,
> conquered by Christ at the time of His first advent,
> and must be passed by the remnant at the Time of the End.

The issues of these three tests are
> **appetite**,
> **independence**, and
> **worship**.

Appetite: the first temptation [Daniel 1]
Daniel passes the test
- Dan 1:5   The king appointed them a daily provision of the king's food and wine
- Dan 1:8   Daniel purposed in his heart that he would not defile himself with the portion of the king's food.
- Dan 1:20   The king...found them ten times better than all the magicians and astrologers

First Adam failed
- Gen 2:17   But of the tree of the knowledge of good and evil, you shall not eat of it.
- Gen 3:1   The serpent said...Has God said, You shall not eat of every tree of the garden?
- Gen 3:6   The woman saw that the tree was *good for food*...she took of the fruit and did eat

Jesus, Second Adam, overcomes
- Matt 4:3   If you are the Son of God, command that these stones be made bread.
- Matt 4:4   Man shall not live by bread alone but by every word that proceeds out of the mouth of God.

Remnant will also overcome
- John 6:35   They resist eating leaven of the Pharisees (church) and Herod (state), but only the Bread of Life
- Rev 21:6   They resist drinking the wine of Babylon, drink only the Water of Life
- Rev 2:7   To him who overcomes will I grant to eat of the tree of life

Independence: the second temptation [Daniel 2]
Daniel passes the test
- Dan 2:13   Daniel, Hananiah, Mishael, Azariah face a decree that the wise men should be slain.
- Dan 2:26   The king said to Daniel...Are you able to make known to me the dream and the interpretation? Daniel could have taken personal credit for explaining the dream, but he didn't.
- Dan 2:28   There is a God in heaven that reveals secrets and makes known to the king...your dream.
- Dan 2:48   Daniel is made ruler over the whole province of Babylon

First Adam failed
- Gen 3:5   The serpent said...In the day you eat thereof...you shall be as gods knowing good *and* evil. The woman saw that the tree...was to be desired *to make one wise*, she took the fruit.
- Gen 3:22-4   And God said...man knows good and evil...Therefore God sent him forth.

Jesus, Second Adam, overcomes
- Matt 4:6   If you are the Son of God, cast yourself down...lest you dash your foot against a stone
- Matt 4:7   You shall not tempt the Lord your God

The dream that Daniel interprets ends with a Stone dashing the feet of an image.

Remnant will also overcome
They resist acting alone: Without me you can do nothing...I am the vine you are the branches.
- Rev 2:10   Be faithful unto death and I will give you a crown of life

Worship: the third temptation [Daniel 3]
Shadrach, Meshach and Abednego pass the test
- Dan 3:5,6   Fall down and worship the golden image or be cast into the burning fiery furnace
- Dan 3:18   Be it known unto you, O king, that we will not serve your gods nor worship the golden image
- Dan 3:25   I see four men loose, walking in the midst of the fire and the fourth is like the Son of God.

First Adam failed
- Gen 3:6   She saw that the tree was...*pleasant to the eyes* (she adored/worshiped the tree and its fruit)
- Gen 3:7,8   And the *eyes* of them both were opened...and they hid themselves.

Jesus, Second Adam, overcomes
- Matt 4:9   All the kingdoms of the world...will I give you if you will fall down and worship me.
- Matt 4:10   You shall worship the Lord your God and him only shall you serve.

Remnant Will also overcome
- Rev 13   They resist worshipping the beast or his image
- Rev 7,14   They receive the seal of God in their forehead.
- Rev 2   He that overcomes will be made a pillar in the temple of God (where they worship continually) and receive a new name...in their forehead.

When You Hear the Sound of the Trumpet

Daniel's prophecies are to be fulfilled "in the latter days" (Daniel 10:14). Just as Daniel was informed as to their meaning, so are we to be illuminated that we may speak out with clarion tones:

> "When the angel was about to unfold to Daniel the intensely interesting prophecies recorded for us who are to witness their fulfillment, the angel said, 'Be strong, yea, be strong (Daniel 10:19). We are to receive the very same glory that was revealed to Daniel, because it is for God's people in these last days, that they may *give the trumpet a certain sound*." *Review and Herald*, Extra, Dec. 24, 1889 (emphasis supplied).

Face the Music
Nebuchadnezzar made an image of gold, 60x6 cubits in size, and "set it up" on the plain of Dura in Babylon. Then he gathered together the princes, governors, captains, judges, treasurers, counselors, sheriffs, and all the rulers of the provinces to attend the dedication of the image. As they stood before the image, an announcement is made. "It is commanded that when you hear the sound of the cornet (trumpet) and other musical instruments, you must fall down and worship the golden image."

At the end of time, circumstances will ultimately lead to a similar worldwide command. The trumpets will sound to announce the call to worship. All will hear it. Nearly all will respond. But as with all prophetic symbols, there is both the physical and symbolic, the secular and spiritual.

Jesus said,

> "My sheep hear my voice, and I know them, and they follow me:
> And I give unto them eternal life; and they shall never perish,
> neither shall any man pluck them out of my hand." John 10:27, 28

Have you heard the voice of Jesus? What does it sound like?
A still small voice? The voice of many waters? A trumpet?

> "I was in the Spirit on the Lord's day, and heard behind me **a great voice, as of a trumpet**, Saying, I am Alpha and Omega, the first and the last." Revelation 1:10, 11

Who is that? Jesus is the Trumpet voice.

> "After this I looked, and, behold, a door was opened in heaven: and **the first voice which I heard was as it were of a trumpet talking with me**; which said, **Come up** hither, and I will show you things which must be hereafter." Revelation 4:1

It seems that trumpets sound whenever Jesus appears. In fact, the very first time trumpets are heard in the Bible... It is associated with the voice of Jesus. When the children of Israel reached Mt Sinai God prepared them to receive His law. Jesus, the Lawgiver, told Moses what to expect.

> "When the **trumpet sounds** long, they shall **come up** to the mount..." And it came to pass on the third day in the morning, that there were thunders and lightnings, and a thick cloud upon the mount, and the **voice of the trumpet exceeding loud**; so that all the people in the camp trembled. And Moses **brought forth the people out of the camp to meet with God**. Exodus 19:13, 16, 17

It's also interesting that whenever Jesus shows up, people "come out" to meet Him.

When He came to Bethlehem, wise men came out of Babylon responding to the invitation, "Come out...my people" When He came to Sinai, the Israelites came out of the camp.

> "And mount Sinai was altogether on a smoke, because the LORD descended upon it in **fire**: and the **smoke thereof ascended** as the smoke of a furnace, and the whole mount **quaked greatly**. And when the **voice of the trumpet sounded long, and waxed louder and louder,** Moses spoke, and **God answered him by a voice**." Exodus 19:18, 19

And what did God say? Exodus 20:1... He spoke to them the Ten Commandments.
After the 10 Commandments were proclaimed from the mountain by the voice of God...
the people begged Moses to speak with God, but they were afraid to hear Him "lest we die."
In Genesis 3:8,9 Adam and Even heard the voice of God walking in the garden...they hid themselves.
Adam explained: "**I heard your voice and I was afraid**" Why? because he had disobeyed

> "Shall **a trumpet be blown in the city**, and **the people not be afraid**? shall there be evil in a city, and the LORD hath not done it? **Surely the Lord GOD will do nothing, but he revealeth his secret unto his servants the prophets**." Amos 3:6, 7

When God blows the Trumpets He is telling us something; He is revealing His secrets.

Trumpet Instructions

God instructed Moses on just how to use Trumpets in the book of Numbers chapter 10.

> 10:2 Make thee **two trumpets of silver**; of a whole piece shalt thou make them: that you may **use them for the calling of the assembly**, and for the journeying of the camps. 10:3 And when they shall blow with them, all the assembly shall assemble themselves to thee **at the door of the tabernacle of the congregation. 10:4** And if they blow but with **one trumpet**, then the **princes**, which are heads of the thousands of Israel, **shall gather** themselves unto thee. 10:5 When ye **blow an alarm**, then the camps that lie on the **east parts** shall go forward. 10:6 When ye blow an alarm the **second time**, then the camps that lie on the **south side** shall take their journey: they shall blow an alarm for their journeys. 10:8 the **priests, shall blow with the trumpets**; and they shall be to you for an ordinance for ever throughout your generations. 10:9 And **if ye go to war** in your land **against the enemy that oppresses you**, then ye shall **blow an alarm with the trumpets**; and ye shall be remembered before the LORD your God, and ye shall be **saved from your enemies**. 10:10 Also **in the day of your gladness**, and in your **solemn days**, and in the **beginnings of your months**, ye shall **blow with the trumpets over your burnt offerings**, and over the sacrifices of your peace offerings;

So...trumpets were used to
1. Call all the people together for worship
2. Call the princes to anoint a king
3. Call to War:
    a. Alarm tones first time moves the Eastern Tribes
    b. Alarm tones second time moves the Southern Tribes
4. Announce special religious events: dedication of temple, day of Atonement, etc.

> "For if the **trumpet give an uncertain sound, who shall prepare himself to the battle**?"
> 1 Corinthians 14:8

In other words, if the trumpet *does* give a *certain sound*, we *shall* be able to prepare ourselves
to gather for worship, for crowning princes, for battle, and for judgment.

Call to Assemble and Worship

"And it shall come to pass in that day, that **the great trumpet shall be blown, and they shall come** which were ready to perish in the land of Assyria, and the outcasts in the land of Egypt, and shall **worship the LORD in the holy mount at Jerusalem**." Isaiah 27:13

"Declare ye in Judah, and publish in Jerusalem; and say, **Blow ye the trumpet in the land: cry, gather together, and say, Assemble yourselves**." Jeremiah 4:5

"**Make a joyful noise unto the LORD, all the earth**: 98:6 **With trumpets and sound of cornet** make a joyful noise before the LORD, the King." Psalm 98:4

In the time of Hezekiah:

"**All the congregation worshipped**, and the **singers sang**, and the **trumpeters sounded**: and all this continued **until the burnt offering was finished**." 2 Chronicles 29:28

Call to Feasts

The Feast of Trumpets

One of the seven annual feasts was dedicated to blaring of trumpets solely for the purpose of drawing attention to the coming Day of Atonement that would follow ten days later.

"Speak unto the children of Israel, saying, In the **seventh month, in the first day** of the month, shall ye have a sabbath, a memorial of **blowing of trumpets**, an holy convocation." Leviticus 23:24, 25

In addition, trumpets were sounded on the first day of every month, called the Feast of the New Moon.

"**Blow up the trumpet in the new moon**, in the time appointed, on our solemn feast day. For this was a statute for Israel, and a law of the God of Jacob." Psalm 81:3

10 days later came the Day of Atonement....and every 49 years the Jubilee

"Then shalt thou cause the **trumpet of the jubilee to sound on the tenth day of the seventh month, in the day of atonement** shall ye make the trumpet sound throughout all your land. And ye shall hallow the fiftieth year, and **proclaim liberty throughout all the land."** Leviticus 25:9, 10

The Spring Feasts, fulfilled at Jesus 1st coming, his death and resurrection, centered on Passover. And yet there is still a future fulfillment:

"And he said unto them, With desire I have desired to eat this **Passover** with you before I suffer: For I say unto you, I will not any more eat thereof, **until it be fulfilled** in the kingdom of God." Luke 22: 15, 16

The final fulfillment of the Passover (being spared when the angel of death passes over us) is still future.

The Feast of First Fruits was fulfilled at Pentecost with the 120 disciples.
And yet there is a final fulfillment in the 144,000:

"These are they which were not defiled with women; for they are virgins. These are they which follow the Lamb whithersoever he goeth. These were redeemed from among men, being the **firstfruits unto God** and to the Lamb." Revelation 14:4

The Fall Feasts are not yet completely fulfilled, but will be at the second coming.

If the Day of Atonement was fulfilled in 1844, then the Feast of Trumpets should have occurred *before* that date. And they were…when each kingdom fell.

> Jeremiah 51:27 Set ye up a standard in the land, **blow the trumpet among the nations, prepare the nations against her, call together against her the kingdoms** of Ararat, Minni, and Ashchenaz; appoint a captain against her; cause the horses to come up as the rough caterpillars. 51:28 **Prepare against her the nations with the kings** of the Medes, the captains thereof, and all the rulers thereof, and all the land of his dominion. 51:29 And the land shall tremble and sorrow: for **every purpose of the LORD shall be performed against Babylon, to make the land of Babylon a desolation** without an inhabitant.

A trumpet with each change of world kingdoms?
Trumpets sounded just before Jericho fell
Trumpets sounded just before Babylon fell
And also at the final fall of the world…

Call for the Dedication of the Temple

at the dedication of Solomon's temple

> 2 Chronicles 5:12 Also the Levites which were the singers, all of them of Asaph, of Heman, of Jeduthun, with their sons and their brethren, being arrayed in white linen, having cymbals and psalteries and harps, **stood at the east end of the altar,** and with them an **hundred and twenty priests sounding with trumpets:**) 5:13 It came even to pass, as **the trumpeters and singers were as one, to make one sound to be heard in praising and thanking** the LORD; and when they lifted up their voice with the trumpets and cymbals and instruments of music, and praised the LORD, saying, **For he is good; for his mercy endureth for ever: that then the house was filled with a cloud,** even the house of the LORD; 5:14 So that the **priests could not stand to minister** by reason of the cloud: **for the glory of the LORD had filled the house of God**.

Like Pentecost in the upper room: 120 disciples were in one accord and the Holy Spirit

Dedication of the Temple 70 yrs later…

> Ezra 3:10 And when the builders **laid the foundation of the temple** of the LORD, they set the priests in their apparel **with trumpets**, and the Levites the sons of Asaph with cymbals, to praise the LORD, after the ordinance of David king of Israel. 3:11 And **they sang together by course in praising and giving thanks unto the LORD; because he is good, for his mercy endureth for ever** toward Israel. And all the **people shouted with a great shout**, when they praised the LORD, because the foundation of the house of the LORD was laid. 3:12 But many of the priests and Levites and chief of the fathers, who were **ancient men**, that had seen the first house, when the foundation of this house was laid before their eyes, **wept with a loud voice**; and many shouted aloud for joy: 3:13 So that the people could not discern the noise of the shout of joy from the noise of the weeping of the people: for the people shouted with a loud shout, and the noise was heard afar off.

30 Prophesy Again! **When You Hear the Sound of the Trumpet**
Call the Princes to the King's Anointing

Absalom planned to use trumpets
    2 Samuel 15:10 But Absalom sent spies throughout all the tribes of Israel, saying, **As soon as ye hear the sound of the trumpet**, then ye shall **say, Absalom reigneth** in Hebron.

But it was a trumpet that was never sounded.

at Solomon's coronation
    "And let Zadok the priest and Nathan the prophet **anoint him there king** over Israel: **and blow ye with the trumpet**, and say, God save king Solomon." 1 Kings 1:34

Jehu is king
    "Then they hasted, and took every man his garment, and put it under him on the top of the stairs, and **blew with trumpets, saying, Jehu is king**." 1 Kings 9:13

Joash is king
    "And when she looked, behold, **the king stood by a pillar, as the manner was, and the princes and the trumpeters by the king,** and all the people of the land rejoiced, and **blew with trumpets**: and Athaliah rent her clothes, and cried, Treason, Treason." 1 Kings 11:14

Jesus is the King of kings! He was crowned after this ascension on Pentecost. In fact…

    "God is gone up with a shout, the LORD **with the sound of a trumpet**." Psalm 47:5

Jesus ascended to heaven for His inauguration as the High Priest. Psalm 22: The angels escorting Him shouted, Open ye gates! Open up ye everlasting doors that the King of glory may come in! The heavenly trumpets sounded His entrance.

And trumpets will be heard when he comes down… at the greatest assembly of all time.

    "And he shall **send his angels with a great sound of a trumpet**, and they shall **gather together his elect** from the four winds, from one end of heaven to the other."

    "For the Lord himself shall **descend from heaven** with a shout, with the voice of the archangel, and **with the trump of God**:" 1 Thessalonians 4:16

    "We shall be changed…In a moment, in the twinkling of an eye, **at the last trump: for the trumpet shall sound, and the dead shall be raised** incorruptible." 1 Corinthians 15:52

The last trump is the 7th trumpet of Rev 11:15. It sounds when the kingdoms of the world become Christ's. Jesus Calls and His sheep hear His voice. "Awake, Awake, ye that sleep in the dust!"

    "The **dead shall hear the voice** of the Son of God (the voice of Jesus, the Trumpet) and **they that hear shall live**… All that are **in the graves shall hear His voice**." John 5:25, 28

That Trumpet will give a certain sound—the sound of eternal life.

Call to War:

Ehud blows a trumpet and the children of Israel join him in fighting the Moabites

Judges 3:27 And it came to pass, when he [Ehud] was come, that he **blew a trumpet in the mountain of Ephraim**, and the **children of Israel went down with him from the mount**, and he before them. 3:28 And he [Ehud] said unto them, **Follow after me: for the LORD hath delivered your enemies the Moabites into your hand**.

Gideon blew a trumpet to gather the tribes to fight the Midianites

Judges 6:33 Then all the Midianites and the Amalekites and the children of the east were gathered together, and went over, and pitched in the valley of Jezreel. 6:34 But the **Spirit of the LORD came upon Gideon, and he blew a trumpet**; and Abiezer was **gathered after him**. 6:35 And **he sent messengers** throughout all Manasseh; who also was gathered after him: and he sent messengers unto Asher, and unto Zebulun, and unto Naphtali; and they came up to meet them.

Gideon gives trumpets to his 300 men

Judges 7:16 And he divided the three hundred men into three companies, and he **put a trumpet in every man's hand** 7:18 **When I blow with a trumpet**, I and all that are with me, then blow ye the trumpets also on every side of all the camp, and say, **The sword of the LORD, and of Gideon**. 7:22 And the three hundred blew the trumpets, and **the LORD set every man's sword against his fellow**

King Saul blew a trumpet to fight the Philistines

1 Samuel 13:3 And **Saul blew the trumpet throughout all the land**, saying, Let the Hebrews hear. 13:4 And all Israel heard say that Saul had smitten a garrison of the Philistines, and that **Israel also was had in abomination with the Philistines**. And **the people were called together after Saul** to Gilgal.

Joab blew a trumpet to stop the fighting

2 Samuel 2:28 So **Joab blew a trumpet**, and **all the people stood still, and pursued after Israel no more**, neither fought they any more.

2 Samuel 18:16 And **Joab blew the trumpet, and the people returned from pursuing after Israel**: for Joab held back the people.

Nehemiah used a trumpet to signal fighting

Nehemiah 4:18 For **the builders, every one had his sword girded by his side**, and so builded. And **he that sounded the trumpet** was by me. 4:20 In what place therefore ye hear **the sound of the trumpet, resort ye thither unto us: our God shall fight for us**.

Rebellion

When **Abijah and Jeroboam** threatened to succeed from the kingdom

2 Chronicles 13:12 And, behold, God himself is with us for our captain, and his priests with **sounding trumpets to cry alarm against you. O children of Israel,** fight ye not against the LORD God of your fathers; for ye shall not prosper. 13:14 And when Judah looked back, behold, the battle was before and behind: and **they cried unto the LORD, and the priests sounded with the trumpets**. 13:15 Then the men of **Judah gave a shout**: and as the men of Judah shouted, it came to pass, that **God smote Jeroboam** and all Israel before Abijah and Judah.

Sheba's Revolt

2 Samuel 20:1 And there happened to be there **a man of Belial**, whose name was Sheba, the son of Bichri, a Benjamite: and **he blew a trumpet, and said, We have no part in David**

32 Prophesy Again! **When You Hear the Sound of the Trumpet**

> 2 Samuel 20:22 Then the woman went unto all the people in her wisdom. And they **cut off the head of Sheba the son of Bichri, and cast it out** to Joab. And **he blew a trumpet**, and they retired from the city, every man to his tent. And Joab **returned to Jerusalem unto the king**.

Trumpets Announce Destructive Judgment

> Jeremiah 4:19 I am pained at my very heart; ...I cannot hold my peace, because thou hast heard, O my soul, **the sound of the trumpet, the alarm of war**. 4:20 **Destruction upon destruction** is cried; for **the whole land is spoiled**:

> Jeremiah 6:1 **blow the trumpet** in Tekoa, and **set up a sign of fire** in Bethhaccerem: for **evil appears out of the north, and great destruction**.

> Jeremiah 42:14 we will go into the land of Egypt, where we shall see **no war, nor hear the sound of the trumpet**, nor have hunger of bread; and there will we dwell:

> Ezekiel 7:14 They have **blown the trumpet, even to make all ready**; but none goes to the battle: for my wrath is upon all the multitude thereof.

> Ezekiel 33:3 If when he [their watchman] sees the sword come upon the land, he blow the trumpet, and warn the people; 33:4 Then **whosoever hears the sound of the trumpet, and takes not warning**; if the sword come, and take him away, **his blood shall be upon his own head**.

> Hosea 5:8 **Blow ye the cornet in Gibeah, and the trumpet in Ramah: cry aloud** at Bethaven, after thee, O Benjamin. 5:9 Ephraim shall be **desolate in the day of rebuke**: among the tribes of Israel have I made known that which shall surely be. 5:10 The princes of Judah were like them that remove the bound: therefore **I will pour out my wrath upon them like water**.

The Day of the Lord

Trumpets are sounded at the final "day of the Lord."

> Joel 2:1 **Blow ye the trumpet in Zion, and sound an alarm in my holy mountain**: let all the inhabitants of the land tremble: **for the day of the LORD cometh**, for it is nigh at hand; 2:2 A day of darkness and of gloominess, a day of clouds and of thick darkness, as the morning spread upon the mountains: a great people and a strong; **there hath not been ever the like, neither shall be any more after it**, even to the years of many generations. 2:3 **A fire devours before them; and behind them a flame burns**: the land is as the garden of Eden before them, and behind them a desolate wilderness; yea, and **nothing shall escape them**.

> 2:17 **Let the priests, the ministers of the LORD, weep between the porch and the altar**, and let them say, Spare thy people, O LORD, and give not thine heritage to reproach, that the heathen should rule over them: wherefore should they say among the people, Where is their God? 2:18 **Then will the LORD be jealous for his land, and pity his people**. 2:19 Yea, the LORD will answer and say unto his people, Behold, **I will send you corn, and wine, and oil**, and ye shall be satisfied therewith:

> Zephaniah 1:15 That day is **a day of wrath, a day of trouble and distress, a day of wasteness and desolation, a day of darkness and gloominess, a day of clouds and thick darkness**, 1:16 **A day of the trumpet and alarm** against the **fenced cities**, and **against the high towers**. 2:1 **Gather yourselves together, yea, gather together**, O nation not desired; 2:2 Before the decree bring forth, before the day pass as the chaff, before the fierce anger of the LORD come upon you, before the day of the LORD's anger come upon you.

> Zechariah 9:12 Turn you to the strong hold, ye prisoners of hope: even to day do I declare that I will render **double** unto thee; 9:13 When I have bent Judah for me, filled the bow with Ephraim, and raised up thy sons,

O Zion, against thy sons, O **Greece, and made thee as the sword of a mighty man.** 9:14 And the LORD shall be seen over them, and **his arrow shall go forth as the lightning**: and **the LORD God shall blow the trumpet, and shall go with whirlwinds** of the south.

Zechariah 9 is entitled The Burden against Hadrach. It lists not only the land of **Hadrach**, (Syria) but also **Damascus, Hamath**, on south to **Tyre and Sidon**, the very sequence of cities conquered by Alexander the Great as he marched down to the Promised Land in 332-331 BC. Tyre was considered unconquerable, an island off-shore that had defied the Assyrians for 5 years and Babylon 13 years! Alexander did it in only 7 months by building a causeway with rubble he scraped from the old city.

When he got down to Jerusalem he had a dream. The high priest, Jaddua, also had a dream.
The Jews, fearful of Alexander's approach, were preparing for a siege, when Jaddua told them his dream: don't be afraid, go out to meet the Greek king and greet him dressed in your best fancy outfits. Meanwhile Alexander remembered his dream: a priest dressed in purple, and scarlet and blue with an entourage in white. The Phoenicians and Babylonians that were in Alexander's army saw the priest and all the people streaming out of Jerusalem, they saw their opportunity to destroy them on the spot. Instead, Alexander personally went out to meet them, went back into the city and had a wonderful time at the temple worshiping Jehovah and reading the book of Daniel.

Jericho Model of a City's Fall

The fortified city of Jericho blocked God's people from entering the promised land.
They were still in their Exodus from Egypt, still in the wilderness – only Jericho was in the way.
Just as the remnant are in the wilderness, in their Exodus from this world, Babylon is in the way.
Jericho fell after 7 blasts of the 7 trumpets. So Babylon will fall after 7 trumpets sound.

> Joshua 6:4 And **seven priests** shall bear before the ark **seven trumpets of rams' horns**: and **the seventh day** ye shall compass the city seven times, and the **priests shall blow with the trumpets**. 6:5 when ye hear the sound of the trumpet, all the **people shall shout with a great shout**; and the **wall of the city shall fall down flat** 6:8 And it came to pass, when Joshua had spoken unto the people, that **the seven priests** bearing the seven trumpets of rams' horns passed on before the LORD, and **blew with the trumpets**: and the ark of the covenant of the LORD followed them. 6:9 And the armed men went before the **priests that blew with the trumpets**, and the rereward came after the ark, the priests going on, and blowing with the trumpets. 6:10 And Joshua had commanded the people, saying, **Ye shall not shout,** nor make any noise with your voice, neither shall any word proceed out of your mouth, **until the day I bid you shout;** then shall ye shout. 6:11 So the ark of the LORD compassed the city, **going about it once: and they came into the camp, and lodged** in the camp.

The 7 priests blew the 7 trumpets each day (7 times)
On the 7th day they blew the trumpets on the 7th time around the city

Revelation 11:19 The temple in heaven was opened and there inside was seen the ark!
When David brought the ark up to Jerusalem he had 7 priests blow 7 trumpets.

34 Prophesy Again! **When You Hear the Sound of the Trumpet**

Bringing the ark to Jerusalem
7 priests

> "And **Shebaniah, and Jehoshaphat, and Nethaneel, and Amasai, and Zechariah, and Benaiah, and Eliezer,** the **priests, did blow with the trumpets** before the ark of God: and Obededom and Jehiah were doorkeepers for the ark. 15:25 So David, and the elders of Israel, and the captains over thousands, went to bring up the ark of the covenant of the LORD out of the house of Obededom with joy. 15:26 And it came to pass, when God helped the Levites that bare the ark of the covenant of the LORD, that they offered seven bullocks and seven rams. 15:27 And **David was clothed with a robe of fine linen**, and all the Levites that bare the ark, and the singers, and Chenaniah the master of the song with the singers: David also had upon him **an ephod of linen**. 15:28 Thus all Israel brought up the ark of the covenant of the LORD **with shouting, and with sound of the cornet, and with trumpets, and with cymbals, making a noise with psalteries and harps.**" 1 Kings 15:24

> "So David and all the house of Israel **brought up the ark of the LORD with shouting, and with the sound of the trumpet.**" 2 Samuel 6:15

We are God's trumpets… (He is the light of the world, we are the light of the world)

> "Cry aloud, spare not, **lift up thy voice like a trumpet**, and **show my people their transgression**, and the house of Jacob their sins." Isaiah 58:1

Some will ignore the message.

> "Also I set watchmen over you, saying, Hearken to the sound of the **trumpet**. But they said, We will not hearken." Jeremiah 6:17

> "They have blown the **trumpet**, even to make all ready; but none goeth to the battle." Ezekiel 7:14

The 7 Trumpets

> "And I saw the seven angels which stood before God; and to them were given seven trumpets. And another angel who had a golden censer came and stood at the altar. He was given **much incense to offer with the prayers of all the saints** on the golden altar. The smoke of the incense, together with the prayers of the saints, went up before God from the angel's hand. Then the angel took the censer, **filled it with fire from the altar, and cast it on the earth**; and there came peals of thunder, rumblings, flashes of lightning and an earthquake." Revelation 8:2, 3

It is the prayers of the saints, ascending with the incense of Christ, which starts the trumpets blaring. When God's people pray, He answers.

> "The cries of the children of Israel came up to God and he sent Moses." Exodus 2:23

Jesus taught us to pray "Our Father in Heaven… Thy will be done in earth as it is in heaven" Now he answers that prayer. Our weapon is prayer. And Jesus will use it.

The trumpet judgments occur because God's people pray for deliverance from suffering.

> "And the seven angels which had the seven trumpets prepared themselves to sound." Revelation 8:6

1st Trumpet: Blood, Fire and Hail

> 8:7 The **first angel sounded**, and there followed hail and fire mingled with blood, and they were cast upon the earth: and the third part of trees was burnt up, and all green grass was burnt up.

This parallels the 7th Plague on Egypt.

> Exodus 9:19 Send therefore now, and gather thy cattle, and all that thou hast in the field; for upon every man and beast which shall be found in the field, and shall not be brought home, the hail shall come down upon them, and they shall die. 9:20 **He that feared the word of the LORD** among the servants of Pharaoh made his servants and his cattle flee into the houses: 9:21 And **he that regarded not the word of the LORD** left his servants and his cattle in the field. 9:23 And Moses stretched forth his rod toward heaven: and the LORD sent **thunder and hail, and the fire ran along upon the ground**; and the LORD rained hail upon the land of Egypt. 9:24 So there was **hail, and fire mingled with the hail**, very grievous, such as there was none like it in all the land of Egypt since it became a nation. 9:25 And the hail smote throughout all the land of Egypt all that was in the field, both **man and beast**; and the hail **smote every herb of the field, and brake every tree of the field**. 9:26 Only in the land of Goshen, where the children of Israel were, was there no hail.

> Psalm 18:12 At the brightness that was before him his thick clouds passed, **hail stones and coals** of fire. 18:13 The LORD also thundered in the heavens, and **the Highest gave his voice; hail stones and coals of fire**. 18:14 Yea, he sent out his arrows, and scattered them; and he shot out lightnings, and discomfited them.

> Isaiah 30:30 And the LORD shall cause **his glorious voice to be heard**, and shall show the lighting down of his arm, with the indignation of his anger, and **with the flame of a devouring fire**, with scattering, and tempest, and **hailstones**. 30:31 For through the voice of the LORD shall the Assyrian be beaten down, which smote with a rod.

God sends the Trumpets, the hail, to get our attention.
He expects us to listen up and hear what He has to say.

> Genesis 49:1 And Jacob called unto his sons, and said, **Gather yourselves together**, that I may **tell you** that which shall befall you in the last days. 49:2 **Gather yourselves together**, and **hear**, ye sons of Jacob; and hearken unto Israel your father.

> Isaiah 18:3 **All ye inhabitants of the world**, and dwellers on the earth, see ye, when he lifts up an ensign (a flag) on the mountains; and **when he blows a trumpet, hear—listen**.

Jesus speaks and His words are hail, fire, blood, cast upon the earth.
Jesus baptized with fire, and shed His blood on Calvary in 31 AD.

1/3 Refined by Fire

Our God is a consuming fire; the final faithful will "abide the day of His coming" because they except the "Refiner's fire" to do its work which is to "purge them as gold and silver." Malachi 3:2, 3. The love of sin and sympathy for the world are burned out of their lives. They place the blood over the door posts of their hearts. The fire falls on the earth where the remnant seed of the woman have fled for protection. These are those who have separated themselves from the Dragon's Beast power. God promises to "bring the third part through the fire" and "refine them as silver is refined, and will try them as gold is tried." Zechariah 13:9.

Isaiah 40:6 ...**All flesh is grass.** 40:7 ...surely **the people is grass.**
The seals affected ¼ of the earth, the trumpets increased the affected territory to 1/3 of the earth
1/3 of the Protestant world (which is helped by the earth) is purified by fire and accepts the blood of Christ.

36 Prophesy Again! **When You Hear the Sound of the Trumpet**
But after seven trumpets, if we still refuse to listen, God will send seven more plagues, the 7 Last Plagues.

>Leviticus 26:18 And if ye will **not yet for all this hearken unto me**, then I will **punish you seven times more** for your sins. 26:19 And I will break the pride of your power; and I will make your heaven as iron, and your earth as brass: 26:20 And your strength shall be spent in vain: for your land shall not yield her increase, neither shall the trees of the land yield their fruits.

After the 7 Trumpets "they repented not" so they got the 7 Plagues

>Deut 4:34 Or hath God assayed to go and take him a nation from the midst of another nation,
>1. by **temptations**,
>2. by **signs**, and
>3. by **wonders**, and
>4. by **war**, and
>5. by a **mighty hand**, and
>6. by a **stretched out arm**, and
>7. by **great terrors**,
>
>according to all that the LORD your God did for you in Egypt before your eyes?

>Deut 4:36 **Out of heaven** he made thee to **hear his voice**, that he might instruct thee:
>and **upon earth** he showed you **his great fire**;
>and **you heard his words** out of the **midst of the fire**.

>5:1 And Moses called all Israel, and said unto them, **Hear, O Israel**, the statutes and judgments which I speak in your ears this day, that ye may learn them, and keep, and do them.

First Commandment

>6:4 **Hear, O Israel**: The LORD our God is one LORD: 6:5 And thou shalt love the LORD thy God with all thine heart, and with all thy soul, and with all thy might.

>Matthew 12:29 And Jesus answered him, The first of all the commandments is, **Hear, O Israel**; The Lord our God is one Lord: 12:30 And thou shalt love the Lord thy God with all thy heart, and with all thy soul, and with all thy mind, and with all thy strength: this is **the first commandment**.

>9:1 **Hear, O Israel**: Thou art to pass over Jordan this day, to go in to possess nations greater and mightier than thyself, cities great and fenced up to heaven,

>32:1 **Give ear, O ye heavens**, and I will speak; and **hear, O earth**, the words of my mouth.
>32:2 My doctrine shall drop as the rain, my speech shall distil as the dew, as the small rain upon the tender herb, and as the showers upon the grass: 32:3 Because **I will publish the name of the LORD: ascribe ye greatness unto our God**.

>Judges 5:3 **Hear, O ye kings; give ear, O ye princes**; I, even I, will sing unto the LORD; I will sing praise to the LORD God of Israel. 5:4 LORD, when thou went out of Seir, when thou marched out of the field of Edom, **the earth trembled, and the heavens dropped, the clouds also dropped water**. 5:5 The **mountains melted** from before the LORD, even that Sinai from before the LORD God of Israel.

>Isaiah 1:2 **Hear, O heavens, and give ear, O earth**: for the **LORD hath spoken**, I have nourished and brought up children, and they have rebelled against me. 1:3 The ox knoweth his owner, and the ass his master's crib: but Israel doth not know, my people doth not consider.

>Isaiah 49:1 **Listen, O isles**, unto me; and **hearken, ye people**, from far; The LORD hath called me from the womb; from the bowels of my mother hath he made mention of my name. 49:2 And he hath made my mouth

like a sharp sword; in the shadow of his hand hath he hid me, and made me a polished shaft; in his quiver hath he hid me; 49:3 And said unto me, Thou art my servant, O Israel, in whom I will be glorified.

But it is our choice to listen. We haven't always.

>Exodus 7:13 And he hardened Pharaoh's heart, that he hearkened not unto them
>Acts 7... Leaders stopped their ears refusing to listen to Stephen

Jeremiah/Ezekiel? 13:10 Because, even because they have seduced my people, saying, Peace; and there was no peace; and **one built up a wall**, and, lo, others **daubed it with untempered morter**: 13:11 Say unto them ...**it shall fall**: there shall be an overflowing shower; and ye, O **great hailstones**, shall fall; and a stormy wind shall rend it.

Ezekiel 38:22 And I will plead against him [Gog] with pestilence and with blood; and I will rain upon him, and upon his bands, and upon the many people that are with him, an **overflowing rain, and great hailstones, fire, and brimstone**. 38:23 Thus will I magnify myself, and sanctify myself; and I will be known in the eyes of many nations, and they shall know that I am the LORD.

I Psalm 105:32 He gave them **hail for rain, and flaming fire** in their land. 105:33 He smote their vines also and their **fig trees**; and **brake the trees** of their coasts.

Job 38:22 Hast thou entered into the treasures of the snow? or hast thou seen the treasures of the **hail**, 38:23 Which I have **reserved against the time of trouble, against the day of battle** and war?

2nd Trumpet: Burning Mountain Turns Sea to Blood

>8:8 And the **second angel sounded**, and as it were **a great mountain burning with fire** was **cast into the sea**: and the third part of the **sea became blood**; 8:9 And the third part of the **creatures** which were in the sea, and had life, **died**; and the third part of the **ships were destroyed**.

This parallels the 1st Plague of Egypt: when water was turned to blood.

Burning mountains have been known throughout history. Some of the more notable volcanoes:
>Vesuvius erupted AD 79, destroyed Pompeii, destroying ships in Naples harbor.
>536 Proto-Krakatau caused the "Dark Ages"
>Krakatau 1883 caused a year of winter (year without a summer).
>Mt St Helens 1980 sloughed a mountain side into Spirit Lake.
>Mt Sinai where God's Law was proclaimed appeared to burn with fire and smoke.
>Babylon a burnt mountain rolled down.

Exodus 19:18 And **mount Sinai was altogether on a smoke**, because the LORD descended upon it in **fire**: and the smoke thereof ascended as the smoke of a furnace, and the whole mount **quaked greatly**. 19:19 And when **the voice of the trumpet sounded long**, and waxed louder and louder, Moses spake, and God answered him by a voice.

Deuteronomy 4:11 the **mountain burned with fire unto the midst of heaven**, with darkness, clouds, and thick darkness. 4:12 And the LORD spoke unto you out of the midst of the fire.

Deuteronomy 12:2 Ye shall utterly destroy all the places, wherein the nations which ye shall possess served their gods, **upon the high mountains, and upon the hills, and under every green tree**: 12:3 And ye shall overthrow their altars, and break their pillars, and **burn their groves with fire**;

38 Prophesy Again! **When You Hear the Sound of the Trumpet**
When Israel forsakes God and worships other gods they are exposed to destructive fire.

> Psalm 32:22 For a fire is kindled in mine anger, and shall burn unto the lowest hell, and shall consume the earth with her increase, and **set on fire the foundations of the mountains**. 32:23 I will heap mischiefs upon them; I will spend mine arrows upon them. 32:24 They shall be **burnt with hunger, and devoured with burning heat, and with bitter destruction**: I will also send the teeth of beasts upon them, with the poison of serpents of the dust.

> Psalm 36:6 **Thy righteousness is like the great mountains**; thy judgments are a great deep: O LORD, you preserve man and beast.

> Psalm 46:1 God is our refuge and strength, a very present help in trouble. 46:2 Therefore will not we fear, though the earth be removed, and though **the mountains be carried into the midst of the sea**; 46:3 Though the waters thereof roar and be troubled, though the mountains shake with the swelling thereof. Selah.

> Psalm 144:5 Bow thy heavens, O LORD, and **come down: touch the mountains, and they shall smoke**. 144:6 Cast forth lightning, and scatter them: shoot out thine arrows, and destroy them. 144:7 Send thine hand from above; rid me, and **deliver me out of great waters**, from the hand of strange children; [great waters = strange children]

> Isaiah 2:2 And it shall come to pass **in the last days**, that **the mountain of the LORD's house** shall be established **in the top of the mountains**, and shall be exalted above the hills; and all nations shall flow unto it. 2:3 And many people shall go and say, Come ye, and let us go up to the **mountain of the LORD, to the house of the God of Jacob**; and he will teach us of his ways, and we will walk in his paths: for out of **Zion** shall go forth the law, and the word of the LORD from **Jerusalem**. [Mount Zion is the Mountain of the Lord, God's people, His Church]

> Isaiah 2:12 For the day of the LORD of hosts shall be upon **every one that is proud and lofty**, and upon every one that is lifted up; and he **shall be brought low**: 2:14 And **upon all the high mountains**, and upon all the hills **that are lifted up**. [High mountains brought low..cast down]

> Isaiah 13:4 The noise of a multitude in **the mountains**, like as of **a great people**; a tumultuous noise of **the kingdoms of nations** gathered together: [Mountains are kingdoms]

> Isaiah 64:1 Oh that thou wouldest rend the heavens, that You would come down, that the **mountains might flow down at thy presence**, 64:2 As **when the melting fire burns**, the fire causes the waters to boil, to make thy name known to thine adversaries, that the nations may tremble at thy presence! 64:3 When thou did terrible things which we looked not for, You came down, **the mountains flowed down at thy presence**.

> Micah 1:3 For, behold, **the LORD** cometh forth out of his place, and **will come down**, and tread upon the high places of the earth. 1:4 And **the mountains shall be molten under him**, and the valleys shall be cleft, as wax before the fire, and as the waters that are poured down a steep place.

> Nahum 1:5 The mountains quake at him, and the **hills melt**, and the earth is burned at his presence, yea, the world, and all that dwell therein. 1:6 Who can stand before his indignation? and who can abide in the fierceness of his anger? his fury is poured out like fire, and the **rocks are thrown down by him**.

> Habakkuk 3:6 He stood, and measured the earth: he beheld, and drove asunder the nations; and the **everlasting mountains were scattered, the perpetual hills did bow**: his ways are everlasting.

> Jeremiah 9:10 For **the mountains** will I take up a weeping and wailing, and for the habitations of the wilderness a lamentation, because **they are burned up**, so that none can pass through them;

Jeremiah 51:24 And I will render unto **Babylon** and to all the inhabitants of Chaldea all their evil that they have done in Zion in your sight, saith the LORD. 51:25 Behold, I am against thee, O **destroying mountain**, saith the LORD, **which destroys all the earth**: and **I will** stretch out mine hand upon thee, and **roll thee down** from the rocks, and will make thee **a burnt mountain**.

Ezekiel 28:16 By the multitude of thy merchandise they have filled the midst of thee with violence, and thou hast sinned: therefore **I will cast thee as profane out of the mountain of God**: and I will destroy thee, O covering cherub, **from the midst of the stones of fire**. [Satan cast out]

Daniel 2:35 Then was the iron, the clay, the brass, the silver, and the gold, broken to pieces together, and became like the chaff of the summer threshing floors; and the wind carried them away, that no place was found for them: and **the stone** that smote the image **became a great mountain**, and **filled the whole earth**.

Zechariah 4:7 Who art thou, **O great mountain**? before Zerubbabel thou **shall become a plain**: and he shall bring forth the headstone thereof with shoutings, crying, Grace, grace unto it.

After cursing the fig tree,

> "Jesus answered and said unto them, Verily I say unto you, If ye have faith, and doubt not, ye shall not only do this which is done to the fig tree, but also if ye shall **say unto this mountain, Be thou removed, and be thou cast into the sea**; it shall be done." Matthew 21:21

Cast into the sea: populated areas, 1/3 of Catholic world is purified by fire and accept the blood of Christ.

3rd Trumpet: Burning Star Makes Rivers Bitter

8:10 And the **third angel sounded**, and there fell a great star from heaven, burning as it were a lamp, and it fell upon the third part of the rivers, and upon the fountains of waters; 8:11 And the name of the star is called Wormwood: and the third part of the waters became wormwood; and many men died of the waters, because they were made bitter.

Great burning Star from heaven: Wormwood, Fell upon rivers & fountains of waters

Num 24:17 I shall see him, but not now: I shall behold him, but not nigh: there shall come *a **Star out of Jacob***, and a Sceptre shall rise out of Israel, and shall smite the corners of Moab, and destroy all the children of Sheth.

Rev 2:28 And I will give him the morning Star. [Jesus, the promise to Thyatira]
Rev 22:16 **I Jesus** have sent mine angel to testify unto you these things in the churches. I am the root and the offspring of David, and **the bright and morning star**.

Gen 15:17 And it came to pass, that, when the sun went down, and it was dark, behold a smoking furnace, and *a burning lamp* that passed between those pieces. [Jesus appeared to Abraham]

Deut 29:18 Lest there should be among you man, or woman, or family, or tribe, whose heart turns away this day from the LORD our God, to go and serve the gods of these nations; lest there should be among you a root that bears gall and *wormwood*;

Jer 23:15 Therefore thus saith the LORD of hosts concerning the prophets; Behold, I will feed them with *wormwood*, and make them drink the water of gall: for from the prophets of Jerusalem is profaneness gone forth into all the land.

Amos 5:7 Ye who turn judgment to *wormwood*, and leave off righteousness in the earth,

Wormwood is the bitterness of sin. It is God's judgment on the Beast's kingdom for its idolatry.

> Jeremiah 9:15 I will make this people eat **bitter food** and drink **poisoned water**.

> Numbers 5:27 And when he hath made her to drink the water, then it shall come to pass, that, **if she be defiled, and have done trespass against her husband**, that **the water** that causeth the curse shall enter into her, and **become bitter**, and her belly shall swell, and her thigh shall rot: and **the woman shall be a curse** among her people.

Only those who are daughters of the Harlot will drink the bitter water and be cursed.
Those who remain loyal to their Husband, Jesus, will not be affected.
Salvation comes for the Remnant because of their loyalty.

> Exodus 15:23 And when they came to Marah, they **could not drink of the waters of Marah**, for they were **bitter**: therefore the name of it was called Marah. 15:24 And the people murmured against Moses, saying, What shall we drink? 15:25 And he cried unto the LORD; and **the LORD showed him a tree**, which when he had **cast into the waters**, the waters were **made sweet**: there he made for them a statute and an ordinance, and there he proved them, 15:26 And said, If thou wilt **diligently hearken to the voice** of the LORD thy God, **and wilt do** that which is right in his sight, and wilt **give ear to his commandments**, and keep all his statutes, I will put none of these diseases upon thee, which I have brought upon the Egyptians: for I am the LORD that heals you.

While wicked wormwood of sin falls on the rivers and makes the waters bitter causing death, the Lord's tree is case into the bitter waters and makes them sweet. This event occurred on the 6th day after leaving Egypt and represents Christ's death which took place on a Friday, the 6th day of the week. Remember, Jesus called Himself a green tree. He was nailed to a tree. He became our Wormwood "to given unto them
beauty for ashes,
the oil of joy for mourning,
the garment of praise for the spirit of heaviness;
that they might be called trees of righteousness." Isaiah 61:3.

> 2 Corinthians 5:21 For *he hath made him to be sin for us, who knew no sin*; that we might be made the righteousness of God in him.

Chernobyl Nuclear Disaster 1986 caught the attention of the physical world. Chernobyl is a Russian word which means "wormwood" or absinthe and is defined in the Concise Oxford Dictionary 6th Edition as "a perennial herb of genus Artemisia with bitter, tonic, and stimulating qualities used in preparation of vermouth, absinth and in medicine."

"In Slavic languages, including the Ukrainian and Byelorussian languages, there is a word 'chernobyl', which means wormwood, bitter grass. This has a striking relevance to the Chernobyl tragedy. I am no fatalist. I do not believe in the blind inevitability of fate, but who can fail to be moved by these tragic and elegiac words from Revelation, which must leave their indelible imprint on the heart."

> Hans Blix, Executive Director of the International Atomic Energy Agency,
> in a speech given before the UN General Assembly on October 23, 1990

Chernobyl is taken from the Russian word 'chernin' which means 'black' because the extremely bitter herb turns their tongues black. It is used as a flea repellant and a de-wormer. It also belongs to the family Asteraceae, which belongs to the order Asterales which, in turn, belongs to the subclass Asteridae. The family, order and subclass names are all formed from 'aster,' which is the Greek and Latin root meaning "star."

On April 25, 1986 reactor 4 at the Chernobyl site failed to recover from a low power test and caused an unplanned power surge that produced a tremendous uncontrolled steam explosion, blowing the 2 million pound concrete container's cap into a thousand pieces, melting a number of control rods, fragmenting radioactive fuel core elements causing a second explosion that set tons of graphite blocks on fire. It took 9 days and 5000 tons of sand, boron, dolomite, clay and lead dropped from helicopters to put it out. All the helicopter pilots died of radiation exposure. Ten times as much radiation was blasted one mile up into the atmosphere than was released by the atomic bomb which exploded over Hiroshima, Japan 41 years earlier.

Winds carried the radioactive fallout to Scandinavia, Northern Italy, Germany, Great Britain and even the east coast of the United States. For five days it rained incessantly, carrying radioactive pollution down the Prypiat river on which Chernobyl sits, into the Dnipro, the 922 square kilometer Kyiv Reservoir supplying drinking water to 30 million people. The deadly rivers carried their poison throughout all Europe.

Chernobyl will not by inhabitable for another 600 years (±3 centuries) and radiation will remain in the area for the next 48,000 years. While only 125,000 died from the direct effects of the catastrophe, 200 million are considered to have excessive exposure to Cesium-137 with a 30-year half-life.

Today, Chernobyl is a ghost town, testifying to the bitter waters of radioactive wormwood.

1/3 of the non-Christian world will accept the blood of Christ and are purified by Divine fire.

4th Trumpet: Sun, Moon and Stars Darkened

> Revelation 8:12 And the **fourth angel sounded**, and the third part of the sun was smitten, and the third part of the moon, and the third part of the stars; so as the third part of them was darkened, and the day shone not for a third part of it, and the night likewise.

This parallels the 9th Plague of Egypt. Exodus 10:21 darkness spread over Egypt that could be felt. Judgment on the worshippers of Ra, the Sun god! God is creator of the Sun, Moon, Stars, Universe!

> Deuteronomy 4:19 And lest thou lift up thine eyes unto heaven, and when you see **the sun, and the moon, and the stars**, even all the host of heaven, should be driven **to worship them**, and serve them, which the LORD thy God hath divided unto all nations under the whole heaven.

42 Prophesy Again! **When You Hear the Sound of the Trumpet**
>Communism, the self-proclaimed center of atheism, fell in 1989.

The trumpets are warning shots. A dress rehersal for the final ultimate judgment of the 7 Last Plagues.

>Revelation 8:13 And I beheld, and heard an angel flying through the midst of heaven, saying with a loud voice, **Woe, woe, woe,** to the inhabitants of the earth by reason of the other voices of the **trumpet** of the three angels, which are yet to sound!

Like the first 4 seals, the first 4 trumpets are limited in scope. But the last 3 will affect all unbelievers.

5th Trumpet, 1st Woe: Bottomless Pit Smokes

>Revelation 9:1 And the **fifth angel sounded**, and I saw a star fall from heaven unto the earth: and to him was given the key of the bottomless pit.

>Luke 10:18 And he said unto them, I beheld **Satan as lightning fall from heaven.**

>Revelation 9:2 And he **opened the bottomless pit**; and there arose a smoke out of the pit, **as the smoke of a great furnace**; and the **sun and the air were darkened** by reason of the smoke of the pit.

The Twin Towers Burn and Fall, 2001. Their smoke darkened the sun and the air.
The abyss, where the devils pleaded with Jesus not to send them. But he did. Now they come up.

>9:3 And there came out of the smoke **locusts** upon the earth: and unto them was given power, as the scorpions of the earth have power. 9:4 And it was commanded them that they should **not hurt the grass** of the earth, **neither any green thing**, neither **any tree**; but only those men which have not the seal of God in their foreheads. 9:5 And to them it was given that they should not kill them, but that they should be **tormented five months:** and their torment was as the torment of a scorpion, when he striketh a man.

Islamic Jihad is launched. The "war on terrorism" is declared. Those who are sealed are protected.

>Luke 10:17-19 Jesus give us authority **to trample on snakes and scorpions** (the Devil and his imps) and to overcome all the power of the enemy; nothing will harm you.

>9:6 And in those days shall men seek death, and shall not find it; and shall desire to die, and death shall flee from them. 9:7 And the shapes of the locusts were **like unto horses** prepared unto battle; and on their heads were as it were crowns like gold, and their faces were **as the faces of men.** 9:8 And they had hair **as the hair of women**, and their teeth were **as the teeth of lions.** 9:9 And they had breastplates, as it were **breastplates of iron**; and the sound of their wings was as the sound of chariots of many horses running to battle. 9:10 And they had tails **like unto scorpions**, and there were stings in their tails: and their power was to **hurt men five months.** 9:11 And they had a king over them, which is the angel of the bottomless pit, whose name in the Hebrew tongue is **Abaddon**, but in the Greek tongue hath his name **Apollyon.** [Destroyer]

Satan is a thief, a destroyer and a murder just as Jesus said he is.
He appears as Christ, but his treachery knows no bounds.
6th Trumpet, 2nd Woe: 200 Million Kill 2 Billion

>9:13 And **the sixth angel sounded**, and I heard a voice from the four horns of the golden altar which is before God, 9:14 Saying to the sixth angel which had the trumpet, **Loose the four angels** which are **bound in the great river Euphrates.** 9:15 And the four angels were loosed, which were prepared **for an hour, and a day, and a month, and a year,** for to slay the **third part of men.**

One third of the world's present population is little over 2 billion people.
The date is set for the death decree on God's faithful remnant.
Instead, God arrives with his army to fight the battle of Armageddon.

> 9:16 And the number of the army of the horsemen were **two hundred million**...
> 9:17 And thus I saw the horses in the vision, and them that sat on them, having **breastplates of fire**, and of jacinth, and brimstone: and the heads of the horses were as the heads of lions; and **out of their mouths issued fire and smoke and brimstone**.

Fire and brimstone are God's weapons.

> 9:18 By these three was the **third part of men** killed, by the fire, and by the smoke, and by the brimstone, which issued out of their mouths.

Instead of 1/3 of the saints dying, 1/3 of the wicked are destroyed,

> 9:19 For their power is in their mouth, and in their tails: for their tails were like unto serpents, and had heads, and with them they do hurt. 9:20 And the **rest of the men** which were not killed by these plagues yet **repented not** of the works of their hands, that they should not **worship devils, and idols** of gold, and silver, and brass, and stone, and of wood: which neither can see, nor hear, nor walk: 9:21 Neither repented they of their **murders**, nor of their **sorceries**, nor of their **fornication**, nor of their **thefts**.

Notice the commandments that are listed here:
    worship devils: 1st commandment
    worship idols: 2nd commandment
    murder: 6th commandment
    sorceries: 9th commandment
    fornication: 7th commandment
    theft: 8th commandment

    but the wicked still do not repent.

44 Prophesy Again! **Seven Heads Rise Again**

The Seven-headed Beast

After the general outline of western world history is presented in Daniel 2, a series of visions (now given to Daniel himself) dominate the last half of Daniel's book (chapters 7-12). Beginning with chapter seven, these visions provide increasing detail as the focus moves ever closer to the end time. The beasts in Daniel 7 are plainly parallel to the metallic image of Daniel 2 and are actually identified as a sequence of empires beginning with Babylon:

Daniel 2	**Gold**	**Silver**	**Brass**	**Iron**
Daniel 7	**Lion**	**Bear**	**Leopard**	**Dreadful beast**
	1 head	**1 head**	**4 heads**	**1 head, 10 horns**
	Babylon	**Persia**	**Greece**	**Rome**

The symbols of this vision, wild predatory animals, also appear in the book of Revelation:

Revelation 12 **A great red dragon** appears in heaven with 7 heads and 10 horns
The dragon is clearly identified as the Devil, that old serpent, Satan (verse 9)
The dragon chases the woman into the wilderness, making war with her remnant.
Revelation 13 **A leopard-bear-lion beast** arises from the sea with 7 heads and 10 horns
One of its heads is mortally wounded and then miraculously healed
Revelation 17 **A scarlet beast**, bearing a woman in the wilderness, also has 7 heads and 10 horns

Babylon, the first of seven empires, initiates the prophetic symbol of **the beast with seven heads**. Notice the beasts of Revelation all have 7 heads and 10 horns, the accumulated characteristics of Daniel 7. But is the scarlet beast the same as the red dragon? Is the beast from the sea the same as the scarlet beast? Context and description determine the identity of each of Revelation's seven-headed beasts.

Four Beasts - Seven Heads

	Pre-Christian Era ← Pagan Empires →		Christian Era ← Pseudo-Christian Powers →	
	Daniel 7	**Revelation 12**	**Revelation 13**	**Revelation 17**
What:	four diverse beasts	a great wonder	a beast	a beast
Where:	from the sea	in heaven	from the sea + earth	in the wilderness
Kind:	Lion, Bear, Leopard	Great red dragon	Leopard, Bear, Lion	Scarlet beast
Heads:	$1 + 1 + 4 + 1 = 7$	7	7	$7 + 1 = 8$
Horns:	10 on 7th head	10	10	10
Crowns:	—	7 on 7 heads	10 on 10 horns	—
Time:	3½ times	1260 days	42 months	one hour
Meaning:	4 kings of the earth	Devil, serpent, Satan	Beast & its Image	7 mountains/kings
	Little Horn emerges	ready to devour child	blasphemy on heads	names of blasphemy
	from 7th head	chases the woman	wounded-healed	carries the woman
	Babylon, Persia,	Pagan Rome	Papal Rome-Satan	rules with 10 kings
	Greece, Rome	Dreadful beast of D7	Little Horn of D7	

Daniel 7:17 These great beasts are **four kings** which shall arise **out of the earth:** *Babylon to Rome*
Eze 21:26,27 Remove the diadem and take off the crown… until He comes whose right it is.
"The *crown was removed from Israel and* "passes successively to the kingdoms
of Babylon, Medo-Persia, Greece, and Rome." *Education* p. 179.

The Metallic Man of Daniel 2

Nebuchadnezzar, king of Babylon,
    "You are this head of gold" Daniel's time. 609-539 BC
    Death decree to those who refuse to worship the image
    God's people captured and exiled
    Temple vessels desecrated with wine and drinking
    Mene,   mene, tekel,   upharsin
    "Counted, counted, weighted, divided"
        Times,   time,   dividing of time

Darius, the Mede & Cyrus, the Persian
    "Chest and arms of silver" 539-331 BC
    Two arms, two combined people groups
    Cyrus is God's "anointed"
    Comes from the East, dries up Euphrates
    Authorizes Jewish return to Jerusalem
    Darius imposes worship with a death decree
    Haman secures a death decree to eliminate Jews

Alexander the Great, king of Greece
    "Belly and thighs of brass" 331-31 BC
    Alexander conquers the world in 12 years
    Comes from the West
    Begins military expansion at river Granicus 334 BC
    2300 years later, 1967, the temple is restored

Julius Caesar of Rome
    "Legs of iron" 31 BC - 330 AD: 360 years – "a time"
    Octavius Augustus Caesar is first Emperor
    He establishes empire by winning Battle of Actium
    Ends Roman Civil War by defeating Mark Antony
    Dan 11 "continue for a time" 360 years
    Two legs, a western and eastern empire
    Constantine moves capitol to Constantinople 330 AD
    Pagan and Papal eras, church & state powers
    Papacy assumes control of western capitol in Rome
    Dan 7: it continues for 1260 years: 538 – 1798

Europe
    "Feet: part of iron, part clay"
    10 toes: Pagan empire fragments into European nations
        Papal empire fragments into Protestant churches

46 Prophesy Again! **Seven Heads Rise Again**

The seven heads are further explained by introducing another symbol: mountains.

7 Mountains
The seven heads are said to be mountains. This is in contrast to "great mountain of the Lord's house"
If the Lord's mountain is a heavenly kingdom, then the seven mountains are earthly kingdoms.

Rev 17:9	The seven heads are **seven mountains** [empires, nations]
Dan 2:35	The stone that smote the image became a **great mountain**, and filled the whole earth.
Zech 4:7	The **great mountain** shall become a plain and the **capstone** shall come forth with shouts of "Grace!"
Dan 2:44	In the days of these kings the God of heaven shall set up **a kingdom**.
Isa 2:2	In the last days, the **mountain of the LORD's house** shall be established in the **top of the mountains** and **all nations** shall flow unto it.

*Christ is the Cornerstone and **Capstone**, the first and the last, the beginning and the end, the ultimate mountain.*
  Phil 1:6   He who began a good work in you shall be faithful to **complete it**.

7 Kingdoms
The seven heads are also interpreted as seven kings or kingdoms. Rev 17:10, "They are seven kings." The fact that both symbols are used, may indicate a dual application. As we have already noted, seven Empire heads are identified among the Daniel 7 beasts: **Babylon, Persia, Greece's 4 heads, Rome.**

Some expositors have been less satisfied with crediting Greece with an allotment of four empire heads. In search of more convincing candidates, there have been many suggestions. One such is:

Babylon	Persia	Greece	Rome	Papacy	Europe	Antichrist

This more logically parallels the symbols of Daniel 2 which also begin with Babylon:

Head	Chest	Belly	Left Leg	Right Leg	Feet	Toes

Lions and Bears, Oh My!
Lions and bears seem to be favored metaphors for depicting the oppression of the wicked against the innocent. For example:

1 Sam 17:34 **David rescued a lamb** from the mouth of **a Lion and a Bear**, when they rose up against him..
Prov 28:15 **A wicked ruler over the poor** people is like a **roaring lion** and a **raging bear**

An interesting listing of these four beasts occurs in Hosea. God uses these beasts as symbols of His judgments on Israel. The world empires that occupied, besieged, and destroyed Jerusalem fulfilled them.

> I will be to them as a **lion**: as a **leopard** by the way will I observe them;
> I will meet them as a **bear** that is bereaved of her whelps, and will rend the caul of their heart
> and there will I devour them like a **lion**: the **wild beast** shall tear them. Hosea 13:7,8

Isaiah also lists a beastly quartet with an even more interesting arrangement and sequence.
The passage is foretelling the time when wild predators and domesticated livestock will coexist peacefully.
Notice the order:

    Wolf with the Lamb, **Leopard** with the Kid, Calf and the **Lion**, Cow and the **Bear**   Isa 11:6,7

The first two pairs name the predator first whereas the second two pairs list them last.
Furthermore, Isaiah presents his first two beasts in reverse order to that of Daniel's order.

    Wolf (dreadful beast) **Leopard** (Greece) – **reverse sequential order of Daniel 7**
    Lion (Babylon)   **Bear** (Persia)   – **forward sequential order of Daniel 7**

Because Babylon ruled in much the same area as Assyria, the two empires appear to be consolidated in the lion symbol by Jeremiah.

    Israel is a scattered flock that **lions** have chased away.
    The first to devour him was the king of **Assyria**;
    the last to crush his bones was Nebuchadnezzar king of **Babylon.** Jeremiah 50:17
    *Actually, the first power to devour the Seed of Abraham was **Egypt***

The consolidation is also seen in Daniel 8 where the goat embodies the combined western powers of Greece and Rome pitted against a ram, the eastern powers of Babylon and Persia. It is commonly acknowledged that Persia inherited, not only the territory, but also the culture of Babylon; and Rome assimilated Greece.

Five are Fallen
In Rev 17 John specifies that five of these seven empires are fallen, one is, one is yet to come.
Rome was in power in John's day, therefore **Rome** is accepted by many to be the king that "is."
If we include Egypt and Assyria and accept Medo-Persia as a single unified power then
the 7 Persecuting Powers are: **Egypt, Assyria, Babylon, Persia, Greece, Rome, Papacy**
    5 fallen would make Rome the "one is"

The only power that "was" in the past but "is not" during Rome's time was Babylon.
Egypt, Syria, Greece, Persia were all still in existence; Babylon was in decay, uninhabited.
The 8th head is "of the seven" because it will be a revived Babylonian empire.

Another view is that the head count begins with Babylon (the empire in existence at Daniel's time) and places the atheistic powers of France and later Russia as the "one that is" making America the 7th head that is to last only a "short time." But is 230 years a short time? Considering the timing of these powers, it is recognized that Russia and America dominate the earth during the same period of time. It appears that they at least overlap.

48 Prophesy Again! **Seven Heads Rise Again**

The important factor is that all the powers included in the Special Seven are persecuting powers that seek to harass, damage, and even destroy the people of God—until the arrival of the 6th head.

worship the image/face the fire	Babylon		Babylon	1.
Haman's death decree	Persia		Persia	2.
Antiochus Epiphanes	Greece		Greece	3.
Christian persecution	Rome		Pagan Rome	4.
Inquisition, Crusades	Papacy	"was"	Papal Rome	5. "five are fallen"
Religious Freedom		"is not"	America	6. "and one is"
Babylon II's death decree	Papacy healed	"yet is"	US/EU/UN	7. "short time"
	Satan as Christ			8. "goes into perdition"

For 1260 years of the Dark Ages, society was divided into Clergy, Nobility, and Peasants. The Church was the glue holding the iron (civil ruling power) and clay (the common people) together. This was the time of the Little Horn, the 5th head, a continuation of Rome as the Papacy.

In 1798 this 5th head (the Papacy) lost its "authority" but was not killed. The 5th head was wounded by the Reformation and France (first by the French Revolution and then by Napoleon). But the wound, while "deadly," was not fatal. By 1799 "**five were fallen.**" Yet, the woman continued to be carried by the kings of Europe, especially Spain, Portugal, and Italy.

Was-Is Not-Will
Revelation 17:8 describes three phases of the woman (Church) as the beast that "was, is not and will come." During the time that the beast **"is not,"** there was no enforcement of Babylonian worship: religious freedom prevailed. **Church and State were separated** during the rise of democracy led by the United States as the 6th **head** of Revelation 17. This was extremely so in Communist Russia where the church was not only separated from the state, it was outlawed altogether. This is the **"One is"** time frame. The beast that enforces religion "is not" while the power that safeguards religious liberty "is." Thus, freedom from Church rule took two paths: democracy and communism. One allowed the free choice of conscience and religious liberty, the other suppressed religion entirely.

Thus,
1. The papacy "**was**" for 1260 years until 1798.   "**Five are fallen**" at this point in time.
2. Then it "**was not**" until 1929.   "**One is**" (America reigns) at this stage.
  Then the Papacy began to be healed. Vatican was formed, the Papal states were restored.
3. It ultimately "**will come**" when fully healed (political-military support from the US/EU/UN superpower).

Because the heads (a la Alexander's generals) are also mountains, there may be a "second phase" of the beast. This sequence of popes since the "healing of the wound" in 1929 brings us to Benedict XVI. Could be.

Head	Prophetic Text	Empire		Pope
1	Revelation 17:	Babylon		Pius XI
2		Medo-Persia		Pius XII
3		Greece		John XXIII
4		Rome		Paul VI
5	"Five have fallen"	Papal Rome	"was"	John Paul I
6	"One is"	Democracy-Communism	"is not"	John Paul II
7	"Yet to come"	US-Papal control	"shall ascend"	Benedict XVI
8	"Goes to perdition"	Global One World Power		"Christ" (Satan)

The 7 Kings of the Beast that "Yet Is"

1.	2.	3.	4.	5.	6.	7.	8.
Pius XI	Pius XII	John XXIII	Paul VI	John Paul I	John Paul II	Benedict XVI	Satan
1922 - 1939	1939 - 1958	1958 - 1963	1963 - 1978	1978	1978 - 2005	April 19, 2005	?
Lateran Treaty 1929				Reigned only 33 days	Seriously Wounded 1981	Rules only a *short* time	Impersonates Christ's 2nd Coming
Five are fallen					**One is**	One yet to come	Goes into perdition

Adapted from Michael Scheifler's Bible Light website on www.aloah.net

1929-1989

Pope Pius XI was reigning when the wound was healed in 1929.
Pope John Paul II transitioned the fall of the 6th head. Born in Communist Poland, he was instrumental in securing the cooperation of the US in the downfall of the Soviet Union and the union of US-Vatican powers. The 6th head is Communism, the power that rose from the godless abyss to challenge Christianity. It's demise came when the union of church and state once again gained control of the world stage.
The 7th head conquered Communism. It is now engaged in defeating Islam, the Church's second foe.

Revelation 17 begins by showing John the "judgment" of the Great Harlot. Since this occurs after 1844 (when judgment began in heaven) we should expect to see five fallen world empires prior to that date. And we do. The 5th power fell in 1798. As the Cold War was ending, the revived Papacy should appear. And it did.

1981 "It was a very good year"

In 1981 the G-7 Summit met on July 20-21 in Ottawa, Canada to determine world policy by the 7 top nations. In the chairman's summary he mentions "the Ten," the ten wealthiest industrialized member States of the International Monetary Fund: Belgium, Canada, Federal Republic of Germany, France, Italy, Japan, The Netherlands, Sweden, the United Kingdom, and the United States

Also in 1981 the European Union admitted it's 10th member, Greece, to join the other nine:
Germany, France, Italy, Belgium, Netherlands, Luxembourg, Denmark, United Kingdom, and Ireland.

1981 was a prophetic year: the Seven Heads and Ten Horns reigned.

50 Prophesy Again! **Seven Heads Rise Again**

Albino Luciani—the Patriarch of Venice—became John Paul I, Pope for 33 days: from August 26, 1978 to September 29, 1978.

His first order of business was ordering an investigation of the Vatican Bank and its American director Bishop Paul Marcinkus. He presided over a mammoth financial scandal that ended with a $244 million Vatican payout to enraged creditors of the Banco Ambrosiano, an institution linked to Bishop Marcinkus that folded amid $3.5 billion in red ink. He went to bed with a copy of his speech terminating the Jesuits and was found dead by his housekeeper the following morning.

Considerable documentation corroborates the Jesuit assassination of not only this pope but also others:
Herman, Edward S. & Brodhead, Frank. *The Rise and Fall of the Bulgarian Connection*. Sheridan Square Press, New York, 1986.

Martin, Malachi. *The Jesuits: The Society of Jesus and the Betrayal of the Roman Catholic Church*. Simon & Schuster, New York, 1989.

Manhattan Avro, *Murder in the Vatican, American, Russian and Papal Plots*, Ozark Books, Springfield, MO. 1985.

Manhattan, Avro. *The Vatican Moscow Washington Alliance*. Chick Pub., Chino, California, 1982.
Tarpley, Webster Griffin, & Chaitkin Anton. *George Bush: The Unauthorized Biography*. ProgressivePress.com.

Yallop, David A. *In God's Name: An Investigation into the Death of Pope John Paul I*. Bantam Books, New York, 1984.

John Paul II does, in this sequence at least, correlate well with the specifications of the Rev 13 beast: It would receive a deadly wound, the wound would be healed, all the world would wonder after him.

October 4, 1979
John Paul II's first visit to the U.S.

The first and last of the Daniel's 4 kingdoms share striking similarities:

Babylon & Rome...
    After invading Israel and besieging Jerusalem (as did all four powers)
    Both destroyed the temple
    Both did it on the 9th of Av
    Both took temple treasures
    Both burned the temple and the city
    Both took Jews as slaves back to their capitols
    Both killed thousands of Jews in the process

The Pattern: destroy the temple then persecute the saints

		70AD	until Constantine		
		Rome	**Rome**		
586BC		Destroyed Temple	Persecutes Saints	Dark Ages	
Babylon	**Babylon**		Martyrs-Catacombs	**Babylon II**	**Babylon II**
Destroyed	Persecuted Jews			Destroyed	Persecutes Saints
Temple	fiery furnace-lion's den			spiritual temple	Inquisition-Crusades

At the end: Rome II will destroy sanctuaries of true worship: economic pressures, tax-exemptions etc.
              Rome II will then persecute the true worshipers: economic boycotts, then death decree

Daniel 7
Daniel's first vision introduces 4 beasts that arise "from the sea."
In verse 17 they are said to be 4 kings "from the earth."

At the time of Christ there were 4 rulers in Palestine.

Luke 3: "Now in the 15th year of the reign of Tiberius Caesar
Pontius Pilate being governor of Judaea, and   (Dreadful beast's Roman representative)
Herod being tetrarch of Galilee, and his brother   (Bear devoured much flesh)
Philip tetrarch of Ituraea and of the region of Trachonitis, (Leopard)
Lysanias the tetrarch of Abilene, (near Damascus)   (Lion)
Annas and Caiaphas being the high priests,   (little horn spoke great words, 1260 days)
the word of God came unto John the son of Zacharias in the wilderness."

Herod, like the bear, "devoured much flesh." Herod murdered his wife, his mother, his father-in-law, Hyrcanus the ex-high priest, and two of his own sons: Antipater and Aristobulus. He was the agent of the Dragon "standing before the woman ready to devour her man child" who ordered the execution of all the infants in Bethlehem. He had ten wives (ten horns). The fact that the Jewish high priests were "set up" by the Roman governor makes the local fulfillment complete as the little horn emerges from Rome. The high priests conspire against the Prince of the covenant, saying great things against Him, accusing Him of being in league with Belzebub, guilty of blasphemy, and worthy of death. Their final success in securing his execution on the cross was the greatest abomination of all time and brought upon their nation it final desolation by the wrath of Rome.

Rome began with an earthquake.
In 31BC a severe earthquake in Palestine marked the beginning of the Roman Empire
Daniel 11 says it would continue "for a time" 360 years.
Constantine moved the capitol from Rome to Constantinople in 330 AD, exactly 360 years later.

Seven Heads Rise Again

The 31 BC earthquake did much damage to Jerusalem, Qumran, Masada and Jericho. The Essenes in Qumran fled their retreat convinced that the end of the world had come. Estimated to be at least 7 magnitude and involving the Jordan valley, it was the strongest quake in 2000 years. Josephus recorded that "30,000 people and many animals [were] killed" early in the reign of Herod the Great on September 2, 31 BC. (Others say it was early spring) "an earthquake in Judea, such a one as had not happened at any other time, and which brought a great destruction upon the cattle in that country... And about thirty thousand persons also perished in the ruins of their houses." (*Antiquities* XV, v.2).

When Jesus died on the cross, in 31 AD, the end of his life was punctuated by a severe earthquake following a strange three-hour darkness covering the land.

Phlegon Trallianus records in his Olympiades: *"In the fourth year of the 202nd Olympiad [AD 32-33], a failure of the Sun took place greater than any previously known, and night came on at the sixth hour of the day [noon], so that stars actually appeared in the sky; and a great earthquake took place in Bithynia and overthrew the greater part of Niceaea."*

Pilate was Roman procurator of Judea from AD 26 through AD 36.
Nisan 14 fell on a Friday only twice in the early 30's AD: April 7 AD 30 and April 3 AD 33.

These events form an interesting set of mirrored dates that illustrate the relations between the end of Pagan Babylon and the beginning of Papal Rome (Spiritual Babylon); between the beginning of the 70 weeks and end of Pagan Rome; between beginning of Pagan Rome (marked by an earthquake) and the ending of the 70 weeks (where an earthquake also marked Christ's death).

```
538     457            31          31            457     538
BC      BC             BC          AD            AD      AD
70 yrs  70 weeks       Rome        70 weeks      Rome    Papal Rome
ending  begins         begins      ending        ends    begins
                       earthquake  earthquake
```

The Wounds of Rome

Revelation 13 describes a wounding and healing of one of the beast's seven heads.
The injury is called a "deadly wound" and its recovery is miraculous: the world wonders.
Ancient Babylon was wounded in the person of Nebuchadnezzar for 7 years.
His wound was healed, and his kingdom was restored.

Ancient Rome was wounded by the triumph of Christ over death. Roman guards could not keep Him in the tomb. Christianity spread despite Rome's fierce opposition.
Ultimately, Christianity prevailed over paganism.

But the Roman wound was healed as Rome adopted Christianity and perverted it into its own image.
Spiritual Babylon was wounded by the triumph of the Word over tradition. Roman Bulls and threats of excommunication could not keep the Bible chained to convent walls. The Protestant Reformation, fueled by the availability of the printed Scriptures in the language of the people, spread despite Rome's fierce opposition.

But the Rome's wound was once again healed as the Bible becomes a forgotten book, as the ecumenical spirit draws the "separated brethren" back to the Mother Church, as the wall of separation of Church and State crumbles from neglect and apathy, as the world once again wonders at the splendor of Rome.

Rome **Wounded**	Papal Rule 3 ½ times 1260 days Wound **Healed**	Papacy **Wounded**	Beast Continued Wound **Healed**
31 – 457 AD	538 – 1798	1517 –1798	1929 -
Christianity Born & spread	Beast continues 42 months Holy city tread under foot 42 months Two witnesses prophecy 1260 days	Reformation Born & spread	Beast continues Holy city tread under foot Two witnesses prophecy
Paganism conquered	Woman flees/flies to wilderness 1260 Holy people shattered 3½ Saints given into little horn's hand 3½	Papacy conquered	Woman flees to wilderness Holy people shattered Saints given to little horn
		1981 John Paul II Deadly Wound	1982 - Time of trouble Persecution Cut Short or no life saved
	Church in the wilderness Inquisition, heretics persecuted Holy Roman Empire – Crusades Church tread underfoot		

History reveals multiple deadly *wounds*: Christ's death, Pagan Rome, the Reformation-Papal Rome, and…

Ronald Reagan shot March 20, 1981

John Paul II shot May 13, 1981

Two leaders
Two gunmen
Two nearly mortal wounds.

In 1981 a repeat "deadly" wound struck the leaders of the new 7th head as it was forming to end the 6th head.

54 Prophesy Again!   Seven Heads Rise Again

Immediately after their mutual healings, the leaders attacked their common foe.

June 7, 1982 was the first meeting between Reagan and John Paul II
"Only President Ronald Reagan and Pope John Paul II were present in the Vatican Library on Monday, June 7, 1982. It was the first time the two had met... In that meeting, Reagan and the Pope agreed to undertake a clandestine campaign to hasten the dissolution of the communist empire...
'This was one of the great secret alliances of all time.'"
                                    Carl Bernstein, "The Holy Alliance,"
                                    Time Feb 24, 1992 p. 28.

It was yet another restoration of Babylon the Great after a passage of "seven times."

In the same year that the leaders of the emerging northern kingdom were wounded in failed assassination attempts, the leader of the southern kingdom (Egyptian President Anwar Sadat) was fatally wounded by a successful assassination attempt on October 6, 1981. Egypt has always been the king of the south. It has always symbolized godlessness. "Who is the Lord that I should obey Him?" The king of the North was once again victorious over the king of the South.

Both wounds healed and Babylon the Great rose as the 7th head, defeating both communism and ancient Babylon (Iraq) in 1991. As America conquered ancient Babylon it acquired the rights and title of Babylon.

Seven Times
Nebuchadnezzar experienced in miniature what would happen to Babylon over the long haul.
In his dream recorded in Daniel 4, Nebuchadnezzar heard the watchers pronounce judgment on him, "Let his mind be changed...and let **seven times pass over him**." Daniel 4:16   A time = 360 years.
Therefore 7 x 360 = 2520 years   539 BC + 2520 = 2520 – 539 + 1 (no zero year) = 1982

Ancient Babylon	Persia – Greece - Rome	Spiritual Babylon	USA	Babylon the Great
605 BC – 539 BC w	w	538 AD – 1798 AD w **1260 years**		w 1982 -
"hew down the tree"	**7 times** = 7 x 360 = **2520 years**			"established in my kingdom"

Seven times indeed passed over ancient Babylon until it was once again established behind the might of the United States in 1982 as these two powers conspired to eliminate their common enemy, a godless empire.

Deadly Wounds
1798 Pius VI by the French Revolution: Papacy falls
1981 Ronald Reagan   March 20
1981 John Paul II   May 13
1981 Anwar Sadat   October 6

Wounds Healed
1929 Mussolini Concordat restored Papal States
1981 European Union adds 10th Nation: Greece
1982 Reagan & John Paul II meet to form 7th head, US backs Afghani Mujehadeen Muslim Militia
1989 Russia pulls out of Afghanistan, Communism/Berlin Wall falls
1991 Iraq War: Babylon dominated, economic sanctions imposed
2001 New York Attacked, Patriot Act, Homeland Security, Afghanistan invaded by US
2003 Sunday Laws established in Europe
2003 Iraq invaded, Babylon speaks as a dragon, TV programming emphasizes Catholicism
   Law and Order, ER, Crossing Jordan, West Wing, American Dreams, Third Watch, Charmed,
   Everwood, Miracles, Revelations, The District, Hack, CSI: Miami, Joan of Arcadia, Without a
   Trace, L.A. Dragnet, The Practice, X-Files, House, Left Behind, The Da Vinci Code
2004 Torture accepted, The Passion is surprisingly popular
2005 Christian Churches Together: church union
2006 Ten Commandments Day

7 Times Part II
Others have pointed to another set of 7 times which began in the time of Haggai.

Haggai 1:15, Ezra 4:24
Temple rebuilt   6th month 24th, 520/521 BC   (Pythagoras left Babylon, died that year)
1260 x 2 (2520 years) later =   (Sep 21/22 2000 if 521 or **Sep 11/12, 2001 if 520**)
Twin Towers in NY fall

Haggai 2:1   **"shaking of all nations"   7th month 21st (Oct 17), 520 BC**
(last day of Feast of Tabernacles)
"In a little while I will once more shake the heavens and the earth, the sea and the dry land"
Hag. 2:6   Hebrews 12:26,27 applies this verse to the second coming of Christ
1260 x 2 (2520 years) later Afghanistan bombed

2520 days = 7 x 360 day-years   (Leviticus 26:18,21,24,28 **seven times punishment**)

607/606 BC Nebuchadnezzar took Zedekiah to Babylon, 10th day 5th lunar month (Jer 52:12,13)
+ 2520 years = **10th day 5th lunar month = Aug 1, 1914 beginning of World War I**.
Dec 9 (24th day of 9th month), 1917 Jerusalem freed from Turkish rule by British Army under General Allenby, from 607 BC is 2520 years.

56 Prophesy Again! **Seven Heads Rise Again**

Although the U.S. had a Charges d'Affaires to the Papal States from the years 1848-1869, the first Ambassador to the Vatican was William A. Wilson, appointed by President Ronald Reagan in 1984.

With the collapse of Communism, the secret crusade of President and Pope seemed to have secured its success. But the Vatican had a secret agenda unknown to even Reagan. The fall of "that evil empire" was only the beginning. It wasn't until early 1990 that Pope John Paul II revealed the Vatican's complete plan. "A united Europe is no longer a dream. It is not utopian memory from the middle ages. The events that we are witnessing show that this goal can be reached." *New York Times*, April 23, 1990.

The Pope aspired to revive the Holy Roman Empire of the Middle Ages when no one dared question the Papacy's claim to be the Kingdom of God on earth. That glorious hour of Papal Rome was written in blood. Historians call it the Dark Ages.

Ancient Babylon and Modern Babylon follow similar courses:

Stage	BC	Ancient Babylon	AC	Modern Babylon
Defeat and Occupation	609 605 597	Siege of Jerusalem. Jewish king stays First captivity. Jewish king removed	1991 2003	Sanctions against Iraq. Saddam remains. US occupies Iraq. Iraqi president removed.
Mental Disorder	570's	Nebuchadnezzar suffers Lycantrophy for 7 years, lived like an animal, long fingernails and long wild hair		Reagan suffers Alzheimer's John Paul II afflicted by Parkinson's disease Saddam lives like an animal in a hole, has long hair, lice when captured
Attack Worship	602 586	Decree to worship golden image (idol) 2nd captivity. Temple destroyed Persians legislate time of worship under penalty of death (den of lions)		Image to the beast worshiped Mark of the Beast enforced Sabbath worship endangered under penalty of death
Last Leader	535	Belshazzar throws drunken party shows disrespect for religion Babylon falls in one night		A drinker, overly confident mixes religion with politics makes nations drunk with immorality
Rescue	535	Kings of the east defeat Babylon Free Israel by drying up Euphrates		Euphrates dried up during 6th plague Kings from east rescue the church

Nebuchadnezzar and Saddam Hussein
Nebuchadnezzar was humbled by God "Is this not Babylon which I have made with my own hands?"
Saddam Hussein was humbled by America. He also boasted of being the second Nebuchanezzar and was actively perusing the restoration of ancient Babylon in defiance of Biblical prophecy.
Iraq was ironically conquered in the same way that Nebuchadnezzar conquered Jerusalem.
But in conquering and occupying Iraq, America becomes Babylon the Great that will meddle with religion.

Ancient Babylon was allowed to conquer Jerusalem and take Judah captive as a punishment to Israel.
Because Judah had become idolaters, the temple was destroyed.
Because Judah did not observe the weekly Sabbath, the city gates were burned.
Because Judah did not observe the 7th year Sabbath, the land was evacuated and allowed to rest 70 years.

Nebuchadnezzar and George Bush
Nebuchanezzar made more than one invasion of Judah.
The first was in 605 BC when he nearly hauled Jehoiakim off to Babylon but instead placed the Jewish king under stiff economic sanctions. When he later rebelled, Nebuchadnezzar returned in 598, besieged the city, killed his son, Jehoiachin (who reigned only part of a year) and installed his uncle, naming him Zedekiah.

Twelve years later in 586 BC he returned, removed the Jewish king, destroyed the temple, and installed his own designated ruler. Zedekiah was blinded, imprisoned, and his sons executed.

The United States made more than one invasion of Iraq.
The first invasion of Iraq in 1991 left Saddam in power but with severe economic restrictions.

Twelve years later in 2003 the US returned, removed Saddam from power, and conducted elections. Saddam's two sons, Udei and Qusay, were killed in a shoot out on July 22, 2003. Saddam was captured Dec 13, 2003 under a rock in a hole in the ground and imprisoned.

The lapse of twelve years, despite three intervening presidential elections and potential changes in government administrations, personnel and policies, expired with a president in power by the same name with key administrative positions filled by the same individuals involved in the first, original invasion. It was like a time warp, as if nothing had changed.

Nebuchadnezzar Strikes Twice
The chronology of the last three kings of Judah has an interesting mirrored symmetry.
From the beginning of Jehoiakim's reign to the beginning of Zedekiah's reign is 12 years.
From the end of Jehoiakim's reign to the end of Zedekiah's reign is 12 years.
Nebuchadnezzar stormed Jerusalem the first time in the 3rd year of Jehoiakim's reign
Nebuchadnezzar be signed the city for the final time 3 years from the end of Zedekiah's reign.

Jehoiakim reigned 11 years
Nebuchadnezzar's first invasion was in Jehoiakim's 3rd year.
Daniel taken to Babylon.
News of his father's death caused Nebuchadnezzar to suddenly return to Babylon.
Jehoiakim was allowed to continued as a "puppet" vassal king.
His last three years were under servitude to Nebuchadnezzar (increased tribute?)
Nebuchadnezzar came and bound him in fetters, carried him and temple vessels to Babylon
Jehoiachin reigned 3 months 10 days
Servants of Nebuchadnezzar came and besieged Jerusalem
"In the eight year of his [Nebuchadnezzar's] reign" 2 Kings 24:12, i.e., 8 years after first invasion.
Nebuchadnezzar sent and brought him to Babylon with goodly vessels of temple, 10K captives, the princes, all the mighty men, craftsmen, smiths and Ezekiel.
He put his uncle, (Jehoiakim's brother?) Mattaniah on the throne and changed his name to Zedekiah
Zedekiah reigned 11 years
Nebuchadnezzar came in the 9th year, 10th month, 10th day surrounded Jerusalem.
The siege lasted parts of three years.
Nebuchadnezzar finally destroyed the temple, broke down the wall, burnt all the palaces

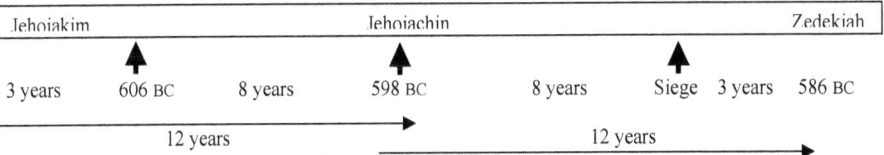

58 Prophesy Again! **Seven Heads Rise Again**

Throughout redemptive history Abomination is always followed by a time of trouble and ultimate desolation as illustrated in the experience of Israel, Spiritual Babylon, future Babylon the Great and Gog-Magog.

Abomination set up Daniel 11:31-39	**Time of Trouble** Daniel 11:40-45	**Desolation** Daniel 12

Israel Falls   31 AD destroyed
    Jesus removed daily
    Israel rejected Christ
	Church persecuted 1260 days?
	 Rome in middle east wars
	 Jerusalem surrounded 66 AD
		Abomination: Jerusalem
		
		 Judgment: Jews Exiled 70 AD

Papacy Falls 538
    Priests replace Christ
    Idolatry, Pagan doctrines
	Heretics persecuted 1260 years
	 Napoleon invades Palestine
	 Signs in heaven and earth
		Abomination: Papacy wounded
		 Judgment: 1798, 1844

Babylon Falls (future)
    Antichrist
    Idol worship
	Beast persecution 1260 days
	 USA in middle east wars
	 Jerusalem surrounded
		Satan, Babylon, Papacy Falls
		 Seven last plagues
		 Second Coming, Resurrection

Gog & Magog (after millennium) Satan loosed to deceive	New Jerusalem surrounded	Hell Fire final destruction

There is also the repeated pattern of Exodus and Deliverance:

Enemy Falls	**Israel Leaves**	**Enemy Rises Again**	**God Rescues**	**Israel goes Home**
Egypt Falls	Exodus	Pharaoh pursues after them	Red Sea	Promised Land
Papacy Falls	Reformation	Papal wound healed	Second Coming	Heaven
Satan Falls	Second Coming	Satan unloosed & attacks	Hell Fire	New Earth

Prophets for the Final Exodus

Jeremiah, Ezekiel	**Daniel**	**Elijah**	**Moses, Ezekiel**
Ate the book	Unsealed	Against idolatry	Leave Egypt, avoid plagues Ex
Tested and mocked	message to Babylon	message to Israel	Message to Egypt, Babylon
Daniel studied	Worship God	Leave Babylon	Get the Mark of God Ez 9
1844 Disappointment	1st Angel's message	2nd Angel's message	3rd Angel's message

World Wonders
2005 John Paul II's funeral coverage

Associated Press 1:33 p.m. ET April 8, 2005
VATICAN CITY – "Presidents, prime ministers and kings joined pilgrims and prelates in St. Peter's Square on Friday to bid an emotional farewell to Pope John Paul II at a funeral that drew millions to Rome."

2005 Benedict XVI calls for a unified Europe and return to Sunday sacredness

60 Prophesy Again! **Seven Heads Rise Again**

First Fulfillment in Prophetic Time
1260 years...Papacy Falls   Wound Healed

Second Fulfillment
1260 days....Babylon Falls

27 AD	1260 days	30 days	1290th day	45 days	1335th day
Jesus Baptized in the Jordan	3½ year witness & ministry of Christ	Transfiguration?	3 ½ days? Last Supper Crucifixion Resurrection DEATH	actually 50 days 40 days of many infallible proofs + 10 in one accord	Pentecost Blessing

1260 period appears again during second half of the 70th week:

31 AD	1260 days	30 days	1290th day	45 days	1335th day
Baptism of the Holy Spirit At Pentecost	Preaching & Witnessing in Jerusalem	Stephen does great wonders and miracles	3 ½ days Trial & Stoning of Stephen 34 AD DEATH	Persecution by Saul Evangelism by Philip	Blessing Bright Light from heaven Saul Converted

66 AD	1260 days	30 days	1290th day	45 days	1335th day
Siege of Jerusalem begins	Jerusalem under siege		3 ½ days? Destruction 70 AD DEATH	1 ½ months	Blessing Cestus withdrew Christians escape

on the larger scale these two are related :

27-31 AD	1260 days	30 days	1290th day	45 days	1335th day
Ministry of Christ	42 years (mo) Peter & Paul Preach & witness	1 year 43rd year Siege of Jerusalem	3 ½ years DEATH 66 – 70 AD Peter & Paul die	1 ½ years	Blessing war ends at Masada 73 AD
	27 + 42 = 69				31 + 42 = 73

Both Solomon's Temple burned in 586 BC and Herod's Temple burned in 70 AD occurred on 9th of Av.

508 AD	1260 days	30 days	1290th day	45 days	1335th day
Papacy rises to power with Clovis' help	Papacy Rules 538 AD begins		3 ½ years French Revolution 1793-1797 **DEATH 1798**	1798+54 = 1843	Blessing Advent Hope Judgment Begins

Finally, The Second Fall of Babylon the Great

	1260 days	30 days	1290th day	45 days	1335th day
Church-State Union Religious Legislation	Persecution Cannot buy/sell Two Witnesses preach & plague	Death Penalty declared	Death Penalty executed Two Witnesses killed 3½ days	7 Last Plagues begin	Blessing Second Coming

History Repeated

> Nebuchadnezzar came against Jerusalem 607 BC, imposing stiff financial demands on them, then finally conquered it 586 BC 10 years later, taking its king Zedekiah captive and killing his sons
>
> U.S. came against Iraq 1991, placed it under severe economic sanctions, but left Saddam in power. then finally conquered it in 2003 12 years later, taking Saddam captive and killing his sons

> Spiritual Babylon has deadly wound, healed and forms Babylon & deceives the world, then burned with fire.
> Satan as Christ has deadly wound at SC, after millennium, healed and deceives again, then burned with fire.

But the harlot that does not repent will come to a sudden end.
"Two things shall come upon you in a moment, in one day: loss of children and widowhood" Isa 47:9.

Euphrates Dries Up

Revelation 17:16-18 tells of a time when the alliance that supports Babylon collapses.
As waters are "nations and languages, tongues and peoples," the waters drying up could speak of the evaporated support from "the coalition."

The waters, of course, could also be the literal Euphrates river. In fact, the real river is drying up. Turkey, from where the headwaters of the Euphrates originate, is engaged in a massive hydroelectric construction project involving some new 22 dams. Two dams have been completed. The Ataturk dam in 1996 and the Belkis dam in April, 2000. These alone have decreased the water flow to 40% of its original levels.

While ancient Babylon built a golden image and imposed a forced worship of it, modern Babylon may perform much the same by legislating a single place, method and time for worship. With news of the proposed WTC memorial and the emotionally charged nature of its historical meaning, there may very well be a literal image that becomes a test of national loyalty and commitment to the war against terrorism.

Revelation 18 accurately describes the Fall of Babylon the Great.
September 11, 2001 the Twin Towers of the World Trade Center fell. "Babylon is Fallen is Fallen"
The towers were a center of commerce. The merchants wail at the sight of the rising smoke.
The two towers fell within one hour of each other, as specified: 9:58AM and 10:28AM.
The events of September 2001 were not the ultimate fulfillment of Revelation 18. That will be a global fall. It was only a prelude, in miniature. Yet it is an important event, nonetheless, arresting the attention of the world and hopefully calling all to reinvestigate Biblical prophecy. It triggered a political upheaval, a religious war, and an economic earthquake. Revelation 18, when it is finally fulfilled will effect all people, all nations, religions and economies.

Now that Modern Babylon has taken over the role of world control, the first order of business will be to establish a universal standardized worldwide religion. Eliminate the factions, the doctrinally diverse, and mandate a single uniform mode of worship.

Notice how events in the political and religious worlds coincide in the following chart and commentary found at teachinghearts.com

Seven Heads Rise Again

	Daniel 11:40 – 12:1	Politics	Religion
War	"At the end time the king of the South will collide with him [king of the north], and the king of the North will storm against him with chariots, with horsemen and with many ships;"	Kuwait and 9-11 attacks	Civil laws changed
Other Countries	"and he will enter countries, overflow them and pass through."	Military Bases established	Concordats
Palestine	"He will also enter the Beautiful Land, and many counties will fall;"	Control	Agreement with Yassir Arafat
Jordan	"but these will be rescued out of his hand: Edom, Moab and the foremost of the sons of Amon."	Friend	Laodicea
Egypt	Then he will stretch out his hand against the countries, and the land of Egypt will not escape. But he will gain control over the hidden treasures of gold and silver and over all the precious things of Egypt.	War with Egypt or Egyptian part of Al-Qaeda	Secularism, media
Libya, Ethiopia	and Libyans and Ethiopians will follow at his heels.	Submission	Ecumenical Alliances
Rumors	But rumors from the East and from the North will disturb him, and he will go out with great wrath to destroy and annihilate many.	Opposition. Another threat	The spread of the Gospel
Israel Occupied	He will pitch the tents of his royal pavilion between the seas and the beautiful Holy Mountain; yet he will come to his end, and no one will help him.	Military Base	Leader of Jerusalem
Persecution	Now at that time Michael, the great prince who stands guard over the sons of your people, will arise. And there will be a time of distress such as never occurred since there was a nation until that time; and at that time your people, everyone who is found written in the book, will be rescued.	Jerusalem surrounded	Mark of the beast persecution

Daniel 11 covers the same period of time that Babylon the Great reigns. It begins when the king of the north is attacked provoking a war against the king of the south. The 9-11 attacks came suddenly, seemingly without warning. But the events before and subsequent to that date are provided to wake us up, like the trumpet blast they are, and give us clues for what is yet to happen.

Egypt has always been the kingdom of the south. But Saudi Arabia is also south of Israel and Iraq. This king of the south attacked the king of the north as prophesied and provokes the war of verse 40. The 9-11 hijackers were mostly Saudi and many were Egyptian. Mastermind and planner for Osama Bin Laden was an Egyptian doctor named Ayman Al-Sawahiri. America, the king of the north, responded with modern chariots: Hummers, tanks and Bradley's, even real horses in the rugged terrain of Afghanistan, and many ships filling the Arabian gulf with aircraft carriers and nuclear subs.

Other countries are involved in the war on terrorism besides Iraq. Prior to 1991 US had military bases in Saudi Arabia, Oman, Bahrain and Yemen. Since 1991 US has established military bases or alliances with Iraq (14 bases), Afghanistan (invaded 2001), Libya (submitted following economic sanctions), Pakistan, Kyrgyzstan, Tajikistan, Uzbekistan, Kuwait, Qatar, Turkey, Djibouti, Somalia, Israel, Jordan, and as of 2005 with the Syrian backed assassination of former president, Rafik Hariri, Lebanon is now freed of Syrian occupation. Only Syria, Iran, Egypt and Ethiopia remain unaligned.

The Beautiful Land
When Israel was established in 1948, United Nations resolution 181 Part III allowed for an international solution for the government of Jerusalem if peace could not be negotiated. On February 15, 2000, Yassir Arafat signed an agreement with Pope John Paul II to have a world capital solution under this resolution placing the Pope as the head and the United Nations as the military force. On July 22, 2003, Shimon Peres indicated his agreement with a "World Capital" solution which would assign the UN Secretary General as major of Jerusalem.

Power	Jerusalem	Worship	Final War
Babylon	Besieged Jerusalem 609, 597, 586	Golden Image vs furnace	Euphrates dried up
Persia	Jews return to Jerusalem	Rebuilds temple	Harman's decree
Greece	Alexander worships at Jerusalem	Antiochus pollutes temple	Macabbean Revolt
Rome	Besieged Jerusalem 70	Destroyed temple	Christian persecutions
Papacy	Crusades to capture Jerusalem 1099	Inquisition	Reformation
Napoleon	Entered Palestine 1799	Removed Pope 1798	Napoleonic Wars
Hitler	Entered Palestine 194?	Forced Fuehrer worship	WWII
US-Vatican	Jerusalem becomes world capital ?	Worship of Beast	Time of Trouble/Plagues
False Christ	Comes to rule from Jerusalem	Worship of Beast's image	Second Coming
Satan	Surrounds New Jerusalem	Bows knee to Christ	Armageddon

Jordan (ancient Edom, Moab and Ammon) maintains friendly relations with the United States. The former queen Noor is also an American.

Egypt was definitely involved in the 9-11 events, supporter of Bin Laden and perhaps even sheltering him. It may foster a new crop of Al-Qaeda fighters. It appears destined to receive the ire of America and its treasures, unlike those looted during Iraq's invasion, to be more carefully controlled when the northern king attacks it. "The land of Egypt will not escape." Al-Qaeda bombed two hotels on October 7, 2004.

On December 19, 2003, **Libya** announced it would cooperate in the destruction of their nuclear, chemical and biological weapons programs after 18 years of economic sanctions. The prophecy states that **Ethiopia** (which includes the modern nations of Eritrea, Djibouti and Sudan) to follow Libya's lead. Sudan, at least, has entered negotiations over its treatment of Christians as of December, 2003, and signed a peace treaty on January 8, 2005, ending twenty years of war.

Rumors from the North-East
This could be threats of WMD or defection of allies. China and Russia pose significant threats to the western powers involvement in Iraq/Iran. China may have its sights on becoming the next superpower, given its growing economic development, after the West exhausts itself with the war on terrorism. This was the career path America took as it emerged following WWII. A further possibility is that the North-East refers to the Northeastern United States and may indicate that another terrorist attack may occur as a preliminary sign of the final fulfillment.

A more likely possibility is Iran, Pakistan or Afghanistan. Pakistan is very risky, supporting the US in spite of its Muslim majority, and possessing nuclear weapons. Iran is already in the cross-hairs for its outspoken ambition for acquiring nuclear capability. It was also, using its alias of Persia, the power that defeated Babylon of old. Iran, though previously at war with Iraq, now shares with the Iraqis a common Islamic ideology. Both have a Shi'a majority and may view the current state of affairs as justification to annex Iraq and consolidate their commonality. In addition to the physical fulfillment, the spiritual will also occur as Christ's coming (from the east and the sides of the north) alarms the wicked.

Persia Frees Israel
Remember that the role of ancient Persia was not a negative one in its relationship with Israel. Cyrus was a type of Christ. He freed the Jews to return to Judah and provided them with funds and authority to rebuild the temple. Rome and Babylon destroyed it. And Greece corrupted its priesthood. Revelation 16:12 tells us that it is the kings of the east who will once again rescue the people of God by drying up the Euphrates. Thus it is possible that in the coming war with Iran, they will employ the Euphrates in some way to defeat the US and liberate the persecuted remnant.

64 Prophesy Again! **Seven Heads Rise Again**

"Four angels bound to the River Euphrates are released to dry it up and make way for the kings of the east."
Physical
As waters are "nations and languages, tongues and peoples," the waters drying up could speak of the evaporated support from "the coalition." The waters, of course, could also be the literal Euphrates river. In fact, the real river is drying up. Turkey, from where the headwaters of the Euphrates originate, is engaged in a massive hydroelectric construction project involving some new 22 dams. Two dams have been completed. The Ataturk dam in 1996 and the Belkis dam in April, 2000. These alone have decreased the water flow to 40% of its original levels.
Spiritual
The waters could be symbolic of those in heaven: the "waters above" placed there at creation.
The heavens will be parted as a scroll as Jesus comes. Perhaps these are the waters of Euphrates.
Revelation 17:16-18 tells of a time when the alliance that supports Babylon collapses.
Thus, the remnant are rescued by the drying up of the Euphrates.

While ancient Babylon built a golden image and imposed a forced worship of it, modern Babylon may perform much the same by legislating a single place, method and time for worship. With news of the proposed WTC memorial and the emotionally charged nature of its historical meaning, there may very well be a literal image that becomes a test of national loyalty and commitment to the war against terrorism.

http://www.whitehouse.gov/news/releases/2006/03/20060307-5.html

President * News * Vice President * History & Tours * First Lady * Mrs. Cheney
YOUR GOVERNMENT   KIDS   ESPAÑOL   CONTACT   PRIVACY POLICY   SITE MAP   SEARCH

The White House
PRESIDENT GEORGE W. BUSH
HOME   EMAIL UPDATES   SEARCH

Executive Order:
Responsibilities of the Department of Homeland Security with Respect to Faith-Based and Community Initiatives

For Immediate Release
Office of the Press Secretary
March 7, 2006

By the authority vested in me as President by the Constitution and the laws of the United States of America, and in order to help the Federal Government coordinate a national effort **to expand opportunities for faith-based** and other community organizations and **to strengthen their capacity** to better meet America's social and community needs, it is hereby ordered as follows:

Section 1. Establishment of a Center for Faith-Based and Community Initiatives at the Department of Homeland Security.

(a) The Secretary of Homeland Security (Secretary) shall **establish** within the Department of Homeland Security (Department) **a Center for Faith-Based** and Community **Initiatives** (Center).

(b) The Center shall be supervised by a Director appointed by Secretary. The Secretary shall consult with the Director of the White House Office of Faith-Based and Community Initiatives (WHOFBCI Director) prior to making such appointment.

(c) The Department shall provide the Center with **appropriate staff, administrative support, and other resources** to meet its responsibilities under this order.

(d) The Center shall begin operations no later than **45 days from the date of this order**.

OFFICIAL NOTICE THAT THE SEPARATION OF CHURCH & STATE HAS ENDED.

Revelation 18 accurately describes the Fall of Babylon the Great.
September 11, 2001 the Twin Towers of the World Trade Center fell. "Babylon is Fallen is Fallen"
The towers were a center of commerce. The merchants wailed at the sight of the rising smoke.
The two towers fell within one hour of each other, as specified: 9:58AM and 10:28AM.
The events of September 2001 were not the ultimate fulfillment of Revelation 18. That will be a global fall. It was only a prelude, in miniature. Yet it is an important event, nonetheless, arresting the attention of the world and hopefully calling all to reinvestigate Biblical prophecy. It triggered a political upheaval, a religious war, and an economic earthquake. Revelation 18, when it is finally fulfilled will effect all people, all nations, religions and economies.

The Beautiful Land
When Israel was established in 1948, United Nations resolution 181 Part III allowed for an international solution for the government of Jerusalem if peace could not be negotiated. On February 15, 2000, Yassir Arafat signed an agreement with Pope John Paul II to have a world capital solution under this resolution placing the Pope as the head and the United Nations as the military force. On July 22, 2003, Shimon Peres indicated his agreement with a "World Capital" solution which would assign the UN Secretary General as major of Jerusalem.

Power	Jerusalem	Worship	Final War
Babylon	Besieged Jerusalem 609, 597, 586	Golden Image vs furnace	Euphrates dried up
Persia	Jews return to Jerusalem	Rebuilds temple	Harman's decree
Greece	Alexander worships at Jerusalem	Antiochus pollutes temple	Macabbean Revolt
Rome	Besieged Jerusalem 70		Christian persecutions
Papacy	Crusades to capture Jerusalem 1099	Destroyed temple	Reformation
Napoleon	Entered Palestine 1799	Inquisition	Napoleonic Wars
Hitler	Entered Palestine 194?	Removed Pope 1798	WWII
US-Vatican	Jerusalem becomes world capital ?	Forced Fuehrer worship	Time of Trouble/Plagues
False Christ	Comes to rule from Jerusalem	Worship of Beast	Second Coming
Satan	Surrounds New Jerusalem	Worship of Beast's image	Armageddon
		Bows knee to Christ	

Jordan (ancient Edom, Moab and Ammon) maintains friendly relations with the United States. The former queen Noor is an American.

Persia Frees Israel
On the other hand, the role of ancient Persia was not a negative one in its relationship with Israel. Cyrus, remember, was a type of Christ. He freed the Jews to return to Judah and provided them with funds and authority to rebuild the temple. Rome and Babylon destroyed it. And Greece corrupted its priesthood. Revelation 16:12 tells us that it is the kings of the east who will once again rescue the people of God by drying up the Euphrates. Thus it is possible that in the coming war with Iran, they will employ the Euphrates in some way to defeat the US and liberate the persecuted remnant.

With the departure of Syria from Lebanon after 29 years of occupation in April 2005, the repeat "fall of Assyria" is once again played out. Assyria fell as ancient Babylon became the world power.

66 Prophesy Again! **Seven Heads Rise Again**

Muslim Prophecies

Because the Islamic faith is based in a large part on the books of Moses, it shares many of the same prophetic teachings regarding events at the end of the world. Muslims believe that the United States is the great satan because it is attacking the Muslim nations on behalf of the Jews as their prophecies predict. Furthermore, the Muslim prophecies say that the war will be in Afghanistan, Baghdad and Syria. But Islam will win the Battle of Qa'im. One very interesting prophecy predicts that the final battle between good and evil will be fought in the holy nation of Iran and that Evil will lose.

Muslim End Time Events:

Muslim prophecies predict the coming of the 12th Imam. Imams are essentially equivalent to the Pope. Both are considered infallible. Both are reputedly manifestations of God on earth. Both hold extreme authority over the faithful. Both favor the union of church and state. Islamic theology teaches that the 12th Imam will appear after an absence of 1000 years to bring universal peace and perfect justice to the world.

Four main characters in Islamic end-time prophecy.
1 Al-Dajjal, Islam's coming evil "antichrist"
2 Jesus will come down and defeat Al-Dajjal, rule for a time, and then die.
3 Mahdi, the 12th Imam Muslim Messiah who will bring peace and utopia
4 Al-Harith ibn Hirath, who will establish Mahdi's government and cause all to serve him.

Dajjal will:
Be an evil antichrist false Messiah
Be blind in one eye
Have the letters "KFR" on his forehead
Appear as a sunrise in the West after a war and a plague
Claim to be a prophet
Work miracles around the world
Travel at high speed
Bring droughts and floods
Places a mark on the people.

Mosque for Fatima in Qom, Iran

Islamic prophecies mention Gog and Magog, destructive powers from the North.
They also believe that Jesus (Isa) will return from heaven to a mosque in Damascus.
But this time under orders from God to confess that He is not God's son as He originally claimed.
He will then call the peoples of the world to Islam (surrender).
He will kill the Daajal and destroys Gog and Magog, and enforces Islamic law.
He will break all the crosses and kill all the Christians and Jews (nonbelievers in Muhammed) who refuse to convert to Islam.

Mahdi will:
Be a young man with black hair
Come from the east
   at the same time that Daajal appears
Ride a white horse
As a conquering hero at the head of a great army
Raised to power by Allah in one day
Bear the full name of Islam's prophet,
   Muhammad ibn Abd-Allah

Descended from Muhammad's daughter, Fatima
Act and talk, but not look like, Muhammad
Have a high forehead and hooked nose
Rule for seven years (or some say 9 or even 19)
Bring peace and distribute great wealth
   to those who serve him.
Appear after a great fire in the sky in Iraq

The Cleansing of the Sanctuary and the Time of the End

In the early 1980's a tremendous time of difficulty and opportunity arose in the Seventh-day Adventist Church. A well-known and respected professor was giving a series of lectures. The context of those lectures fueled a revival in many quarters and a division in others. The context of the message was threefold.

- **First**, that the church had misunderstood the cleansing of the sanctuary. Christ, in fact, did not go to the most holy Place as taught by Adventist theologians. This, according to the lecturer, took place in 31 AD when Jesus ascended to His throne.
- **Second**, the day year principle of prophecy as taught by the Seventh-day Adventist Church was flawed. Because of this, when Daniel 8:14 speaks of two-thousand three hundred days it was really meant only 1150 days and this spoke of Antiochus Epiphanies.
- **Thirdly**, the sanctuary message of the Seventh-day Adventist Church depended too much on the writings of Ellen White and not enough on sound Biblical principles.

This was a unique turn around for this man who just a few years before had written his own book on the meaning of Daniel. This lecturer, of course, was Desmond Ford. One of my favorite non-biblical authors, writing almost 80 years earlier, said the following. "Be not deceived; many will depart from the faith, giving heed to seducing spirits and doctrines of devils. We have now before us the alpha of this danger. The omega will be of a most startling nature." (*Selected Messages* vol. 1 page 197).

If you were to follow Mr. Ford in his theology to some logical conclusion, one would be startled and amazed. For example, by making 1844 a non-effectual day in biblical teaching would be a major mistake. For what it would do is take away concepts such as Righteousness by Faith as seen in the Sanctuary service. Further, this opinion also seems to call for elimination of the process of Sanctification. It would in essence seem to be saying that once you accepted Jesus Christ as Lord and Master that you could never be lost. In other words, "Once saved always saved." Nothing could be further from the truth. We know that man must cooperate daily with his Creator, Redeemer, and Sustainer, Jesus Christ. Man must yield to Him through the indwelling power of the Holy Spirit. In many ways the "New Theology" makes of non-effect the power of the cross and the perfect substitutionary sacrifice provided for mankind.

Thus we want to affirm that we hold true all the fundamental teachings and truths as presented by the Seventh-day Adventist church. We believe that the historical model is the most correct of all models of biblical prophecy. We also believe, however, that there are yet prophetic details to be more fully understood as the nearness of the second coming approaches. In *Christ's Object Lessons* the inspired author wrote on page127 the following: "In every generation there is a new development of truth, a message of God to the people of that generation. The old truths are all essential, new truth is not independent of the old, but an unfolding of it. It is only as the old truths are understood that we can comprehend the new."

What are these old truths that we speak about in Daniel 8? Let us try to give a thumbnail sketch in our review. In this chapter we are introduced to several different symbols. Most notable is a ram, a goat, and a little horn power. This little horn power seeks to destroy the truths of salvation. Gabriel himself interpreted the vision to Daniel when he tells him that the ram with two horns were the Medes and the Persians. The He-goat which he saw was Greece. We know that historically the symbol for Greece was in actuality a goat. For many years tradition has held that Caremus the first king of Macedon (later known as Greece) followed a herd of wild goats to Edessa where it is said that he established his capital city of Aege or the "goat city." The Aegean Sea, surrounding the Greek isles, is known as the "goat sea."

68 Prophesy Again! **Cleansing the Sanctuary**

We also know that Alexander eventually became ruler of the emerging Greek Empire until his death when it was divided among his four generals. The great horn was broken.

Next we see the little horn power. In Chapter seven Daniel told us that this little horn power came up through secular Imperial Rome but was distinctly religious in nature.
- It speaks great words against the Most High.
- It wages are against the saints.
- It seeks to change times and laws.
- It blasphemes God's name and those that dwell in heaven.

This little horn power was none other than spiritual Rome.

Another interesting characteristic of all three of these symbols is how their final destination is to reach the pleasant land, which is in Israel, specifically Jerusalem.

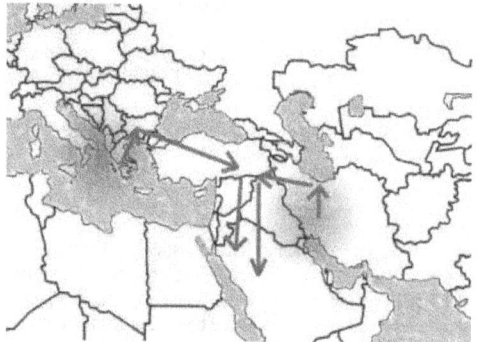

No review of Daniel 8 would be complete without mentioning verses 13 and 14. These wonderful verses uphold and support the investigative judgment which began in 1844. It further teaches all three aspects of salvation. These three aspects are justification, sanctification and glorification—none of which could take place without the shedding of the blood of the unblemished lamb, a symbol of Jesus. See John1:29. The 2300 day prophecy of Daniel 8:14, then, ended in 1844 and is a true way mark in Adventist history.

But while it closes the door of History for the church we must ask the question, "Does it open another door on exciting new discoveries?" In the coming pages we will seek to give a secondary opinion on these texts—not one which is dogmatic, but exploratory in nature. We do this in conjunction with the inspired author who wrote the following in the Review and Herald December 20th 1892:

> "There is no excuse for anyone taking the position that there is no more truth to be revealed and that our expositions of scripture are without error. The fact that certain doctrines [not our fundamental beliefs] have been held as truth for many years by our people is not a proof that our ideas are infallible."

An example of this, we believe, can be seen in the way many of the evangelists in the 1920's and 1930's taught that Israel would never be a nation again based upon their interpretation of prophecy. The Old Testament passages which painted a victorious picture of Israel becoming the center of the world, leading other nations to the worship of Jehovah, were identified as conditional prophecies which were invalidated by the rejection of Christ at the end of the 70 weeks. That Israel *did* become a nation in 1948 is today an undisputable fact of history. The importance of this event, however, must be properly understood from a theological and eschatological point of view. A sobering admonition on just this point comes again from the pen of inspiration in *The Great Controversy* pages 36 and 37:

> "The Saviour's prophecy concerning the visitation of judgments upon Jerusalem is to have another fulfillment, of which that terrible desolation was but a faint shadow. In the fate of the chosen city we may behold the doom of a world that has rejected God's mercy and trampled upon His law. Let men beware lest they neglect the lesson conveyed to them in the words of Christ. As He warned of Jerusalem's destruction, giving them a sign of the approaching ruin that they might make their escape, so He has warned the world of the day of final destruction and has given them tokens of its approach, that all who will may flee from the wrath to come."

Together let us re-examine then chapter 8 of Daniel.
Some of the questions we must ask are:
- What nations represent the symbols of Daniel 8 today?
- Are the meanings suggested today consistent with Adventists Theology?
- Does history actually repeat itself? .

One of these questions leads us to Verses 13 and 14. Certainly it is true that the end of the 2300 day year prophecy terminated in 1844. This was known then and today as one of the anchor points for ushering in the "Time of the End." Yet we know that this was a time of "Great disappointment" amongst the early pioneer believer who thought Christ would return in 1844. It was only when they read Revelation 10:8-11 that they understood the reason for their experience. Verse 11 said they must continue to prophesy. This is consistent with one of those early pioneers who wrote in the small book *Testimonies to Ministers* page 113: "The light that Daniel received from God was given especially for these last days. The visions he saw by the banks of the Ulai and the Hiddekel, the great rivers of the Shinar, are now in process of fulfillment, and all the events foretold will soon come to pass."

Therefore, simply stated, we believe that an examination of what has transpired since 1844 is entirely consistent with fundamental Adventist theology. One would not have to look far to secure possible answers. Let's go back and look at these symbols once again The ram which had two horns in today's society can only be two nations: Iraq and Iran.

Iraq historically was the nation of Media while the Iranians were known as the Persians. There has been a love-hate relationship for thousands of years between these two neighbors. Some commentators suggest that Cyrus and Darius were in some way related. Though in many ways their cultures stay united through religious means, Persia, and now Iran, has held the superior hand. Even as the Medes had their hand in world powers historically so the Iraqi's had their time in the spotlight as well.

After the Shah of Iran fell from power in 1978 and was replaced by Islamic fundamentalists under the Ayatollah Khomeini, the United States did everything it could to keep Iran from becoming a force in the Middle East. The United States even sent large amounts of weaponry to support the opposition. Some commentators and historians even believe that certain types of weapons of mass destruction were supplied. There is no doubt, however, that when the conflict between these two neighbors came to an end they both continued exporting terrorism. Iraq under the leadership of Saddam Hussein tried to control the rest of the Middle East by force. Iran on the other hand tried to control the rest of the Middle East through her brand of Islamic fundamentalism. To the west this has become known as Jihad or holy war.

Notice, now, which direction the ram is pushing. It is going westward, northward, and southward. It is heading toward the same territory at which the little horn power is aiming. Both of these powers are trying to export something they have. What is it that they both possess in common. The answer is a false religion or definition of God.

Both of them think they are the greatest religion.
Both are based on working your way to heaven.
Both have a totalitarian form of government.
Both favor the union of church and state.
Both have the goal of world domination.

The ram's power is said to be great
while the little horns power is exceedingly great.

But here the similarities end. In verse five of chapter 8 it tells us that another power from the west which is very great and smashes the ram. Daniel describes this power as a goat with a horn. While historically we recognize this was Greece, we ask the question in all sincerity and humbly, is there an animal or kingdom described as a he-goat in Revelation which is described in its youth as Lamb-like. The answer, of course, is yes—the United States of America.

Now back to verse five.
The United States has attacked this region twice.
The purpose for this is threefold.

- **First,** Islam as a religion is exporting terror around the world because it is based upon world domination. Many scholars are trying to tell us that Islam is a religion of peace. In our opinion, this is far from the truth. As you read the Koran you do not read about mans duty to his fellow man, because of his relationship with God. There is no Golden Rule; no Ten Commandments. The Koran simply tells you that "Allah," is better than all other gods.
- **Secondly**, the United States knew that Iraq had weapons of mass destruction because they either shared the technology with her or provided the actual weapons themselves. We know for certain that the United States was funneling everything but nukes to Saddam as he fought Iran for eight years. When they finally signed a peace accord it worried our leaders in Washington.
- **Thirdly,** as much as we would try and ignore it, we have a national interest in this part of the world—oil. To deny otherwise would continue to make us the laughingstock of the rest of the world.

Verses 5 and six describe the kind of "Shock and Awe" firepower fury by which we attacked.

Someone may be asking however, as they read these words, "in your context how does this western power or the United States come to an end, with the four notable winds?" This is a valid question. First we believe, as the inspired pen writes, that the time is coming when our influence as a nation will be far less than it is now. Why? because the beast power will eventually be in greater control of the world. Further we know, according to the same source, that

> "Legislators will yield to the demand for a Sunday law. …By the decree enforcing the institution of the papacy in violation of the law of God, our nation will disconnect herself fully from righteousness. …As the approach of the Roman armies was a sign to the disciples of the impending destruction of Jerusalem, so may this apostasy [Sunday law] be a sign to us that the limit of God's forbearance is reached, that the measure of our nation's iniquity is full, and that the angel of mercy is about to take her flight never to return." 5T 451

> "It is at the time of national apostasy [when the national Sunday law is passed], when acting on the policy of Satan the rulers of the land will rank themselves on the side of the man of sin—it is then the measure of guilt is full; the national apostasy is the signal for national ruin." II *Selected Messages* 373

Further, throughout scripture, wind has meant a variety of things such as heat and torture. It has been a symbol for war and destruction as seen in Jeremiah 18:17. But here we believe that it is the four corners of the earth which takes note as to who is losing power (the U.S.) and who is gaining power (the beast).

We believe this is consistent with traditional Adventist theology. Why? Because we know that this little horn power is going to attack the sanctuary and everything for which it stands.
We believe that this little horn power is going to try and replace God's seal with its mark.
We believe that this little horn power will rule with an iron-fist in the near future just as she has in the past.
We believe that this little horn power will war against the Prince of princes—Christ Himself.
We believe that this vision was not only historical in nature but will be repeated for "the time of the end."
We believe the little horn power is growing stronger every day and will continue to prosper until Christ Himself brings it to an end.
We believe that until that time he will magnify himself and try to eliminate God's people as he has done historically.

In conclusion we believe that we are standing on the threshold of eternity. God is calling for all to make decisions for Him today. These winds of strife will only be held back for so long. It is our desire and our prayer that each person will accept the invitation of the "Spirit and the bride" and come to Jesus today—the day of salvation.

Double Talk

"The secrets of wisdom... are double to that which is" Job 11:6.

Prophetic symbols may often be figurative and literal, spiritual and physical, heavenly and earthly. Scripture identifies this important concept of double application, double significance, double occurrence. It is first demonstrated in the dreams of Pharaoh interpreted by Joseph.

> Behold, there come seven years of great plenty throughout all the land of Egypt: And there shall arise after them seven years of famine... And for that the dream was doubled unto Pharaoh twice; it is because the thing is established by God, and God will shortly bring it to pass. Genesis 41:29-32

If saying the dream was "doubled...twice" seems a bit redundant, recall that Pharaoh had two dreams: the seven fat-seven lean cows and the seven fat-seven lean ears of corn. But notice that not only are there two types of subjects (cows and corn), there were also two sets of each (seven and seven *plus* seven and seven). The reason for the doubling, Joseph explains, is that it is "established by God" and that it will "shortly come to pass."

It is quite fascinating that God frequently says and does things twice. For example, the law of the Hebrew slave is first mentioned in Exodus 21. It is the first ceremonial law recorded, immediately following the Ten Commandments. It concerns the fate of any Hebrew who is sold into slavery. He is to work for only six years. He is released to go free in the seventh year. But if he finds a wife and has a family during his tenure with his master, he has a choice: go free alone or stay with his family and become a slave for life. To seal the latter transaction, his ear is pierced as a symbol of his irrevocable decision. This beautiful precept is itself a prophecy of Christ's decision to become a love slave forever, having His hands, His feet and side pierced for us.

But the account is then repeated in Deuteronomy 15 where additional detail is provided.

> And also unto thy maidservant thou shalt do likewise. It shall not seem hard unto thee, when thou sendest him away free from thee; for he hath been worth a double hired servant to thee, in serving thee six years. Verses 17, 18.

This was the experience of Jacob. He worked 7 years for Leah and then 7 years for Rachael. No wonder Joseph understood Pharaoh's dreams! The double seven-year concept was very clear to him. The first seven years of Jacob's servitude brought many sons from the fertile Leah, but the second seven years, which gained for him the hand of Rachael, were mostly barren.

> "For God speaks once, yes twice, yet man perceives it not." Job 33:14.

Jacob had his time of trouble. He struggled with God through the night, refusing to let go, holding on until he received the assurance of God's blessing. Morning brought deliverance. But others shared the same experience. David had his time of Jacob's trouble. Elijah had his. Daniel faced the lions and was delivered. Jesus struggled with the cup and persevered in faith to victory over death.

> "Wherefore do I see every man with his hands on his loins, as a woman in travail, and all faces are turned into paleness? Alas! For that day is great, so that none is like it: it is even the time of Jacob's trouble, but he shall be saved out of it." Jeremiah 30:6

The remnant saints will also face a time of Jacob's trouble. Only by clinging to the arm of God with the faith of Jesus will they, too, experience deliverance. We should pay special attention to the repetitions of God. Let us now examine the longest repeition in prophecy: the 2300 days.

The Dating Game: Certainty and Confirmation

Consider the accepted interpretation of Daniel 8 and 9.
The pivotal anchor dates of 457 BC, 27, 31 and 34 AD bound the 70 weeks of Daniel 9.
1844, a particularly unique Adventist date, marks the end of chapter eight's 2300 day prophecy.
Many other interpretations pick alternative dates: 444BC for the decree and 30 or 33 AD for the crucifixion, all in an attempt to move the 70th week down to the end of time for use as an imagined 7 final years of tribulation.

But why should the dates chosen by the traditional Adventist interpretation be any better? Are we just as guilty in choosing 457BC (which is part of the Daniel 9 vision) because we have a need to tie it into 1844 (which is derived from the Daniel 8 vision)? With careful study, the two *do* appear to be connected. The 70 weeks are "cut off" from the 2300 days. But the connection is less than obvious, it would seem, to many of our critics. Admittedly, the 1260 years of papal supremacy *do* seem to end convincingly on 1798 with the deposing of pope Pius VI, a symbolic and essentially literal deadly wound, even though 538 AD is less conspicuous in its historical significance since the Ostrogoths continued to terrorize Rome for another 40 years.

The relationship between all these dates, however, is greatly strengthened and confirmed by recognition of their jubilee connections. When it is discovered that the super-jubilee period of the 70 weeks (490 years or 10 jubilees) sets the pace for the other time periods, confidence in our original interpretation is greatly bolstered.
Far from 1844 being a "non-event," there is no question that it has tremendous prophetic significance.

Beginnings and Endings
The time interval from the end of the 70 weeks (34 AD) when Israel's probationary time of opportunity to fulfill their mission as God's chosen people came to an *end on earth*, until the end of the 1260 years of papal supremacy in 1798 when the Roman Church's allotted time of dominance over the saints came to an *end on earth*, is exactly 36 jubilees (36 x 49 or 1764 years).

    457BC   70 weeks-490 years-10 jubilees   34 AD ◄——— 36 jubilees-1764 years ———► 1798
                                                     Ends on earth   Ends on earth

Similarly, the time from the ***beginning in heaven*** of Christ's mediation as our High Priest in the Holy Place of the heavenly sanctuary in 31 AD, until the ***beginning in heaven*** of His ministry in the Most Holy Place at the start of the antitypical Day of Atonement in 1844, is exactly 37 jubilees (37 x 49 or 1813 years).

    27AD   31 AD ◄——— 34AD ——— 37 jubilees-1813 years ———► 1844
               Begins in heaven   Begins in heaven

One further jubilee connection remains, but sadly never materialized. From the time that Jesus ***began on earth*** His 3½ year ministry (27 AD) as a witness to the truth about His Father's character of love, until the time when His people could have ***begun on earth*** their final witness to the world of God's loving character through a demonstration of His righteousness by faith, could have been the next logical sequence: 38 jubilees (38 x 49 or 1862 years) ending in 1889. The time was ripe for God to move the Church to its climax. Sunday law legislation was pending before Congress. The stage was set, conditions were right.

    27AD ◄——— 31AD ——— 34AD ——— 38 jubilees-1862 years ———► 1889
   Begins on earth   Begins on earth

74 Prophesy Again! **Double Talk**

But God's people did not respond. Failure to embrace and proclaim the magnificent and life-changing truths of the 1888 message of Righteousness by Faith, rendered 1889 the real "non-event" of Adventist history. Yet, even here God's impeccable control over time and history is forcefully demonstrated.

Such precision is simply more than coincidental. These mathematical relationships interlinking the principle prophecies of Daniel were *not* the basis for the original pioneer Adventist position on accepting these dates. The events associated with these dates, which occurred in heaven, were in each case attended by a display of God's Spirit poured out upon His waiting people *on earth*. Christ began His holy place ministration with His inauguration as our High Priest in the *heavenly* sanctuary. The disciples waiting in an *earthly* upper room received simultaneous confirmation of the event as they witnessed the outpouring of the Holy Spirit on the day of Pentecost. Likewise, Christ began His most holy place Day of Atonement activities *in heaven* with a similar shower of the Spirit manifested by an appearance of the prophetic gift at the same time in 1844 *on earth*.

2300 Again

It should be of no surprise, then, that the 2300 year time period appears in another historical setting—that of Daniel 8! This is not to say that the original interpretation is no longer valid. The double jubilee linkage between the two terminal dates of the jubilee prophecy of Daniel 9 illustrated above should remove any doubt that these dates are correct. The fact that this interval shows up in more than one place only confirms it's prophetic importance. The restoration of the heavenly temple from spiritual desolation is appropriately mirrored by a matching restoration of the earthly temple from physical desolation. God, who is in control of the affairs of man, who sets up kings and takes down kings, has determined the times beforehand. It is a tribute to His marvelous wisdom that truth can be identified in every age.

Daniel's second vision in chapter 8 takes place in what is now southern Iran, near Basra. We find Daniel standing on the bank of the Ulai River. In vision he sees a ram with horns, one higher than the other, and the higher one comes up last. The ram is also standing on the bank of a river. The description, so far, of this dual-power symbol with a delayed development of its dominant phase is clearly parallel to the bear of Daniel 7, his first vision. Both are later identified as the co-regency of the Medes and Persians. The ram is "pushing" north and south and west. This aptly describes the historical expansion of the Persian Empire.

Greece   Medo-Persia   Medo-Persia

Cyaxares the Mede originally teamed up with Nebuchadnezzar the Babylonian to topple Nineveh and the Assyrian Empire. Later, Darius the Mede joined forces with Cyrus the Persian to overthrow the Babylonians. The ram, therefore, is representative of imperial forces spanning the time frame from Babylon to Persia, the first two world empires, paralleling the Lion-Bear and Gold-Silver symbols of Daniel's previous visions.

Chapter 8 has been a puzzle for many who don't see this parallel. Daniel 2 features a sequence of 4 empires. Daniel 7 repeats these same 4 empires. Revelation 13 alludes to them as well in a composite manner. Then why does Daniel 8 only feature two? In reality, it combines all four in these two symbols of the goat and the ram.

Goat	Ram
Rome and Greece	Babylon and Persia

Interestingly, the goat powers arise chronologically after the ram powers and they come from the west to confront the ram in the east. This has always been the case.

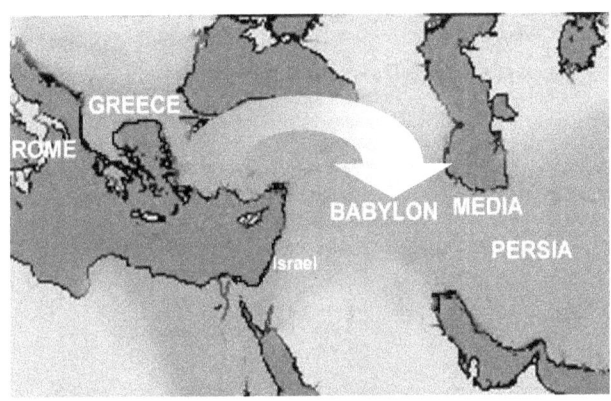

Daniel observed a "rough he goat" with a single prominent horn between its eyes, charging on with amazing speed, literally flying over the earth without touching the ground. The he-goat is a frequent symbol in mythological literature to epitomize masculine virility. It, like the ram, was a sacrificial animal. But, when contrasted with sheep separated on the right hand of favor, the goats on the left symbolize the lost.

The goat and ram have many applications. Besides the original roles of Greece and Persia, the goat and ram emerge throughout history in both physical and spiritual representations. Christ, the Ram, comes from the east and confronts the goat-devil who charges from the west, filled with "cholar." Islam rises from the east and wages war with the Christian west throughout the Middle Ages. And still today the clash of ideologies burns between the modern powers of Persia (Iraq and Iran) and the leading western nations (America and Britain).

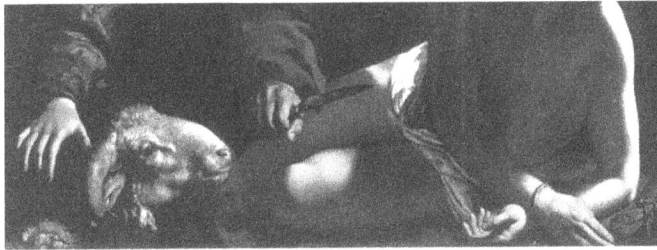

The Other Ram
At the time of the first Advent, these two symbols were realized in the struggle between Christ and Satan. Jesus was the Ram caught in the thicket of this world (Genesis 22:13).

He was the "Lamb of God" with the two horns of divinity and humanity (Son of God and Son of man). He stood on the shore of the river Jordan where He was baptized and began His ministry. John 1:29; Mark 1:5. Jesus stood in the East and reached out to the north (Galilee), west (Tyre, Samaria), South (Egypt as an infant). "Him hath God the Father sealed" John 6:27. Jesus, the Word of God, is the book sealed with seven seals. First seal: White horse going forth to conquer. Jesus egan His mission announcing, "The kingdom of

God is at hand" Such a following grew that the Jewish leaders feared "the world is gone after him!" John 12:19.

The Other Goat

Then the goat, Satan, attacks the Ram. The goat is even today the satanic symbol of devil worshippers. Jesus revealed this when He exposed the plans of the Jewish leaders to kill Him. "You are of your father the Devil...[who was] a murderer from the beginning." John 8:44 And though they should destroy His body temple in AD 31, He would raise it up again in three days. He arose Himself; His church was raised up at Pentecost; the heavenly temple was restored as well. This is the spiritual fulfillment of Daniel 8.

At the time Pilate crucified Christ, **Pan, the half-man half-goat, god** of the forests perished. Pan is the only god whose reputed death has been historically recorded. The event took place during the reign of the Roman emperor Tiberius and was related by the Greek philosopher Plutarch in his 'Why Oracles Are Silent'. An Egyptian sailor, Thamus, whose ship was bound for Italy via the island of Paxos, heard a divine voice calling out his name and telling him to 'proclaim that the great god Pan is dead'. The early orthodox Christians reasoned that Pan died at the exact moment of Christ's crucifixion because his divine martyrdom heralded the extinction of the false gods. Gradually, Pan became identified as the Great Satan whose domain was hell, depicted as the devil possessing a forked tail, horns and hooves.

In Leviticus 16, the Day of Atonement ends with the accumulated sins of the entire year being transferred from the sanctuary to the head of the scape goat, Azazel, who is then led out into the wilderness to perish alone. The devil will ultimately experience isolation in the wilderness of this depopulated earth for a thousand years during the millennium. I'm curious if the Islamic epithet of "the Great Satan" cast upon the United States is intentional or unwitting application to America's role as the end time he-goat from the west.

The Original Greek Goat

Daniel is told that the goat is Greece and that the great horn is its first king, Alexander the Great (8:20). It is coming from the west and is aimed straight at the ram. As the ram in Daniel 8 parallels the bear of Daniel 7, so the goat in Daniel 8 parallels the leopard of Daniel 7. The Leopard was fast but the Goat is mad, angry and infuriated. He strikes the ram head-on at the bank of the river, throwing him to the ground and breaking his horns. The goat and the little horn that rises from it historically represent the empires of Greece and Rome.

Alexander the Great's amazingly rapid advance through Asia Minor is demonstrated in the timing of the first three major battles waged against the Persian Empire. All three where engaged at a river:

    334 BC June Battle at the river Granicus where his 20,000 men faced 40,000 Persians,
    334 BC November Battle at the river Pinarus near Issus against a force of 500,000, and the final
    331 BC October Battle at the river Bumodus near Arbela against an estimated one million troops.

After inheriting the Macedonian kingdom, Alexander the Great led his army east, across the Hellespont and along the Black Sea, with the goal of driving the Persians from Asia Minor. In early June of 334 BC Alexander reached the Granicus (Granikos) River, near the Sea of Marmara, where he made his first encounter with a Persian army outnumbering his forces 2:1. Though Alexander was nearly killed as he led the charge across the river, the Battle was a spectacular victory for Greece and a crushing defeat for Persia. The Macedonians completely routed their enemies and took 2,000 prisoners. This overwhelming triumph opened western Asia and gave control of the Aegean Sea to the Greeks. (John Mixter, "Alexander's First Great Victory," *Military History*, December 1997).

Paratroopers stand in awe beside the western wall

2300 years
-334 B.C. late May/early June
1966 A.D.
+1 (no year zero)
1967 A.D. June 5-10
terminates with the year and month of Israel's Six Day War
"Milhemet Sheshet Hayamim"

The allusion in Daniel's vision to the battle of Granicus, where Alexander the *Great*'s first battle against Persia was a face-off across a river, is unmistakable. This event begins another long period of the 2300 days specified in Daniel 8, which will end with the restoration of the sanctuary to its rightful position. It is in the context of the ram-goat confrontation that the little horn arises and the question is asked, "How long shall the sanctuary be trodden under foot?" Palmoni, the wonderful numberer (pele is wonderful in Isaiah 9:6, mene is numbered in Daniel 5:25), provides the answer: 2300 days. Then shall the sanctuary be cleansed from its ignominy.

The circumstances of this conflict are striking. Israeli forces conquered all the Arab armies of Egypt, Jordan, Iraq and Syria, capturing the West Bank, the Gaza Strip, the Golan Heights, the Sinai Desert, the Old City of Jerusalem and the Temple Mount.

The Ram Returns

2540 years ago the Old Testament prophet Daniel was introduced to the first Persian Empire on a night in 536 BC when the world's first superpower came to its end. While the Babylonian King Belshazzar partied, the Medes and Persians invaded the capitol city and conquered it. Persia thus became the world's second superpower and held that position for the next two hundred years.

Iran (modern Persia) is the land of the Aryans, who appeared in the southern shores of the Caspian Sea from the Caucasus Mountains around 2000 BC, the time of Abraham. They were first known as Elamites, descendants of Elam, one of the sons of Shem and a grandson of Noah. After conquering the area of today's Iraq and Iran, the Elamites established their capital in Shushan (Susa, or modern Shush, some 240 km above the Persian Gulf). It was from here that King Chedorlaomer led a coalition of eastern kings on a military raid of Palestine where Lot and his household, residing in Sodom, were taken captive. Genesis records the daring rescue by Abraham who secured the assistance of three allies. The story is a template for many future wars between Jews and their neighbors.

Shushan became the favorite capitol for a string of Persian rules. Cyrus the Great (550-529 BC), Darius the Great (521-486 BC), Artaxerxes II (404-359 BC featured in the book of Esther) all ruled from ancient Susa. It was here that Daniel received the vision of the goat and ram in chapter 8.

The battles between Alexander the Great and Persia that began in 331 BC were the initial historic fulfillment of the Daniel 8 vision of the goat-ram confrontation. Yet Daniel describes not only conditions of ancient history, but also a recapitulation of these events at the end of time. Daniel 8 specifically locates the time that the vision is to take place in verse 17 as "at the time of the end" and in verse 19 as "the last end." Since the beginning of the Christian era, the sequence has been repeated several times. Daniel 11 predicted a total of four major eastern empires to rise from the area of ancient Persia, cross the Euphrates, and challenge the spread of Christianity.

Following the death of Alexander the Great in 323 BC, the Greek Seleucids, based in Syria, took control for about 100 years until the Parthians declared independence around 220 BC and controlled Persia for the next 400 years. Outside powers eclipsed Persia for half a millennium. But its return was prophesied. And each time the eastern ram would keep pushing west only to meet the western goat head on.

Persia Returns
1. Finally, in 224 AD, a Persian prince from Fars, Ardeshir I, defeated the Parthians and established the first neo-Persian empire under the Sassanian Dynasty. The Sassanians expanded significantly reaching its peak under Khosrow II Parviz when his realm reached all the way to Jerusalem and even Constantinople.

The Sassanid dynasty made Zoroastrianism its state religion, moved west-ward across the Euphrates, conquering Syria, Palestine, Egypt and most of Turkey. They even captured Jerusalem fulfilling the prophecy of Isaiah 27:8, which predicted that the City of Peace, left desolate by the dispersion, would be, handed over to the "east wind."

But the Sassanians over-extended themselves. Taking on too many battlefronts simultaneously and over-taxing the people rendered them vulnerable to the Byzantines under Emperor Heraclius who easily took over the area of modern Iraq with little resistance. Constantinople, headquarters of the eastern Christian church, fought back and finally drove the Persians out of Asia Minor. The final blow came in 636 AD when the new power in the region, Arab Muslims, swept into the Iraq-Iran territories changing overnight the religious-political ideology of Persia from Zoroastrianism to Islam.

Muslim Persians

2. In 632 AD the prophet Mohammed from Arabia in the south lead Media and Persia to invade all the lands around them expanding into a second vast eastern empire that stretched from India to Spain. Jerusalem, once again, fell to the invading Mohammedans. And once again, the east wind blew over-whelming the west with lightening speed. This second Persian Empire engulfed most of North Africa, vast areas around the Mediterranean, advancing all the way to the Atlantic. After conquering Spain, the Muslims pushed into France where Christians at the city of Tours finally defeated them.

THE
ARAB-MUSLIM EMPIRE
632 C.E. - 750 C.E.

By the eighth century, the eastern Christian church in Constantinople eventually repelled the Muslim forces that then turned their attention to the western Church, conquering the island of Sicily and even successfully invading Italy, almost taking Rome itself in 860 AD.

Seljuk Turks

3. In the 11th century, Islamic people in the north from central Asia, the Seljuk Turks, invaded and conquered most of Asia Minor, took Constantinople which they renamed Istanbul. This third Persian Empire, renamed their new territory Turkey, after themselves, subjecting a great many Greek Christians to Muslim rule and controlling all seven of the cities to which the Book of Revelations was addressed. The Turkish invaders came from Asia, but occupied once again the same general area of ancient Media and Persia. Eventually, the Ottoman Empire crossed the Bosporus, invaded central Europe until they were finally stopped during the First World War.

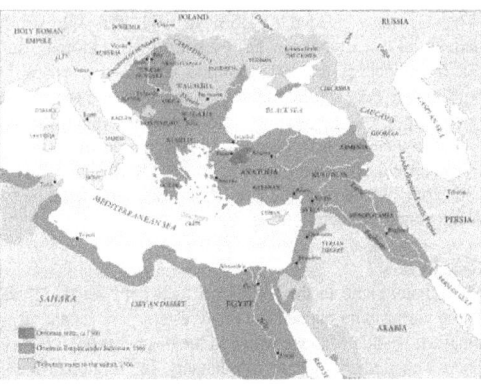

The British and Lawrence of Arabia established the nations of Saudi Arabia and Iraq in order to drive a wedge into the Muslim world dividing it East and West across the river Euphrates.

80 Prophesy Again! **The Ram Returns**
Radical Muslim Fundamentalists
4. A fourth Persian power now extends from Russia to Iran, from Turkey and the Black Sea across Kazakhstan, Uzbekistan, Indonesia and Africa. This expanded fourth Persian Empire is today taking on the Western powers.

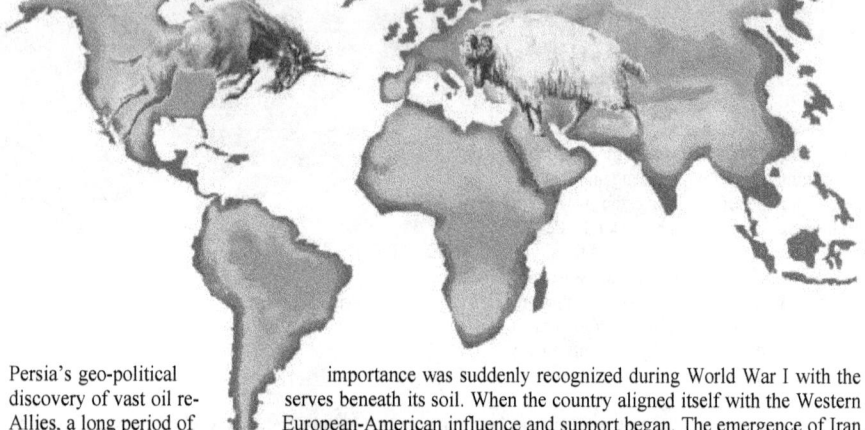

Persia's geo-political importance was suddenly recognized during World War I with the discovery of vast oil reserves beneath its soil. When the country aligned itself with the Western Allies, a long period of European-American influence and support began. The emergence of Iran as a modern nation began with the 1921 military coup of Rezah Khan who declared himself hereditary Shah ("Shah for life") and established the Pahlevi dynasty. He formed a European-styled parliament and finally changing the country's name to Iran in 1935.

When Germany invaded the USSR in 1941, Iran sided with the Allies in providing a route to USSR for the delivery of war supplies by British and American forces. But when Russia was not granted access to Iranian oil, it engineered the 1945 political revolts that established Soviet bloc nations along Iran's northern borders: the People's Republic of Azerbaijan and the Kurdish People's Republic. And when Soviet troops remaining in Iran showed no signs of leaving, Iran asked for American and British protection. In 1947 the United States and Iran began a 25-year period of cooperation as America supported the development of Iran's oil industry. With the creation of the Baghdad Pact, Iran began to receive vast amounts of military and economic aid from the US, which was squandered by the Shah on opulent palaces while economic and social conditions deteriorated.

Role Reversal
The climax came in the form of a feud between the Shah's autocratic monarchy and autocratic Islamic Shiite clerics who blamed the pro-Western policies and denounced the growing secularization. In 1979 the fanatical Islamic Mullahs whipped the disenchanted Iranians into spark the Islamic Revolution, deposed the Shah who fled the country on January 16. Ayatollah Khomeini returned from exile in France, declared himself "Imam," created a new Constitution that turned Iran into a Shiite Islamic Republic, banned all western influences, and announced that April 1 was "the first day of God's government." He declared war on the Great Satan (America) and on November 4 incited university students to seize the US Embassy in Tehran and hold 52 Embassy workers hostage for the next 444 days. Among the young student revolutionaries was a brilliant engineering student named Mahmoud Ahmadinejad who, 25 years later, would become the President of Iran.

Today

The kingdom of Media is inhabited by the Kurdish people in Syria and northern Iraq.
The kingdom of Persia is called the nation of Iran, the center of the Islamic Revolution and global terrorism.
The kingdom of Greece is today the Christian nations of Western Civilization, especially America.
Thus the goat-ram conflict is actually a clash of civilizations, a battle between Christian and Islamic forces.

Today the Islamic Revolution targets the demise of Israel and the United States, is spreading world-wide with Al Qaeda cells throughout Asia, the Philippines, South America, Europe and Africa.

Iraq & Iran

1991 and 2003 the Persian Ram was struck
by the American Goat...twice, 12 years apart.
The first horn is smaller than the second
which comes up "higher"
Iran is three times the size of Iraq.
While all other Middle East Islamic nations speak Arabic,
Iran retains its own Farsi language
and Shia version of Islam.
Iran is now daring and defying America
in its goal of acquiring nuclear arms.
Iran calls for the elimination of Israel (Little Satan) as a nation
and U.S. (Great Satan) for supporting her.

The first Persian Gulf War between a U.S.-led coalition of western nations against the 4th Persian kingdom of modern Iraq was, as wars go, a small but immeasurably important conflict between east and west. Positioned at the Euphrates River, it was in the right place, at the right time, and it follows the prophetic template specified by Daniel: A western army, its president (the single majestic horn) enraged with Iraq, *"crossing the earth with his troops without touching the ground,"* crushes the Ram of the East at the Euphrates. Not just once, but twice, in succession!

Two Horns, Two Battles

Daniel indicated that this war would have two parts and that the greater of these would be the second segment. The Ram had two horns, the higher one came up last.

Gulf War II

This means a second Gulf War greater than the first occurring in the same Middle East region of the Euphrates. The second Gulf War (pitting the west against the second horn of the eastern ram in Daniel's prophecy) began on March 19, 2003 at 4 A.M. Baghdad time. The Bush Administration would cite an earlier date: September 11, 2001, which triggered the invasions of Afghanistan and Iraq, two fronts in a wider Middle-Eastern war.

84 Prophesy Again! **The Ram Returns**
"And the rough goat is the king of Grecia: and the great horn that is between his eyes is the first king." Daniel 8:21

       1991   2003   1991   2004
American Greek-Roman Western Superpower   takes on   Iraqi Babylonian-Persian Eastern Power

Goat-Ram I
334 BC the Grecian Goat defeated the Persian Ram at the river Granicus.
2300 years later the Jews defeated the Arabs to restore Jerusalem's temple area in 1967.

Goat-Ram II
1991 the American and European Goat defeated the Iraqi Ram at the river Euphrates in the Persian Gulf.
2003 the Goat power struck the Ram's first horn again. There is still another horn: Iran.

For the first time in the history of the world, an alliance of 28 nations under the banner of the United Nations lead by the U.S. and Britain came from the west by air and sea "without touching the earth" to attack Iraq from Kuwait near the Ulai river. This fulfillment of Daniel 8 is far more complete and precise than the Greco-Persian encounters which took place 23 centuries ago, hardly "at the time of the end."

1989 marked the end of the Cold War. With the fall of the Soviet Union, **Dick Cheney, Colin Powell, and Paul Wolfowitz** produced the 'Defense Planning Guidance' report calling for the U.S. to maintain military dominance around the globe (make itself 'absolutely powerful') and prevent the emergence of any new rivals from challenging our superpower position through 'preemptive' strikes and military 'forward presence.'

Cheney, Powell and Wolfowitz knew that the military budget would quickly fade away without a plan to fill the 'threat blank.' On **August 2, 1990 President Bush called a press conference** to report that the threat of global war had significantly receded, but in its wake a new unforeseen threat to national security could come from anywhere. **By a remarkable coincidence, Iraq invaded Northern Kuwait later the same day.**

Cheney et al. were out of political power for the eight years of Clinton's presidency. During this time the neo-conservatives founded the **Project for the New American Century (PNAC).** The most influential product of the PNAC was a report entitled "Rebuilding America's Defense," which called for U.S. military dominance and **control of global economic markets**. See www.newamericancentury.org.

With the election of George W. Bush, the authors of the plan were returned to power: Cheney as vice president, Powell as Secretary of State, and Wolfowitz in the number two spot at the Pentagon. The lapse of twelve years, despite three intervening presidential elections and potential changes in government administrations, personnel and policies, expired with a president in power by the same name with key administrative positions filled by the same individuals involved in the first, original invasion.

It was like a time warp, as if nothing had changed.

Operation Desert Storm 1991

July 17, 1990 Saddam Hussein accuses Kuwait of oil overproduction and theft from the Rumailia Oil Field.
July 25, US Ambassador to Iraq, April Glaspie, assures Hussien that the Iraq/Kuwait dispute is an Arab affair and that the United States is not affected.
August 2, Hussein invades Kuwait. President Bush immediately freezes Iraqi and Kuwaiti assets.
The United Nations calls on Hussien to withdraw.
August 6, Economic sanctions authorized.
August 7, Secretary of Defense Cheney visits Saudi Arabia, dispatches 82nd Airborne and fighter squadrons.
August 8, Iraq annexes Kuwait.
August 9, UN declares the annexation invalid
August 12, USA announces interdiction of all Iraqi ships, starts build-up of forces in the Persian Gulf
August 22, President Bush authorizes the call up of reserves
August 25, UN authorizes military interdiction
September 14, Iraqi forces storm diplomatic missions in Kuwait City
November 8, Bush orders additional deployments
November 20, Democrats file suit to require the President to get Congressional approval
November 22, President Bush visits troops for Thanksgiving
November 29, UN Security Council authorizes force by January 15 if Iraq doesn't pull out

1991:
January 9, Baker and Aziz meet in Geneva for 6 hours without resolution.
January 12, Congress votes to allow US troops engage in offensive operations
January 15, Deadline for UN Resolution 678: Iraq doesn't withdraw.
January 16, US announces Operation Desert Storm, the "liberation of Kuwait," has begun
Air war started January 17 2:38 a.m. local time (January 16, 6:38 pm EST)
January 17, Iraq launches first SCUD missile attack
January 30, US forces reach 500,000
February 6, Jordan King Hussein lashes out against American bombings and supports Iraq
February 13, US Bombers destroy a Baghdad bunker killing nearly 300 citizens.
February 17, Tariq Aziz travels to Moscow to discuss a negotiated end to the war.
February 22, President Bush issues ultimatum for Iraqi troop withdrawal
February 23, Ground war begins: Marine, Army, Arab forces enter Iraq and Kuwait
February 25, Iraqi SCUD missile hits US barracks in Saudi Arabia
February 26, Kuwait City controlled
February 27, President Bush orders cease-fire effective midnight Kuwaiti time.
February 28: General Schwartzkopf ordered the armies advancing on Baghdad to stop.
February 28: Purim, celebration of Jewish victory over threat of Haman in Persia.

Operation Iraqi Freedom 2003

March 19, 2003 U.S. led coalition invades Iraq following a 24 hour ultimatum for Saddam Hussein to leave. The sweeping victory is short-lived despite the initial celebrations in the street.
Fierce resistance is protracted, popular opinion shifts in the months to follow.
Free elections are ultimately held, a constitution is crafted, and a government is established.
Escalating insurgency sponsored by Iran leads to waning support in the US and a precipitous drop in polls.
Saddam Hussein goes on trial but dominates and obstructs the proceedings.
All the while Iran, under the leadership of the newly elected firebrand President Ahmadinejad, defies the world in escalating its determination to attain nuclear power status and alleged weapons capability.
Israel voices its mountain apprehension of Iran and its intention to make good on its threat to "wipe Israel off the map." When Ariel Sharon is incapacitated by a devastating stroke, the hawks in the Knesset counter threat to eliminate Iran's nuclear program single-handedly.

That Which Has Been Shall Be
The Prophecies of Esther

Esther is a timeless story of drama, intrigue, courage, justice and deliverance. It has the distinction of being one of only two books in the Bible to not even mention the name of God. And it is not mentioned or quoted by any other book of Scripture. Yet Esther remains a valuable sampling of primordial history, a rich source of behind the scene divine activity, and a preview of the final judgment.

The setting is the royal Persian palace where king Ahasuerus banishes a stubborn, independent queen. Similar issues prevailed with Lucifer's rebellion in heaven and his later eviction. Ahasuerus (Hebrew) or Xerxes (Greek) is a type of God the Father. Queens Vashti and Esther, his wives, are types of Israel who was married to God and of New Jerusalem who is prepared as a bride for her Husband. Haman "the adversary and enemy" (Esther 7:6) is a type of Satan, our "adversary the devil, [who] as a roaring lion, walks about, seeking whom he may devour" (1 Peter 5:8).

In the third year of his reign, Ahasuerus made a feast for all the princes of his provinces to show "the riches of his glorious kingdom and the honor of his excellent majesty" for 180 days—six months. And when the days where finished, he made another feast for just those at his Shushan palace that lasted for seven days.

The timing of these feasts compliments the liturgical calendar followed by Israel beginning with Passover at full moon (mid-month) at the start of the church year. The last feast of the year occurred exactly six months later at full moon (mid-month) in the seventh month.

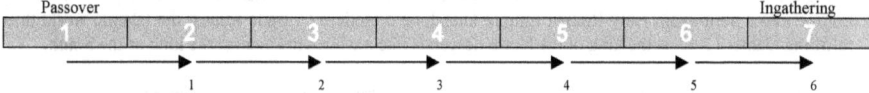

This party lasted seven days and was held "in the court of the garden of the king's palace." Likewise, the Feast of Tabernacles or Ingathering began on the 15th day of the seventh month and lasted seven days. It was a celebration that commemorated Israel's freedom from Egypt but also the joys of the new earth when the harvest of the world takes place at the Second Coming and when Adam receives the Garden of Eden restored.

The royal wine was in abundance and they drank "according to the law; none did compel." The king had appointed that "all should do according to every man's pleasure." God never coerces his subjects but allows full freedom of choice to every creature.

Vashti, the queen, conducted a rival feast for the women in the royal house. The queen held her own competing event apparently in defiance of and certainly not in respect for the king and his feast. On the final seventh day, the king decides to show off his trophy wife to his seven princes and seven chamberlains "for she was fair to look on" Esther 1:11. He specifically asks her to come in wearing the royal crown, but her highness refuses. The decree, after a brief consultation, is made: "Let the king give her royal estate unto another that is better than she." Esther 1:19.

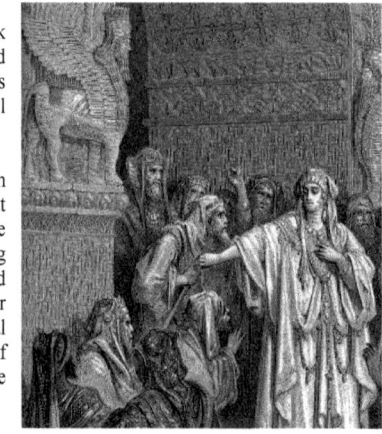

Operation Desert Storm 1991

July 17, 1990 Saddam Hussein accuses Kuwait of oil overproduction and theft from the Rumailia Oil Field.
July 25, US Ambassador to Iraq, April Glaspie, assures Hussien that the Iraq/Kuwait dispute is an Arab affair and that the United States is not affected.
August 2, Hussein invades Kuwait. President Bush immediately freezes Iraqi and Kuwaiti assets.
The United Nations calls on Hussien to withdraw.
August 6, Economic sanctions authorized.
August 7, Secretary of Defense Cheney visits Saudi Arabia, dispatches 82nd Airborne and fighter squadrons.
August 8, Iraq annexes Kuwait.
August 9, UN declares the annexation invalid
August 12, USA announces interdiction of all Iraqi ships, starts build-up of forces in the Persian Gulf
August 22, President Bush authorizes the call up of reserves
August 25, UN authorizes military interdiction
September 14, Iraqi forces storm diplomatic missions in Kuwait City
November 8, Bush orders additional deployments
November 20, Democrats file suit to require the President to get Congressional approval
November 22, President Bush visits troops for Thanksgiving
November 29, UN Security Council authorizes force by January 15 if Iraq doesn't pull out

1991:
January 9, Baker and Aziz meet in Geneva for 6 hours without resolution.
January 12, Congress votes to allow US troops engage in offensive operations
January 15, Deadline for UN Resolution 678: Iraq doesn't withdraw.
January 16, US announces Operation Desert Storm, the "liberation of Kuwait," has begun
Air war started January 17 2:38 a.m. local time (January 16, 6:38 pm EST)
January 17, Iraq launches first SCUD missile attack
January 30, US forces reach 500,000
February 6, Jordan King Hussein lashes out against American bombings and supports Iraq
February 13, US Bombers destroy a Baghdad bunker killing nearly 300 citizens.
February 17, Tariq Aziz travels to Moscow to discuss a negotiated end to the war.
February 22, President Bush issues ultimatum for Iraqi troop withdrawal
February 23, Ground war begins: Marine, Army, Arab forces enter Iraq and Kuwait
February 25, Iraqi SCUD missile hits US barracks in Saudi Arabia
February 26, Kuwait City controlled
February 27, President Bush orders cease-fire effective midnight Kuwaiti time.
February 28: General Schwartzkopf ordered the armies advancing on Baghdad to stop.
February 28: Purim, celebration of Jewish victory over threat of Haman in Persia.

Operation Iraqi Freedom 2003

March 19, 2003 U.S. led coalition invades Iraq following a 24 hour ultimatum for Saddam Hussein to leave.
The sweeping victory is short-lived despite the initial celebrations in the street.
Fierce resistance is protracted, popular opinion shifts in the months to follow.
Free elections are ultimately held, a constitution is crafted, and a government is established.
Escalating insurgency sponsored by Iran leads to waning support in the US and a precipitous drop in polls.
Saddam Hussein goes on trial but dominates and obstructs the proceedings.
All the while Iran, under the leadership of the newly elected firebrand President Ahmadinejad, defies the world in escalating its determination to attain nuclear power status and alleged weapons capability.
Israel voices its mountain apprehension of Iran and its intention to make good on its threat to "wipe Israel off the map." When Ariel Sharon is incapacitated by a devastating stroke, the hawks in the Knesset counter threat to eliminate Iran's nuclear program single-handedly.

Rise of the Ram - Act 2

September 22, 1980 Iraq invaded Iran starting an eight-year war that left a million dead, all because of the Persian Gulf's disputed Shatt al Arab waterway. The US supported Saddam Hussein while Russia aided Iran. The war ended in a dismal stalemate with both nations financially exhausted. But the chemical weapons supplied by the US and deployed by Iraq caused a backlash of anti-American sentiment and galvanized the Arab-Muslim world against the United States.

When the Soviets invaded Afghanistan, America supported the Afghani Mujhadeen rebels. Both attempts by the U.S. to buy favor in the Arab world backfired. When the Russians ultimately pulled out of Afghanistan, the Taliban took advantage of the resulting power vacuum and installed radical islamic rule while providing a safe haven for Al Qaeda to setup training camps and plan their attack on America under the guidance of Osama bin Laden, a disgruntled Saudi prince with hundreds of millions of dollars to bank roll his visions of terror.

With the fall of the USSR, Russia began to market their surplus military hardware as a way to raise some badly needed cash. In 1989, flush with new oil money, Iran seized this opportunity to purchase numerous combat aircraft, a fleet of diesel-powered submarines, and an $800 million nuclear power reactor to be constructed in the southern Iranian town of Bushehr.

The following year, Iraq realized they needed to ante up. So it was that in early 1990 Saddam Hussein, looking for additional oil revenues to rebuild his war machine, decided to make Kuwait his 19th province. Suddenly, the world was faced with the first post-Cold War crisis and, for the first time in 40 years there was not an American-Russian conflict of foreign policy opinion. Russia, desperate for America's economic aid, was surprisingly agreeable. Both President Bush and Mikhail Gorbachev declared the Persian Gulf crisis "a test-case for the New World Order" and an opportunity for cooperation between Washington and Moscow.

Meanwhile, the Islamic Revolution in Iran was quietly gaining power and ambition. When Mohammed Khatami was elected President in 1997, the European Union applauded the change in the Iran's internal power base as a possible move away from the repressive religious regime. The EU began to renew economic relations while the US continued economic sanctions for Iran's role in international terrorism. But it was the Bushehr reactor project that drew the most critical Western attention. Suspicions mounted that Iran's nuclear aspirations were linked in some sinister way to their open confession that Israel and America must be destroyed. Thus it was that in President Bush's State of the Union Address in January, 2002, in the wake of 9-11, Iran was fingered as a member of the Axis of Evil.

The repeat of history in the two Gulf Wars is noteworthy in more than just the fact they were both waged under a Bush Presidency. The foreign policy of Middle East dynamics is much the same. Prior to the 1991 invasion, America was deeply involved in supporting Saudi Arabia, the Shah of Iran and Saddam Hussein with the aim of securing pro-Western client states in the midst of the Muslim world. With that having failed, the US is now determined to achieve the same outcome through the use of military force. But the price has been expensive.

After the invasion of Iraq in 2003, Iran-US relations rapidly deteriorated. Iran allied with Syria and stepped up its support of Islamic Jihadists, Shiite militants, and suicide bombers in Iraq. By the end of 2005 the US was facing off with Iran in a nuclear showdown. With the prospect of fanatical Muslim fundamentalist zealots soon possessing nuclear-tipped missiles, the US and Israel (the undeniable targets) pressured the International Atomic Energy Agency to assess the activities of nuclear weapon production within Iran. Although Germany began the initial construction of Iran's nuclear reactor, they repented when they, too, began to suspect that Iran's intentions were beyond simply that of domestic energy. Russia stepped in and is currently completing the project. Not surprisingly, the Russians have been unusually aggressive in trying to work out an external uranium enrichment program that would allow Iran to save face, avoid a confrontation with the West, and protect their cash cow.

When Iran's Defense Minister, Ali Shamkhani, revealed that Iran's new North Korean Nodong-based Russian-modified Shahab-3 missile could now reach targets up to 810 miles away, Israel was quick to push the panic button. But the Arab world defends Iran's position pointing out that Israel has no right to object since they already have a large nuclear arsenal themselves. Iran's lust for nuclear parity was clearly seen when the Shahab-3 was deployed in July, 2004 with great fanfare, parading their six missiles through the streets of Teheran bearing large posters stating, "We will crush America under our feet!" and "We will wipe Israel from the face of the earth!"

"Israel must be uprooted and erased from history" inscribed on a Shahab 3 ballistic missile in a military parade in Teheran (September 22, 2003)

Israel is not ignoring these sentiments as simply rhetoric. She has decided to prepare for unilateral military intervention as was executed previously in dealing with the Iraqi nuclear threat when the Israeli Air Force bombed the Osiraq reactor near Baghdad in 1982. An indication that Israel is serious about the prospects of a repeat performance on Iranian soil is her 2005 shopping list totalling $319 million in weapons purchased from the United States which include:
    2,500 one-ton bombs
    1,000 half-ton bombs
    500 quarter-ton bombs
    500 one-ton "bumker buster" bombs (capable of penetrating 6-foot thick concrete walls).
The BLU-109 bunker busters are satellite-guided ordinances that can be fired from the new fleet of 102 long-range F-16 fighter jets purchased from the U.S. in 2004.

America is also planning ahead for their next operation. An article by Pulitzer Price-winning journalist Seymour M. Hersh entitled "The Coming Wars" (*New Yorker*, January 24-31, 2005) claimed "the next strategic target [is] Iran." Hersh reported that "The Administration has been conducting secret reconnaissance missions inside Iran" working "with Israeli planners and consultants to develop and refine potential ...targets inside Iran." When asked for confirmation a month later while visiting NATO, President Bush declared that such a notion that the US was getting ready to attack Iran "is simply ridiculous." But then he added: "Having said that, all options are on the table."

But one year later, essentially the same article again in *New Yorker* creates an international outcry!

To Washington, Iraq has always been but a stepping-stone to Iran which was never punished for removing the U.S.'s puppet, the Shah, and seizing the American Embassy in Tehran.

88 Prophesy Again! The Ram Returns

Despite mounting pressure from the world community, Iran maintains its right to become a nuclear power, or as Ayatollah Khameni put it, "join the club." Iran is willing to defy the United Nations, the IAEA, to risk international economic and political isolation. In turn, it threatens to pull out of the NPT (nuclear non-proliferation treaty), stop producing oil (translation: spark a global financial collapse), and bring "harm and pain" to Israel and America. Since Iran houses the second largest pool of untapped petroleum in the world and sits in a position to wreak serious damage to the world economy by simply turning off the taps. Furthermore, Iran controls the Strait of Hormuz which it could close and shut off 40% of the world's oil supply from leaving the Persian Gulf. "Oil, Geopolitics, and the Coming War with Iran," Michael T. Klare, April 11, 2005.

Then Mahmoud Amadinejad was elected President of Iran. He wastes no time in telling his vision for Iran and the world. After his address to the UN in September 2005 Ahmadinejad was told that "One of our group...saw a light around me, and I was placed inside this aura. I felt it myself. I felt the atmosphere suddenly change, and for those 27 or 28 minutes, the leaders of the world did not blink...they were rapt. It seemed as if a hand was holding them there and had opened their eyes to receive the message from the Islamic Republic."

The Iranian president believes he is being influenced by a spiritual force, guided by an unseen mystical power, that he has been chosen to prepare the way for the Mahdi. Even his name, Ah-MADI-nejad, inspires him in his devotion to the coming Mahdi. He sees himself as an Islamic John the Baptist who must create global mayhem as a prerequisite for the 12th Imam's return which he is fervently convinced will occur in as little as two years. He believes it to be an angel, perhaps Allah himself. The western world sees a more sinister force at work, demonic, perhaps Satan himself.

President Ahmadinejad is "a Holocaust-denying, virulently anti-Semitic, aspiring genocidist, on the verge of acquiring nuclear weapons of the apocalypse, [who] believes that the end is not only near but nearer than the next American presidential election. ... This kind of man would have, to put it gently, less inhibition about starting Armageddon than a normal person" (Charles Krauthammer, Washington Post, Dec. 16, 2005).

It is quite clear that Iran is hell-bent on engaging the US, the EU, the world in an all-out Armageddon-styled conflagration regardless of the intense collateral damage that Iran would certainly suffer in a nuclear exchange. From Teheran's viewpoint, it would be well worth the price just to exterminate Israel once and for all.

Speaking to a crowd on January 5, 2006 in the holy city of Qom, Iran's President Ahmadinejad said, "Islam is a universal ideology that leads the world to justice...Islam is ready to rule the world." Mehran Riazaty at RegimeChangeInIran.com

Tensions escalated in early spring as Passover neared. The International Atomic Energy Agency reported to the UN Security Counsel that Iran was not cooperating with inspections, they had cut the seals to their reactor and resumed uranium enrichment. At the same time, Islamic riots erupted around the world in protest to Danish cartoons of Mohammed. Paris cities burned in separate riots over unemployment for Muslim immigrants.

Then Iran announced in early April, 2006 that they had successfully produced uranium hexafloride gas with a concentration of 3.5% enough to fuel a reactor and proudly claimed membership in the "Nuclear Club." While the US and the EU called for sanctions and even mentioned chapter 7 (UN authorized use of force), a stalemate was brewing with both Russia (profiting handsomely with Iran's expensive defense contracts) and China (very much dependant on Iranian oil) strongly opposing any sanctions

In rapid fire, the headlines are spelling doom and gloom for the he-goat. The prominent horn is about to break.

OIL STOCK EXCHANGE TO BE LAUNCHED IN IRAN

(Asia Pulse Businesswire Via Thomson Dialog NewsEdge)TEHRAN,
April 27 Asia Pulse - Oil Minister Kazem Vaziri Hamaneh said on Wednesday that the Oil Stock Exchange will be launched in Iran in the **next week.**

The long expected euro-based Iranian oil burse is finally opening its doors for business. The stampede to unload US dollars will follow shortly thereafter. This may be the prelude to the fall of the he-goat. On the same day, Iran receives its first shipment of Russian-made BM-25s long-range missiles from North Korea.

Iran has missiles that put Europe in range
Thu. 27 Apr 2006
JERUSALEM (Reuters) - Iran has received a first shipment of missiles from North Korea that are capable of reaching Europe.

With the IAEA's 30 day deadline expired on April 28 and a report not favorable to Iran, Tehran began making threats of double the retaliation if any military action is directed their way. At the same time, Russia announces (in spite of US demands) the lucrative sale of 29 anti-missile systems to Iran. All the ingredients of a major confrontation are now present.

The ram in the East is once again pushing at the West. Daniel 8 tells us that the goat power will charge with all its furry and stomp on the ram breaking both of its horns. Will it be led once again by the United States? If so the cost will bankrupt America. Will Europe lead the charge? There are some who see the growing strength of Germany at a time when the world's eyes are following a German Pope as a recipe for unifying Europe into a born-again Holy Roman Empire launching a modern Crusade against the Islamic world thus fulfilling Daniel 11:40 as the king of the North descends like a whirlwind against the king of the South.

Only as the final battle actually plays out will we know for sure as prophecy prophesies again.

That Which Has Been Shall Be
The Prophecies of Esther

Esther is a timeless story of drama, intrigue, courage, justice and deliverance. It has the distinction of being one of only two books in the Bible to not even mention the name of God. And it is not mentioned or quoted by any other book of Scripture. Yet Esther remains a valuable sampling of primordial history, a rich source of behind the scene divine activity, and a preview of the final judgment.

The setting is the royal Persian palace where king Ahasuerus banishes a stubborn, independent queen. Similar issues prevailed with Lucifer's rebellion in heaven and his later eviction. Ahasuerus (Hebrew) or Xerxes (Greek) is a type of God the Father. Queens Vashti and Esther, his wives, are types of Israel who was married to God and of New Jerusalem who is prepared as a bride for her Husband. Haman "the adversary and enemy" (Esther 7:6) is a type of Satan, our "adversary the devil, [who] as a roaring lion, walks about, seeking whom he may devour" (1 Peter 5:8).

In the third year of his reign, Ahasuerus made a feast for all the princes of his provinces to show "the riches of his glorious kingdom and the honor of his excellent majesty" for 180 days—six months. And when the days where finished, he made another feast for just those at his Shushan palace that lasted for seven days.

The timing of these feasts compliments the liturgical calendar followed by Israel beginning with Passover at full moon (mid-month) at the start of the church year. The last feast of the year occurred exactly six months later at full moon (mid-month) in the seventh month.

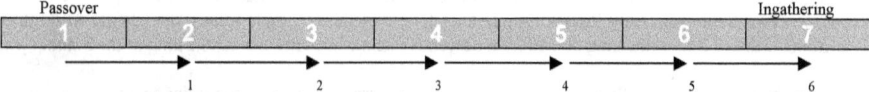

This party lasted seven days and was held "in the court of the garden of the king's palace." Likewise, the Feast of Tabernacles or Ingathering began on the 15th day of the seventh month and lasted seven days. It was a celebration that commemorated Israel's freedom from Egypt but also the joys of the new earth when the harvest of the world takes place at the Second Coming and when Adam receives the Garden of Eden restored.

The royal wine was in abundance and they drank "according to the law; none did compel." The king had appointed that "all should do according to every man's pleasure." God never coerces his subjects but allows full freedom of choice to every creature.

Vashti, the queen, conducted a rival feast for the women in the royal house. The queen held her own competing event apparently in defiance of and certainly not in respect for the king and his feast. On the final seventh day, the king decides to show off his trophy wife to his seven princes and seven chamberlains "for she was fair to look on" Esther 1:11. He specifically asks her to come in wearing the royal crown, but her highness refuses. The decree, after a brief consultation, is made: "Let the king give her royal estate unto another that is better than she." Esther 1:19.

It is of interest to note the nations throughout history which have employed the eagle as their national symbol. Obadiah identified Edom (Esau/Amalek) as one. Others included ancient imperial Rome, the Holy Roman Empire, the Hapsburgs, the Third Reich, and the United States.

When Mordecai left the palace with the king's new decree, "the city of Shushan rejoiced and was glad…And many of the people of the land became Jews; for the fear of the Jews fell upon them." Esther 8:15, 17.

Zechariah foretells a time when all the nations will join the remnant in worshiping the God of heaven.
"**Ten men** out of all the languages of the nations shall take hold of the skirt of a Jew and say, We will go up to Jerusalem with you to pray, for we have heard that God is with you." Zechariah 8:23.
The great ingathering of the final Pentecost is here foreshadowed.

Polluting the Sanctuary

Daniel chapter 8 continues with the aftermath of the goat-ram collision. Out of the goat's single horn come four. And then a little horn arises in the later times of the four horns. It stands up against **the Prince of princes.** Daniel 8:25. Who is this Prince of princes?

> "And from **Jesus Christ**, who is the faithful witness, and the first begotten of the dead, and **the Prince of the kings of the earth**." Revelation 1:5

Then what is the little horn? It is said to arise at the time of the four horns. Most who read this passage assume that the little horn sprouts from one of these four horns. But the text is ambiguous. According to http://69.10.163.110/tempest/seventhunders/daily-3.htm here is what it actually says:

> "Therefore the he goat waxed very great: and when he was strong, the great horn was broken; and for it came up **four notable ones** [masculine] toward the four **winds** [feminine] of heaven." Daniel 8:8.

אַרְבַּע תַּחְתֶּיהָ, לְאַרְבַּע רוּחוֹת הַשָּׁמָיִם.

Paul spoke about "every wind of doctrine." This is referring to the beliefs of a church which are symbolized by a woman in scripture. Thus, the he-horns are political powers whereas the she-winds are spiritual powers.

These four horns extend outward in all four directions, north, south, east and west. Notice that the horns are he-horns from the he-goat and they grow toward the four she-winds. These powers become worldwide in scope and extent. Now Daniel continues in the next verse:

> "And out of **one** ["achath" feminine] **of them** ["hem" masculine] came forth **a little horn**, which waxed exceeding great, toward the south, and toward the east, and toward the pleasant *land*." Daniel 8:9.

וּמִן-הָאַחַת מֵהֶם, יָצָא קֶרֶן-אַחַת

Daniel clearly indicates, through his explicit use of Hebrew gender, that the little horn came from one of four she-winds, since the pronoun "them" and the winds are both feminine. Therefore it would not arise form Greece directly but from one of the regions into which Greece would expand. Many identify the late Greek-Selucid king Antiochus Epiphanes as the little horn. And, indeed, he was an example of a vile, abominable, tyrant that desecrated the temple around 172 BC. However, a better fulfillment was recognized by Peter when he identified this power in Acts 4:26-28:

> "For of a truth against thy holy child Jesus, whom thou hast anointed, both Herod, and Pontius Pilate, with the Gentiles, and the people of Israel, were gathered together. For to do whatsoever thy hand and thy counsel determined before to be done."

Herod stood up against the "holy child Jesus" and issued a decree to destroy all the infants in Bethlehem.
Pilate was Roman Governor of Judea in the reign of Tiberius Caesar, Emperor of Rome.
He stood up against Christ by pronouncing a sentence of death on our Saviour.
The Gentile soldiers and officers stood up against Jesus by executing the sentence.
The people of Israel, through the Sanhedrin, stood up against Christ by demanding His death.
Zechariah 1:18-21 speaks of four horns "the horns of the Gentiles" which scattered Judah.
The modern nations of Western Civilization owe the legacy of their foundation to the kingdom of Greece.

> He magnified himself even to the Prince of the host
> and "from him" the daily was taken away
> and the place of his sanctuary was cast down.

Taking away the Daily
Many different ideas have been entertained over the centuries as to what the "daily" really meant. The Jews believed it was the Babylonians who took away their daily sacrifices by destroying their temple. Early Christians believed it was Christ's earthly ministry that was taken away by Rome in ordering His crucifixion. Later Christians believed it was pagan sun worship that took away the true daily worship of the Son of God. Then with Papal Rome's appearance, they saw its false earthly human priesthood as the abomination that took away the daily ministration of Christ in the heavenly sanctuary. Next, when Muslims threatened to invade Europe, Rome identified the Mohammedans as the abomination that would take away Christianity and make the world desolate. Finally, Rome pointed the finger at the Protestant Reformers and blamed them for taking away the daily mass. But when the papacy came to its end in 1798, suddenly attention was directed once again back to Rome. It was the "power, seat and great authority," taken way from the Caesars of Imperial Rome and given to the Popes that was now understood to be the "daily."

The Hebrew word for "daily" is Tamid. It means "to stretch" and is translated as "always" (Exodus 27:20), "continually, day by day" (Exodus 29:38, 42; Numbers 4:7), perpetual and "ever" (Psalm 25:15). In each of these instances it is a modifier of something else. Continual burning lamps, continual burnt offering, continual bread, etc. But in Daniel 8, 11 and 12 Tamid is prefixed with the definite article "the." This is the only occurrence of this in scriptures. In Daniel Tamid is a noun, not a modifier. This is why the King James version indicates, by placing the word "sacrifice" in italic typeface, that it has been added. Unfortunately, because it makes "daily" become a modifier when it should not be.

Daniel 8:12 "And an host was given against the Daily by reason of transgression"..."to finish the transgression" The Hebrew is B' Fa-sha. B' is the second letter of the Hebrew alphabet. It is the first word of the Bible: "**In** the beginning." Daniel's verse should read: "...was given against the Daily **in** transgression." Deuteronomy 13:2 describes a illegitimate birth as Fa-sha Israel "a vile transgressor in Israel." Thus, this daily is an evil power, a sinful force, and a transgression.

Verse 11: "He magnified himself even to the Prince of the host, and from him the Daily was taken away." From whom was the Daily taken? It is either the little horn or the Prince of the host. But since the Daily is evil, and there is nothing evil in Christ the Prince to be taken away, then the evil Daily must be taken away from Rome.

The little horn emerges from Rome. Like the two legs of iron in the image of chapter 2, it had two stages of development: pagan and papal.

    1 Pagan Rome was a system where the State controlled religion, its visible head was the Emperor.
    2 Papal Rome was a system where religion controlled the State, its visible head was the Pope.

Paganism conducted its worship in temples filled with images and marked by festivals.
Papal worship didn't change this arrangement, and both were centered in the city of Rome.
The little papal horn took away Paganism and the place of its sanctuary, setting up its own instead.

The most famous sanctuary of Roman Paganism was the Pantheon, where "all the gods" (pan-theo) were assembled and on display for public adoration. It was originally built between 27 and 25 BC by Marus Agrippa (whose name is seen inscribed over the entrance) as a temple to the seven planets, the seven deities of the Roman state religion. It is the best-preserved and oldest building in the world that has been in continuous use since its erection over 2,000 years ago.

98 Prophesy Again! **Polluting the Sanctuary**

When Hadrian restored it in 125 AD, it was intended to be an ecumenical gesture to the subjects of the empire as a repository for all the gods in the Roman realm that the imperial armies conquered and brought back to the capitol. It was converted into a Roman Catholic church in 608 and renamed the Church of Mary and the Martyrs. Masses are still held there for weddings and funerals. The history of the Pantheon, then, illustrates the continuation and transfer of title over the city of Rome, from pagan to papal control.

Daniel 11:31 adds: "they shall pollute the sanctuary of strength, and take away the Daily, and place the abomination that makes desolate." Then Daniel 12:11 specifies that this would be "from the time that the Daily shall be **taken away** and the abomination that makes desolate set up..."

Thus, the pagan Daily made way for the papal abomination of desolation.
Daniel 8:13 includes "the Daily and the transgression of desolation" as the parties responsible for giving "both the sanctuary and the host to be trodden under foot."

This passage can be read in one of two ways:
  (the Daily) and (the transgression of desolation) where only one is a desolating power
or
  (the Daily and the transgression) of desolation. where both are desolating.

If these are both referring to Rome, then both are desolating powers.
  1. the Daily desolation (3 Arian horns) that was taken away (by Pagan Rome) makes room for...
  2. the transgression of desolation (Papal Rome) that takes its place.

1 2 3 ⬅ 4 5 6 7 8 9 10

When the Roman Empire disintegrated into the 10 barbarian nations of Europe, three accepted the teachings of Arius, that Christ was a created being. This heresy became a fighting issue for the emerging little horn. The Papacy could incorporate nearly every pagan concept into its teachings, but not this one. Seven of the 10 horns would turn on these three (Visigoths, Ostrogoths and Vandals) and uproot them.

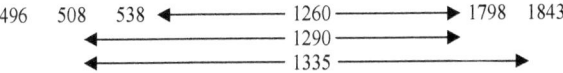

Historically, the work by Pagan Rome to eliminate the Arian problem, began with the conversion of Clovis, king of the Franks in 496 AD. Then, in 508 Clovis fought his first battle for the Pope against the Visogoths of Spain. The last of the three horns was uprooted by Justinian's general Belisarius in 538. This began the 1260 years of Papal supremacy which ended in 1798. 1290 years extended from 508. But blessed were they who waited unto the 1335 years of 1843 when the glorious prospect of the second advent thrilled the hearts of expectant believers during the climax of the Great Advent Awakening.

The desolation continues. Uprooting of three powers has occurred in other phases of Rome as well.
Pagan Rome conquered: North Africa (Carthage, led by Hannibal), Gaul to the north, and Greece to the east.
Modern papal Rome will defeat: Atheism (Soviet Union), Protestantism (United States), and secularism.

Moses originally received the details and specifications for building the first earthly sanctuary. The one he built in the wilderness was modeled after what he saw while face to face with God on Mt Sinai. Ezekiel later was given considerable detail for the construction of another sanctuary and its services. But this temple was never built. In the New Testament, Paul spent much time in the book of Hebrews, describing the sanctuary and its services with attention directed to the heavenly sanctuary where Christ now acts on our behalf.

With the coming of the "falling away" into apostate Papacy and Protestantism, the truth regarding the real purpose of Christ's heavenly ministry as our High Priest was again cast to the ground. But the time finally came, in the mid 1800's when a renewed understanding of the heavenly sanctuary and its role in the salvation of mankind made clear what had long been forgotten. The sanctuary was restored.

> "For **the mystery of iniquity does already work**; only he who now letteth will let, **until he be taken out of the way, and then shall that wicked be revealed**." 2 Thessalonians 2:7-8

Paganism, secular, godless, pleasure-seeking, worldly paganism stands in the way of letting the Papacy be fully revealed. When it is taken out of the way, then the Universal Church can take over.

Las Vegas epitomizes the Daily today. It goes non-stop, night and day, day in and day out, constant, continual, excitement and entertainment.

So, Rome stood up against Jesus Christ, crucified Him, and "from him" the constant pagan activities were taken away "and the place of his sanctuary was cast down." The word for "sanctuary" here is ***miqdash*** which can mean a palace, a chapel, a temple (for Jehovah or idols), an asylum, a sanctuary. It is a general term that can sacred or secular usage. This is quite different from the word used for sanctuary in verses 13 and 14.

> "How long shall be the vision concerning the daily, and the transgression of desolation, to give both the **sanctuary** and the host to be trodden under foot? And he said unto me, Unto two thousand and three hundred days; then shall the **sanctuary** be cleansed." Daniel 8:13, 14.

Here "sanctuary" is the Hebrew word ***qodesh*** which can only mean a sacred place, consecrated, dedicated, hallowed, holy, sanctuary. It is reserved exclusively for God's house, His dwelling. This distinction strongly suggests that the sanctuary back in verse 11 is not God's sanctuary, but that of Pagan Rome.

100 Prophesy Again! **Polluting the Sanctuary**

So, Rome stood up against Jesus Christ, crucified Him, and "from him" the constant pagan activities were taken away and the place of the Pagan sanctuary was cast down. Pagan Rome's sanctuary was the capitol city of Rome. It was prophesied to rule for 360 years, "a time" in prophecy, from 31 BC to 330 AD.

The Vatican museum has, in the Sala di Costantino, on display a huge painting by Gianfrancesco Penni of Sylvester I receiving a small statue of a warrior known as Roma Aeterna (eternal Rome) from Constantine as he is leaving Rome. It is entitled, "The Donation of Rome from Constantine to the Pope."

The message symbolized in this exchange was this: the Pope, representing the papacy, is now the little power, the little horn. The place of his sanctuary was **taken away** to Constantinople. This happened in 330 AD.
The dragon gave his seat, his power, and authority to the beast. Revelation 13:2.

And what authority it was! As Paul predicted, "that man of sin be revealed, the son of perdition; who opposeth and exalteth himself above all that is called God, or that is worshipped; so that he as God sitteth in the temple of God, showing himself that he is God" 2 Thessalonians 2:3, 4. The Pope gradually assumed to be infallible in matters of faith and practice when speaking "ex cathedra" (from the cathedral) when sitting on the throne of Peter. Every Catholic is bound to accept his words when, as the Vicar of Christ, the Pope speaks from Peter's chair, in the Cathedral of God, declaring himself to be infallible in defining and declaring unbiblical doctrines which he claims to be essential to salvation as though he were God!

Evidence that the wound of 1798 was healing is seen in these words contained in Pope Leo XIII's, Encyclical Letter, "On the Chief Duties of Christians as Citizens," dated January 10, 1890:

> But the supreme teacher in the Church is the Roman Pontiff. Union of minds, therefore, requires, together with a perfect accord in the one faith, complete submission and obedience of will to the Church and to the Roman Pontiff, as to God Himself.

This was translated in *The Great Encyclical Letters of Pope Leo XIII* (New York: Benziger, 1903), p. 193.

Taking the Daily Again

In the early 1900's, the prophecy of Daniel 11 was singled out as important to the end times:

> "We have no time to lose. Troublous times are before us. The world is stirred with the spirit of war. Soon the scenes of trouble spoken of in the prophecies will take place. **The prophecy in the eleventh of Daniel has nearly reached its complete fulfillment. Much of the history that has taken place in fulfillment of this prophecy will be repeated.**"

Then verses 30-36 are quoted:

> "In the **thirtieth verse** a power is spoken of that 'shall be grieved, and return, and have indignation against the holy covenant: so shall he do; he shall even return, and have intelligence with them that forsake the holy covenant. And arms shall stand on his part, and they shall **pollute the sanctuary of strength, and shall take away the daily** *sacrifice,* **and they shall place the abomination that maketh desolate**...'"

Here, again we encounter the sanctuary, the daily and the desolating abomination. It is this that is going to be repeated in our day. We should, therefore, understand clearly the history of the original fulfillment. This history began with the conversion of Clovis in 496 AD. Is this an important date? The *National Catholic Register*, September 8, 1996 thought so:

> PARIS-John Paul II is coming to France this month-his fifth visit since becoming Pope in 1978-to celebrate the 15th centenary of the baptism of Clovis, the first Western Christian king and founder of the modern French nation. It was as a result of that baptism-traditionally believed to have taken place in Reims in 496 A D.-that France glories in the title of the "eldest daughter of the Church.". .. It was in Reims that Clovis, pagan leader of the Salian Franks, was baptized by St. Remi, the bishop of Reims, in the presence of all the kings' nobles. He was to give to France (then still known as Gaul) its name, its capital, its first royal dynasty (the Merovingians, named after his grandfather, Merovec), and its official faith.
>
> Some have suggested that Clovis' baptism was also the baptism of France. ... The kings baptism did, however, mark the first official recognition of Christianity in a country still dominated by paganism and Arianism (the early Christian heresy which denied the divinity of Christ). The history of France and of Europe, and indeed the history of the Catholic Church would not have been the same if this baptism had not taken place. ... Celebrating Clovis baptism endorse the traditional view that his conversion marked the actual founding of France. "By celebrating the baptism of Clovis, the French republic is unilaterally endorsing a certain Christian image of France," he wrote. "To remember Clovis is to recall monarchic religious and the divine rights of kings. ..."

Though President Jacques Chirac was uncertain about the political fallout of attending the Papal celebration, the article was certain that "General Charles de Galle, would have gone. 'For me,' de Galle said, 'the history of France begins with Clovis. My country is Christian and I begin to count the history of France from the arrival of a Christian king bearing the name of the Franks.'" It is clear that the Catholic church understands their history quite well indeed. If 496 is an important date to them, it should be to us as well.

Polluting the Sanctuary

Babel Paganism begins....... Babylon Persia Greece Rome...... Paganism continues... **Dragon**
Papacy................. **Beast**
Protestantism........... **False Prophet**

Mohammed founded the religion of Islam (622) about the same time that the papacy was beginning (538). The one member of the united three-fold evil trinity that had continuous existence throughout all history is paganism, sun worship, spiritualism at the end. It is the "continual" force of evil on earth.
Each of these powers have a spiritual and political aspect, a union of church and state:

Power	Spiritual	Political
Dragon	spiritualism, pantheism, Hinduism, Buddism, Shintoism, Mohammedism	socialism, communism, nazism, fascism, etc.
Beast	Catholicism, Papacy	monarchy, divine right of kings
False Prophet	Protestantism	Democracy

Revelation 16:13 features the evil trio at the very end: the dragon, the beast, and the false prophet.
But the three-fold union has occurred throughout redemptive history.

Following the Exodus it was the Midianites, the Moabites, and Balaam (the false prophet).
In the time of Gideon it was the Midianites, the Amalekites, and the children of the East. (Judges 7:12)
Jehoshaphat faced the tribes of Edom, Moab, and the children of Ammon (2 Chronicles 20:23)
Daniel 11:41 mentions these same three again as not escaping out of the hand of the king of the north.

Now, consider the three progressively greater powers of Daniel 8: the great power, the greater power, and the exceeding great power. Today we see Iran, the ram, becoming a great power. A greater power, the American he-goat, opposes and attacks it. But the exceeding great power, the little horn of the revived Papacy united under Europe, will step in to bring peace. In the end, Babylon (the great city) will be divided into three parts.

Remember, prophetic symbols have both positive and negative, physical and spiritual applications.
The daily or continual has, therefore, both an evil (paganism) and holy (Christ's intercession) meaning.
The Papacy removed the threat of paganism in 508 AD with the baptism of Clovis.
At the end of time, the Three-fold Union will remove the Law, taking it captive, and replace it with a substitute.

Five verses in the book of Daniel detail the circumstances surrounding the "taking away of the daily:"
- Daniel 8:11 Little horn magnifies himself to the prince of the host,
  by him the daily was taken away, casts down the place of sanctuary
- vs 12 Because of transgression, a host against the daily is given to him to cast the truth to the ground
- vs 13 the transgression of desolation gives the sanctuary and host to be trodden under foot
- Daniel 11:31 arms shall take away the daily and place the desolating abomination
- Daniel 12:11 from the time the daily is taken away, and the abomination that makes desolate set up shall be 1290 days.

The interpretation of these verses is based on either viewing the daily as:
> something good (Christ's intercession) and its taking away as a sacrilege or as
> something bad (abomination) and its taking away as a historical fact.

Prophetic symbols have both positive and negative realities in both the physical and spiritual realms.

The Evil Daily
God's people are exposed to a daily dose of evil influence, temptation, and conflict with the Law of God. But Divine intervention will make a way of escape for them by removing this "evil daily."

For example, the **imagination of men's hearts** were **evil continually** in the days of Noah. Genesis 6:5 When were the continual evil imaginations taken away? At the flood, at their destruction.

The enemies of God's people "reproach" them "while they say **daily**...where is thy god?" Psalm 42:10. This was demonstrated when the king's servants spoke with Mordecai "**daily** unto him" asking him "why do you transgress the king's commandment?" Esther 3:3, 4. A later command brought them deliverance.

When Daniel arrived in Babylon, the king "appointed them a **daily** provision of the king's meat." Daniel 1:5. This diet was defiling them. Meat and wine from the king's table represented Babylonian doctrine, teaching. But Daniel purposed to have this daily provision "taken away" and replaced with pulse—sprouted vegetables. He was "proved" for 10 days and when Melzar saw that they were "fairer and fatter" he "**took away** the [**daily**] portion of their meat, and the wine" verse 16. They desired to feed instead on the pure Word of God.

The Good Daily
Parallel to the evil daily that is taken away by God, is the good daily that is taken away by evil forces. In fact, it is a response to the "putting away of sin" and the purification of the saints that Satan attacks.

Isaiah 58:2 God says that His professed followers "seek me daily, and delight to know my ways, as a nation that did righteousness, and forsook not the ordinance of their God." It is when **they cease to seek God daily,** when they **no longer delight to know His ways**, when the nation **ceases to do righteousness**, when it **forsakes the ordinance of God,** that the "daily" is taken away.

Sacrifices are offered on the altar "**day by day continually**" Exodus 28:38
"A **continual** burnt offering" vs 42
They are "the **daily** meat offerings" Numbers 4:16 which they were to "offer **daily**" Numbers 28:24
It is "the **daily** burnt offering" Numbers 29:6. When were the sacrifices taken away?
When Jesus, the daily Teacher, was taken away and crucified on Calvary, the sacrificial system ended.
Jesus said, "I was **daily with you in the temple teaching**, and you **took me not**" Mark 14:49.
But, when His "hour was come," Judas came with the mob and "took him away."

	"taken away"	
Eden sacrificial system began and continued until **CALVARY**		70AD
		Abomination that resulted in **desolation**
		lies 3 days in tomb

The high priest bore the names of Israel upon his breastplate when he went into the most holy place as a "memorial before the Lord **continually**" Exodus 28:29. "And Aaron shall **bear the judgment of the children of Israel** upon his heart before the Lord **continually**." vs 30. Melchisedec, "king of Salem, priest of the Most High God...abideth **a priest continually**." Hebrews 7:1-3
When will the continual judgment of Israel be taken away?
When Jesus leaves the most holy place, when the judgment ends.

1844: Most Holy Place Mediatorial Work of Intercession **ENDS**	
	SET UP Abomination of desolation
	Satan as "Christ"

104 Prophesy Again! **Polluting the Sanctuary**

When the wicked solidify their rejection of God and the saints seal their loyalty to God, the judgment ends. As the saints "shine as the stars," Satan appears as "an angel of light" claiming in abomination to be Christ.

The same thing happens at the end in the experience of the Two Witnesses. As their daily testimony ends and they are taken away, the abomination of their execution is followed by the destruction of Babylon.
The **two witnesses** in Revelation 11 are identified as the two lamp stands which "stand before the Lord **continually**" Leviticus 24:4. The **lamps in the holy place** were to "burn **continually**," verse 1.
Their daily illumination will be taken away at the end of their 42 months of witnessing. This was modeled during the French Revolution, when the Scriptures (and all things sacred) were burned in the streets of Paris. This abomination also resulted in desolation: the deadly wound of the papacy in 1798.

French Revolution
Two Witnesses testify in sackcloth 1260 days until **SLAIN**
Abomination that results in **desolation**
lies 3 days in street

The **twelve cakes of shewbread** were set in order "before the Lord **continually**." vs 8.
"Every sabbath" they were placed in the holy place. "Give us this day our **daily** bread" Matt 6:11
When will this Sabbath Bread, this "**continual** bread" (Numbers 4:7) be taken away?
When the image to the beast is set up and worship of a false sabbath is commanded.

Sunday Law
Continual Sabbath shewbread set before Lord until **Taken Away**
Abomination that results in **desolation**
"made void Thy law"
"time to act"

"So shall I **keep thy law continually** for ever and ever" Psalm 119:44
"I will have respect unto thy statutes continually" vs 117
"Keep thy **father's commandment**, and forsake not **the law of thy mother**:
Bind them **continually** upon thine heart." Proverbs 6:20.
But when the world decides to end the observance of God's law, when the Sunday Law is passed, the Lord will begin to work, the time will have come. "It is time for thee, LORD, to work: for they have made void thy law." Psalm 119:126.

Therefore:
Little horn magnifies himself to the prince of the host (secular political power)
Because of transgression a host against the daily is given to him (the armies of France, later Europe)
the transgression of desolation gives the sanctuary (capitol) and host (nation) to be trodden under foot
the host (given to the little horn) casts the truth to the ground, casts down the place of sanctuary
arms (Clovis' and Justinian's armies) shall take away the daily (political administration),
by him the daily was taken away (transfer of governmental power from Imperial to Papal Rome)
arms (Justinian's forces) shall place (in Rome) the abomination (papacy) that makes desolate
from the time the daily is taken away and the abomination that makes desolate set up shall be 1290 days.

But, in addition to the historical fulfillment, there will be a final repetition at the end of time.
The daily rule by national governments will be taken away as the kings of the earth unite with the woman to form Babylon the Great, thus setting up the final abomination that will lead to global desolation. A great crisis will make this final alliance a strategic necessity, a matter of survival for the Christian West as it faces the threat of an Islamic East in its quest for world domination.

Job's Take Away

Job experienced the literal taking away of his oxen, asses, and camels by marauding bandits and the loss of his sheep and children by "acts of God" for whom he sacrificed and sanctified continually, daily. After the "taking away" he was afflicted with a grievous sore from head to foot—the same attacks the world at the end of time when the first of seven last plagues begin to fall.

1:2 And there were born unto him **seven sons** and **three daughters**.
1:3 His substance also was **seven thousand sheep**, and **three thousand camels**, and five hundred yoke of **oxen**, and five hundred she **asses**, and a **very great household**; so that this man was the greatest of all the men of the east.
1:4 And his sons went and feasted in their houses, **every one his day**; and sent and called for their three sisters to eat and to drink with them.
1:5 And it was so, when **the days of their feasting were gone** about, that Job sent and sanctified them, and rose up early in the morning, and offered burnt offerings according to the number of them all:...
Thus did Job **continually.**

1:13 And there was a day when his sons and his daughters were eating and drinking wine in their eldest brother's house: 1:14 And there came a messenger unto Job, and said, The **oxen** were plowing, and the **asses** feeding beside them: 1:15 And the Sabeans fell upon them, and **took them away**; yea, they have slain the servants with the edge of the sword; and I only am escaped alone to tell thee.

1:16 While he was yet speaking, there came also another, and said, The **fire of God is fallen from heaven**, and hath **burned up the sheep**, and the servants, and consumed them; and I only am escaped alone to tell thee.

1:17 While he was yet speaking, there came also another, and said, The Chaldeans made out three bands, and fell upon the **camels**, and have **carried them away,** yea, and slain the servants with the edge of the sword; and I only am escaped alone to tell thee.

1:18 While he was yet speaking, there came also another, and said, Thy sons and thy daughters were eating and drinking wine in their eldest brother's house: 1:19 And, behold, there came **a great wind from the wilderness**, and smote the four corners of the house, and it fell upon **the young men, and they are dead;** and I only am escaped alone to tell thee.

1:20 Then Job arose, and rent his mantle, and shaved his head, and fell down upon the ground, and worshipped, 1:21 And said, Naked came I out of my mother's womb, and naked shall I return thither: the LORD gave, and **the LORD hath taken away**; blessed be the name of the LORD.

2:7 So went **Satan** forth from the presence of the LORD, and **smote Job with sore boils** from the sole of his foot unto his crown.

106 Prophesy Again! **Polluting the Sanctuary**

Alexander Engages the Persians
Mosaic from Pompeii

The restoration of the temple involves both the heavenly and earthly versions.

- The heavenly sanctuary, obscured for centuries by papal substitution, began its return to men's attention with the first fulfillment of the first 2300-day prophecy in 1844.
- The earthly sanctuary, held hostage for centuries by Muslim domination, began its promise of return with the second fulfillment of the 2300-day prophecy in 1967.

The 1260 Connection
Interestingly, 1967 is connected to prophetic times in yet another way.

The Dome of the Rock was built between 687 and 692 AD by the Umayyad caliph 'Abd al-Malik on top of the Temple Mount in Jerusalem, is a site sacred to Jews, Muslims and Christians. The existence of this Umayyad mosque and a second, the al-Aqsa Mosque, built by caliph al-Walid, both on the Temple Mount, have a long enduring history. Destroyed by at least five earthquakes, the Al-Aqsa mosque was last restored in 1035 AD.
Muslims began construction on the Al-Aqsa Mosque in 707 AD and completed it in 710. This structure is near the Dome of the Rock, famous icon of the city's skyline. Al-Aqsa is the largest mosque in Jerusalem; about 5,000 people can worship in and around the mosque.

Muslims worshipping at the mosque have, at times, hurled rocks down at Jews praying below at the Western Wall. A group of Jews known as the Temple Mount Faithful actually have plans to rebuild the ancient Jewish Temple in this area.

Exactly 1260 years later, in the year 1967, it and the Old city of Jerusalem returned to Israeli rule.

Daniel 9

This chapter has an interesting number of occurances of the words Lord and LORD. Count them:

9:1 In the first year of Darius the son of Ahasuerus, of the seed of the Medes, which was made ki over the realm of the Chaldeans; 9:2 In the first year of his reign I Daniel understood by books the number of the years, whereof the word of the LORD came to Jeremiah the prophet, that he would accomplish seventy years in the desolations of Jerusalem.
9:3 And I set my face unto the Lord God, to seek by prayer and supplications, with fasting, and sackcloth, and ashes: 9:4 And I prayed unto the LORD my God, and made my confession, and said, O Lord, the great and dreadful God, keeping the covenant and mercy to them that love him, and to them that keep his commandments; 9:5 We have sinned, and have committed iniquity, and have done wickedly, and have rebelled, even by departing from thy precepts and from thy judgments: 9:6 Neither have we hearkened unto thy servants the prophets, which spake in thy name to our kings, our princes, and our fathers, and to all the people of the land.
9:7 O Lord, righteousness belongeth unto thee, but unto us confusion of faces, as at this day; to the men of Judah, and to the inhabitants of Jerusalem, and unto all Israel, that are near, and that are far off, through all the countries whither thou hast driven them, because of their trespass that they have trespassed against thee.
9:8 O Lord, to us belongeth confusion of face, to our kings, to our princes, and to our fathers, because we have sinned against thee.
9:9 To the Lord our God belong mercies and forgivenesses, though we have rebelled against him;
9:10 Neither have we obeyed the voice of the LORD our God, to walk in his laws, which he set before us by his servants the prophets.
9:11 Yea, all Israel have transgressed thy law, even by departing, that they might not obey thy voice; therefore the curse is poured upon us, and the oath that is written in the law of Moses the servant of God, because we have sinned against him.
9:12 And he hath confirmed his words, which he spake against us, and against our judges that judged us, by bringing upon us a great evil: for under the whole heaven hath not been done as hath been done upon Jerusalem.
9:13 As it is written in the law of Moses, all this evil is come upon us: yet made we not our prayer before the LORD our God, that we might turn from our iniquities, and understand thy truth.
9:14 Therefore hath the LORD watched upon the evil, and brought it upon us: for the LORD our God is righteous in all his works which he doeth: for we obeyed not his voice.
9:15 And now, O Lord our God, that hast brought thy people forth out of the land of Egypt with a mighty hand, and hast gotten thee renown, as at this day; we have sinned, we have done wickedly.
9:16 O Lord, according to all thy righteousness, I beseech thee, let thine anger and thy fury be turned away from thy city Jerusalem, thy holy mountain: because for our sins, and for the iniquities of our fathers, Jerusalem and thy people are become a reproach to all that are about us.
9:17 Now therefore, O our God, hear the prayer of thy servant, and his supplications, and cause thy face to shine upon thy sanctuary that is desolate, for the Lord's sake.
9:18 O my God, incline thine ear, and hear; open thine eyes, and behold our desolations, and the city which is called by thy name: for we do not present our supplications before thee for our righteousnesses, but for thy great mercies.
9:19 O Lord, hear; O Lord, forgive; O Lord, hearken and do; defer not, for thine own sake, O my God: for thy city and thy people are called by thy name.
9:20 And whiles I was speaking, and praying, and confessing my sin and the sin of my people Israel, and presenting my supplication before the LORD my God for the holy mountain of my God
9:21 Yea, whiles I was speaking in prayer, even the man Gabriel, whom I had seen in the vision at the beginning, being caused to fly swiftly, touched me about the time of the evening oblation. [last sacrifice of the day: close of probation]

Lord (Adonai) occurs 10 times, an allusion to God's Law, the Ten Commandments.
LORD (self-existent, eternal Jehovah) occurs 7 times as a prelude to the 7 elements listed by Gabriel (verse 24) in his interpretation of the chapter 8 vision that will be accomplished within the 70 weeks by the Messiah.

108   Prophesy Again!   **70 Weeks**

Gabriel now explains in further detail the perplexing aspects of the 2300 day prophecy.

> 9:22 And he informed me, and talked with me, and said, O Daniel, I am now come forth to give thee skill and under-standing. 9:23 At the beginning of thy supplications the commandment came forth, and I am come to shew thee; for thou art greatly beloved: therefore understand the matter, and consider the vision.
>
> 9:24
> 1   **Seventy weeks are determined** upon thy people and upon thy holy city,
> 2   to **finish the transgression**, and
> 3   to make **an end of sins**, and
> 4   to make **reconciliation for iniquity**, and
> 5   to bring in **everlasting righteousness**, and
> 6   to **seal up the vision** and prophecy, and
> 7   to **anoint the most Holy**.
>
> 9:25 Know therefore and understand, that from the going forth of the commandment to restore and to build Jerusalem unto the Messiah the Prince shall be seven weeks, and threescore and two weeks: the street shall be built again, and the wall, even in troublous times.
> 9:26 And after threescore and two weeks shall Messiah be cut off, but not for himself: and the people of the prince that shall come shall destroy the city and the sanctuary; and the end thereof shall be with a flood, and unto the end of the war desolations are determined.
> 9:27 And he shall confirm the covenant with many for one week: and in the midst of the week he shall cause the sacrifice and the oblation to cease, and for the overspreading of abominations he shall make it desolate, even until the consummation, and that determined shall be poured upon the desolate.

These last three verses 9:25-27 form a perfect Hebrew chiasm or mirror. Notice how the themes of Construction, Destruction and Messiah are balanced in these three sequential verses. This assists in identifying the "He" of verse 27 as that of the Messiah who is cut off after 69 weeks.

Construction: 25 "restore and build Jerusalem"
    Messiah: "unto Messiah the Prince shall be 7 and 62 weeks"
        Construction: "street shall be build again, and the wall"
            Messiah: 26 "Messiah cut off, but not for himself"
        Destruction: "destroy the city and the sanctuary"
                "end…with a flood and…desolations"
    Messiah: 27 "He shall confirm the covenant with many for one week"
Destruction: "sacrifice and oblation cease"
        "abominations shall make it desolate"

Two Seventies

Daniel 9 opens with the aging prophet perplexed over the puzzling vision of the 2300 days. The sanctuary was destined to be "trampled under foot" and subjected to an abomination of desolation! How could this be? The 70 years foretold by Jeremiah were nearly expired. Now it appears that the temple's restoration would be postponed for a dreadful double millennial delay. Daniel turns again to examine the scroll of Jeremiah. Yes, it *did* specify 70 years. Then Gabriel arrives to explain. After 70 years of punishment, 70 weeks of forgiveness would be determined to usher in the Messiah.

To Daniel, a figure like 70 years would naturally suggest a Sabbath theme. After all, 70 is a sabbath decade. But 70 weeks was an even stronger Sabbath symbol composed of 7 tens and 7 days. 70 years, 70 weeks, they must be related. 70 weeks of 7 days total a 490 day period of time. And this number speaks of forgiveness. It was this very figure to which Jesus referred when Peter asked Him about how many times one should forgive:

"Then came Peter to Him and said, Lord, how oft shall my brother sin against me and I forgive him? till seven times? Jesus saith unto him, I say not unto thee, until seven times, but until seventy times seven."
Matthew 18:21, 22

Forgiveness is the essence of the Sabbath in all of its variations. And 490 speaks of a complete jubilee of forgiveness. Jesus was very much aware of the 70 week prophecy and its implications for the Jewish nation.

Jubilee: rest, release, restoration
Moses first used the term jubilee in the details he provided in his five volume epic work, the Pentateuch. The jubilee was the culmination of a trilogy of Sabbath concepts, the climax of rest, release and restoration. Beginning in the beginning, God established the Sabbath as His holy day of rest and celebration of a perfect creation.

"And on the seventh day God ended his work which he had made; and he rested on the seventh day from all his work which he had made. And God blessed the seventh day, and sanctified it: because that in it he had rested from all his work which God created and made." Genesis 2:2,3.

Then, when God created the Hebrew nation and gave them rest from their slavery, He instituted a sabbath of years.

"When you come into the land which I give you, *then shall the land keep a sabbath* unto the Lord. Six years you shall sow your field, and six years you shall prune your vineyard, and gather in its fruits; but in the seventh year shall be a sabbath of rest unto the land...you shall neither sow your field nor prune your vineyard." Leviticus 25:2.

Furthermore, this was a year of release for the Hebrew servants who had sold themselves into slavery because of debt. They were to be forgiven one year out of seven. So after every six days man would rest from his weekly labor and after every six years the land would rest or lay fallow, and man would rest from his yearly cultivating chores while bond servants were freed to take a "sabbatical." But this wasn't all. After every six sabbatical years of land rest, a super sabbath, the jubilee, was to be celebrated.

"You shall number *seven sabbaths of years*...seven times seven years...*forty and nine years*. Then shall you cause the trumpet of the *jubilee* to sound (throughout all your land) on the tenth day of the seventh month, in the *day of atonement*." Leviticus 25:8.

Property values were restored to their original levels, lands were restored to their original owners, and all debts were erased.

Seven days	=	a *week* ending with the *Sabbath day*
Seven years	=	a sabbatical *year of land rest*
Seven sabbaticals	=	a *jubilee*

"And you shall hallow *the fiftieth year* and *proclaim liberty* throughout all the land: it shall be *a jubilee* unto you." Leviticus 25:10.

The jubilee was to be celebrated for an entire year and it was a time of liberty and forgiveness of debt.

The Sabbath Sentence
Israel had been punished with 70 years of Babylonian exile because they refused to observe the law of the sabbatical and jubilee years. Every seventh year Hebrew slaves were to be given one year of sabbatical rest. And after every seventh sabbatical year, in the year of Jubilee, all debts were to be erased. But greed

prevented these sabbath rests from being realized. After years of disobedience, the nation faced the threat of captivity. As the Babylonians were poised for attack, the Lord gave Israel one last chance. And they took it.

> "This is the word that came unto Jeremiah from the Lord, after that the king Zedekiah had made a covenant with all the people which were at Jerusalem: to proclaim liberty unto them, That every man should let his manservant, and every man his maidservant, being an Hebrew or a Hebrewess, go free; ...then they obeyed and let them go." Jeremiah 34:8-10

Their obedience worked! Now God could step in and protect them, turn the Babylonians back, and be their fortress—because they had once again chosen to obey His statues. But their reform was short-lived. In the very next verse we read,

> "But afterward they turned, and caused the servants and the handmaids, whom they had let go free, to return, and brought them into subjection for servants and for handmaids." Jeremiah 34:11

Like the unforgiving servant in Christ's parable of Matthew 18, though forgiven by God of a staggering debt that had grown into a 70 year prison sentence, the nobles couldn't forgive their own servants for a single year! As a consequence they, too, would be cast into captivity until their debt was fully paid. "If you forgive not men their trespasses, neither will your heavenly Father forgive yours." Matthew 6:15.

Double Land Sabbath

The jubilee was also noted as a second land sabbath. Leviticus 25:11 instructed the people, "You shall not sow, neither reap...for it is the jubilee; it shall be holy unto you." Two years of sequential land rest would have been devastating to the agricultural prosperity of Israel except for God's miraculous intervention. God said,

> "Then I will *command my blessing* upon you in the *sixth year*, and it shall bring forth *fruit for three years.* And you shall sow the eighth year, and eat yet of old fruit until the ninth year; until her fruits come in you shall eat of the old store." Leviticus 25:21.

So, every seven years a land sabbath, and after 49 years (ending in a seventh land sabbath) the jubilee would come as a second year land sabbath in a row, occurring as the 50th year and also the first year of the next seven year cycle. Grouped around the double land sabbaths were three years of blessing.

```
71234567123456712345671234567123456712345671234(6712)34567...
     1        2       3        4       5        6     ( 7J )    1
                                                       BBB
```

While the land was to lay fallow once every seventh year, it was to rest for two consecutive years when a jubilee came around. This double land sabbath was a rare event in the Biblical record. But one such episode is recorded in both Isaiah 37 and 2 Kings 19 (two chapters that are also unique in being exactly reproduced word for word. Pay attention when God repeats something.). These passages recount the threatened attack by Sennacherib, king of Assyria, and God's miraculous deliverance during the reign of Judah's king Hezekiah.

Hezekiah described it as "a day of trouble" "and blasphemy". He called on Isaiah to "lift up prayer for the remnant that are left." God's people are faced with eminent annihilation. And then God says, "This shall be a sign unto you, you shall eat this year such things as grow of themselves, and in the second year that which springs of the same; and in the third year sow and reap and plant." This was a jubilee double land sabbath.

A jubilee meant deliverance. And a jubilee deliverance is awesome. Sennacherib loses his entire army and retreats back to Nineveh where his own sons assassinate him. This is reminiscent of another "king of the north" who sets up his headquarters "between the seas" (Mediterranean, Black and Caspian seas) and yet "comes to his end, and none shall help him." Daniel 11. The last king of the north will act during the final remnant of time, when God's final remnant will be facing the threat of death, but will be delivered at the Jubilee of jubilees.

Sennacherib's Last Stand occurred in 702 BC, a known jubilee. Notice how this date fits into future 49-year jubilee anniversaries, two of which we recognize as important prophetic dates in Daniel 9:

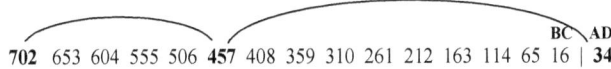

702 653 604 555 506 **457** 408 359 310 261 212 163 114 65 16 | **34**

Counting 49-year intervals from 702 BC, five jubilees later (5 x 49 = 245) falls exactly on 457 BC, the starting date for Daniel's 70 week prophecy which would last 490 years or 10 jubilees. This was a sevenfold expansion of the 70 years of Babylonian exile, the punishment for not observing the law of the land sabbaths.

How was the 70 year sentence determined? The dispensational proponents take a superficial position that this was based on a lapse on Israel's part for observing the sabbatical land rests that occurred every seven years. They consequently arrive at a 490 year period which would contain 70 sabbatical years. But they neglect to recognize the Jubilee years in this same period which occur every 49 years and also demanded the land to rest from agricultural pursuits. This reduces the number of years of neglect to 430 in which 70 land sabbaths were ignored: 61 sabbatical years and 9 jubilee years. Ezekiel explicitly foretold these 430 years. He was instructed to "bear the iniquity of the house of Israel" by laying on his left side for 390 days to represent "the years of their iniquity" Ezekiel 4:5. "I have appointed thee each day for a year" Ezekiel 4:6. He was then to lay on his right side for another 40 days "to bear the iniquity of the house of Judah." Together, the total years of iniquity was 430 years and accounted for the 70 sabbatical and jubilee years of land rest which together, they were responsible to keep but failed to observe.

After 70 years of punishment, the Lord was now offering to give them 70 weeks of forgiveness, a time of probation, a grace period. Each year on the Day of Atonement God would forgive the nation. He would forgive them on 490 Atonements, and give them 490 years in which to learn their lesson. If they didn't, He would bring the ultimate judgment—not just captivity, but total destruction. Once again, the issue was Sabbath observance. Would Israel this time accept the ultimate living Lord of the Sabbath?

The Sabbath Messiah
Daniel prophesied that after 69 weeks the Messiah would come. The time period is expressed as a separate time periods of 7 weeks and 62 weeks. The 7 weeks are stated separately at least to emphasize the jubilee aspects of the prophecy. As we already noted, Leviticus 25:8, states that "seven Sabbaths of years" was to mark off each jubilee time period. In addition, 7 weeks identifies the period of time from Passover to Pentecost, from the wave sheaf offering of the first fruits to the encounter with God at Sinai and the receiving of His covenant law.

The pattern of 7 + 62 + 1 where the final week is divided parallels that of the 1260 days, 42 months, and 3½ years.

"A time, times and dividing of times," as specified in Daniel 7, also parallels "mene, mene, tekel, upharsin." The formula, re-sequenced, is: "weighed, numbered-numbered, divided."

70 Weeks

Right on time, in the fall of AD 27, "in the fullness of time" Galatians 4:4, Jesus was baptized and began his ministry at the beginning of the 70th week, the 7th decade of weeks. This is Sabbath symbology. Jesus, in fact, is the true living Sabbath. In Matthew 11:28 he makes the great invitation, "Come unto me all ye who labor and are heavy laden and I will give you *rest*." Jesus is Holy and He was anointed. The Sabbath day is holy and it is blessed. But the "most holy" time period of all is the Jubilee. It was a convergence of Jesus, the Holy One, anointed on the "holy" Sabbatical year before the 50th Jubilee from the Exodus, the "most holy" time, which begins on the Day of Atonement, the only time when the High Priest enters the "most holy" place.

When Jesus read from the scroll of Isaiah, there in Nazareth as recorded in Luke 4, he was announcing "the acceptable year of the Lord," the Jubilee year that brings release to the captives, reconciliation and restoration to the poor. When Jesus came to the Jordan for baptism 69 x 7 years later, in 27 AD, it was a sabbatical year.

It is no wonder that following His baptism Jesus proclaimed "the time is fulfilled" Mark 1:15.
He was announcing the start of the final seven year count down to the final jubilee.

7 Sabbatical	1	2	3	4	5	6	7 Sabbatical	1 Jubilee
27 AD Baptism	28	29	30	31 Passover	32	33	34 Stephen	35

↑Fall   ↑Spring   ↑Fall

The 70 weeks span the events of Israel's final period of probation marked by seven significant events:

    1 Jerusalem, the street, and the wall will be built and restored
    2 The coming of Messiah the Prince
    3 Covenant shall be confirmed with many
    4 The Messiah shall be "cut off" for someone else
    5 Sacrifices and oblations will cease
    6 The city and the temple are destroyed
    7 Following a war of desolations

During the 70 weeks seven items were to be accomplished:

    1 They are **determined** upon Daniel's people and his holy city,
    2 to **finish the transgression**, and
    3 to make **an end of sins**, and
    4 to make **reconciliation for iniquity**, and
    5 to bring in **everlasting righteousness**, and
    6 to **seal up the vision** and prophecy, and
    7 to **anoint the most Holy**.

Determined
The 70 week prophecy uses this term three times in Daniel 9:

    24: **70 weeks are determined** upon Daniel's people
    26: unto the end of the war **desolations are determined**
    27: and **that determined shall be poured** upon the desolate (desolator)

Time is determined in Scripture as a limit, a boundary which is certain and fixed, set to occur by appointment:

Job 14:1,5 Man that is born of a woman is of few days and full of trouble...Seeing **his days are determined, the number of his months** are with thee, **thou hast appointed his bounds** that he cannot pass.

Job 14:14 If a man die, shall he live again? **all the days of my appointed time will I wait**, till my change come.

Acts 17:24, 26 "God that made the world and all things therein ...hath **determined the times before appointed**, and the **bounds** of their habitation."

Daniel is particularly focused on appointed time:

    Daniel 8:19 "**at the time appointed the end shall be.**"
    Daniel 10:1 "**the time appointed was long.**"
    Daniel 11:27 "the end shall be **at the time appointed.**"
    Daniel 11:29 "**At the time appointed** he shall return."
    Daniel 11:35 "the time of the end:...**is yet for a time appointed.**"

Scripture uses these words, determined and appointed, to indicate that the end results, the final consequences are determined by the initial actions:

2 Samuel 13:32 [the death of Amnon] "**by the appointment of Absalom has been determined from the day** that he forced his sister Tamar."

Daniel 11:36 "**that that is determined shall be done.**"

Matthew 22:22 "And truly the Son of man goes, **as it was determined.**"

Genesis 18:14 "**At the time appointed** I will return unto thee, according to the time of life."

Exodus 9:5 "**the LORD appointed a set time.**"

Exodus 23:15 "Thou shalt keep the feast of unleavened bread:...**in the time appointed**"

Numbers 9:3 "In the fourteenth day of this month, at even, ye shall keep it **in his appointed season.**"

1 Samuel 13:8 "And he tarried seven days, **according to the set time that Samuel had appointed.**"

1 Samuel 24:13, 15 "Shall seven years of famine come unto thee in thy land? or wilt thou flee three months before thine enemies...? or that there be three days' pestilence in thy land? So the LORD sent a pestilence upon Israel from the morning even **to the time appointed.**"

Psalm 81:3 "Blow up the trumpet in the new moon, **in the time appointed**, on our solemn feast day."

Proverbs 7:19 "**the good man is not at home, he is gone a long journey:**…and **will come home at the day appointed.**"

Jeremiah 5:24 "God…giveth rain, both the former and the latter, in his season: he reserves unto us **the appointed weeks of the harvest.**"

Jeremiah 8:7 Yea, the stork in the heaven **knoweth her appointed times;** and the turtle and the crane and the swallow **observe the time of their coming**; but my people know not the judgment of the LORD.

Jeremiah 33:25 "Thus saith the LORD…**I have…appointed the ordinances of heaven and earth**."

Ezekiel 4:6 "**I have appointed thee each day for a year.**"

Habakkuk 2:2 "Write the vision, and make it plain upon tables,…For **the vision is yet for an appointed time**…**it will not tarry**…but the just shall live by his faith."

Acts 17:30 "God…**has appointed a day, in the which he will judge the world.**"

An interesting parallel exists between Daniel 9:24 and Isaiah 61, which Jesus quoted in Nazareth. Each scripture contains seven points, listed in a nearly mirrored reverse order to each other:

Daniel 9:24	Isaiah 61 / Luke 4:18, 19
70 weeks (of years) are determined	to preach the acceptable **year of the Lord**
to **finish the transgression**, and	to preach the **gospel to the poor**
to make **an end of sins**, and	to preach **deliverance to the captives**
to make **reconciliation** for iniquity, and	to **heal the brokenhearted**
to bring in **everlasting righteousness**, and	to **set at liberty** them that are **bruised**
to seal up the **vision** and prophecy, and	the **recovery of sight** to the blind
to **anoint** the most Holy.	the Spirit of the Lord..has anointed **Me**

The **"most holy"** that was to be anointed, was not only a place but a Person—Jesus:

- Luke 1:35 "The holy thing..shall be called the son of God"
- Acts 3:14 Peter called Him "the Holy One"
- 1 John 2:20 John called Him "the Holy One"
- Mark 1:24 Demons called Him "the Holy One of God"
- Acts 2:27 David said that God's "Holy One" would not see corruption
- Rev 3:7 Christ is called "Holy"

Peter affirmed that Jesus was "the holy one" that the Lord **"anointed"** Acts 4:27
Yes, "God anointed Jesus of Nazareth with the Holy Ghost" Acts 10:38

Jesus, the Messiah (which means "anointed" in Hebrew), was "anointed" by the Holy Spirit at His baptism. "And Jesus, when he was baptized, went up straightway out of the water: and lo, the heavens were opened unto him, and he saw the Spirit of God descending like a dove, and lighting upon him: And lo, a voice from heaven, saying, This is my beloved Son, in whom I am well pleased. This was the incident in the life of Jesus by which *he was manifested* to Israel." Matthew 3:16, 17. His first message in Nazareth announced the purpose of His mission: "the Spirit of the Lord…has anointed Me" Luke 4:22

Remember, the Sabbath was the very reason that Israel had been taken into Babylonian exile. Their failure to let the land rest every 7th year and every jubilee resulted in their forced evacuation of the land so that "it might keep sabbath 70 years." 2 Chronicles 36:21. Following this 70 year period, Daniel is told that the Jewish people would be given a 70 x 7 year period (10 jubilees) in which to accomplish that which was determined. They started "the transgression" by rejecting the sabbath days and the sabbath years. Now they would "finish" it by rejecting and killing the Living Sabbath Himself as Jesus said, "Fill...up then the measure of your fathers" Matt. 23:32.

Thus, the 70 weeks would **"finish the transgression."** On the cross, Jesus cried out, "It is finished."
"He was wounded for our *transgressions*, bruised for our iniquities" Isaiah 53:5

Then **"shall Messiah be cut off."** "He was cut off out of the land of the living" Isaiah 53:8.
But not for Himself: He didn't die for His own sins, for He was sinless. He died for the sins of the world.

The Messiah, "in the midst" of the 70th week, **"shall cause the sacrifice and oblation to cease"**
Jesus was *the* "Lamb of God". After His death "There remaineth no more sacrifice for sins" Heb 10:18, 26.
The temple veil was supernaturally rent from top to bottom indicating this end. Matthew 27:50, 51.
This came after 3½ years of ministry in the middle of the last 7 years. Eusebius in the fourth century wrote:

> "Now the whole period of our Saviour's teaching and working of miracles is said to have been three-and-a-half years, which is half a week. John evangelist, in his Gospel makes this clear to the attentive." (Eusebius, *The Proof of the Gospels*, book 8, chapter 2).

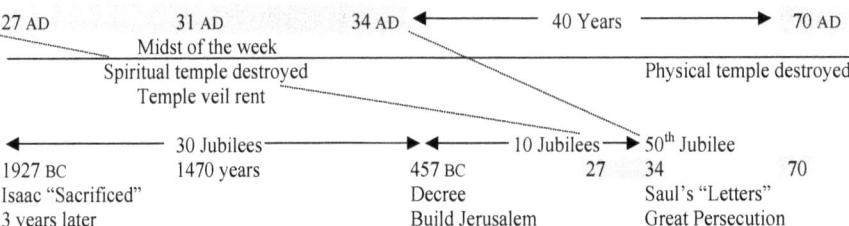

30 Jubilees before the 70 weeks (40 jubilees before Calvary), Isaac modeled the Messiah's sacrifice on Jerusalem's Mount Moriah. 40 years after the 70 weeks and the final rejection of the Messiah, the nation and its temple was destroyed. The 70 weeks end with "a great persecution against the church" at the hands of Saul (Acts 8:1) who is authorized with "letters" from the high priest "breathing out threatenings and slaughter." Acts 9:1. Thus, the important jubilee boundaries are marked by significant decrees affecting God's people. This will be repeated at the end of time.

Next, the 70 weeks were **"to make an end of sins"**
Jesus came "to save his people from their sins" Matthew 1:21.
He was "the Lamb of God, which taketh away the sins of the world" John 1:29.
"Christ died for our sins" 1 Cor 15:3, and "bare our sins in his own body on the tree" 1 Peter 2:24.
He "put away sin by the sacrifice of himself" Hebrews 9:26.
"He was manifest to take away our sins" 1 John 3:5.

The 70 weeks were **"to make reconciliation for iniquity"**
Jesus, "our merciful and faithful high priest" made *"reconciliation* for the sins of the people" Hebrews 2:17
"Having made peace through the blood... *to reconcile* all things unto himself" Col 1:20-22
"You that were sometimes alienated... has he *reconciled*." Ephesians 2:16
"God was in Christ, *reconciling* the world unto Himself, not imputing their trespasses unto them;
    and has committed unto us the word of *reconciliation*" 2 Cor 5:19
"He gave himself for us, that he might redeem us from all *iniquity*" Titus 2:14
Because "the Lord hath laid on him the *iniquity* of us all" Isaiah 53:6
"He is faithful and just to cleans us from all *iniquity*." 1 John 1:9

The 70 weeks were **"to bring in everylasting righteousness"**
God promised in Isaiah 53 "My righteous servant shall make *many righteous*"
"By the righteousness of one... shall *many be made righteous*" Romans 5:17-21
Jesus told John the Baptist that He came "to fulfill *all righteousness*" Matt 3:15
Christ was "set forth to be a propitiation through faith in his blood
    to declare *his righteousness* for the remission of sins" Romans 3:21-26
"For he has made him to be sin for us, who knew no sin;
    that we might be *made the righteousness* of God in him" 2 Cor 5:21
"By his own blood he entered in once into the holy place,
    having obtained *eternal redemption* for us" Heb 9:12.

The Messiah **"shall confirm the covenant with many for one week"**
At the last supper, Jesus said, "This is my blood of the new testament (new covenant)
    which is shed *for many* for the remission of sins" Matt 26:28.
"For this cause he is the mediator of the new testament (new covenant)" Heb 9:15.
He is "the mediator of the *new covenant*" Heb 8:6 "the *messenger of the covenant*" Malachi 3:1
He shed "the blood of the *everlasting covenant*" Heb 12:24 Which covenant?
"the covenant, that was *confirmed* before of God in Christ" Galatians 3:17.

But, some may object, Jesus only confirmed the covenant for half a week. He acknowledged this.
His entire 1260 day mission was limited to the Jewish nation because of the covenant made with Israel.
He came "that [He] should be made *manifest to Israel*" John 1:31.
Jesus said, "I am not sent but unto the lost sheep of the *house of Israel*" Matt 15:24.
He directed His disciples to "go rather to the lost sheep of the *house of Israel*" Matt 10:5,6.
Even after His death, the gospel continued to go "to the *Jew first*" Romans 1:16.
To "the children of the prophets, and of the covenant...*first* God... sent him *to bless you*" Acts 3:25.
"It was necessary that the word of God should *first* have been spoken *to you*" Acts 13:46.

For another 3½ years was "the Lord working with them, and *confirming the word* with signs" Mark 16:20
But, with the stoning of Stephen, the gospel went to the gentiles. Peter went to Cornelius, Paul was
converted. Supernatural events occurred in both of these apostles' lives because the "time was fulfilled."
Peter had a vision, Cornelius was visited by an angel, and Paul met the Lord on the Damascus road.

On Schedule
Jesus fulfilled every aspect of salvation history by the events of His life.
He began His 3½ year journey with baptism just as the children of Israel did in passing through the Red Sea.
Christ's baptism by John at Jordan's edge was a preview of His death, burial and resurrection. Romans 6.
Thus His mission began with a symbolic portrayal of the literal destiny that would mark its close.
It was also a forecast of the Holy Spirit's descent on Pentecost as the symbolic dove rested above His head.

This anointing baptism would have taken place on the 15th of Tishri, the start of the Feast of Tabernacles—itself a reminder of Israel's wilderness wanderings which was commemorated by living in booths for one week.

Jesus then spent 40 days in the wilderness to mirror Israel's 40 years in the Sinai desert.
Christ was led there by the Holy Spirit even as Moses led the Israelites on their desert trek.
1260 days later (based on a 360 day year) His mission *ended* on Passover, the 14th of Nissan, the date on which ancient Israel *began* their Exodus from Egypt.

Mission Begins	The Mission	Mission Ends
Baptism	3 ½ years	Death, Burial, Resurrection
Tishri 15 (middle of month full moon)	1260 days	Nissan 14,15,16 (middle of month full moon)
Feast of Tabernacles (Booths)	42 months	Passover, Unleavened Bread, Wave Sheath

The Coming of His Hour
Christ was on schedule throughout His 1260 day, 42 month, 3½ year ministry from beginning to end.
"They sought to take him: but no man laid hands on him, because *his hour was not yet come*" John 7:30
Jesus repeatedly said, "*Mine hour* is not yet come" John 2:4, "*My time* is not yet come" (7:6)
But in Gethsemane as the mob was approaching, he said, "*My time* is at hand" Matt 26:18
Finally, he announced, "*The hour* is come" John 17:1; Matt 26:45; Mark 14:41.
He was placed on the cross at *the third hour*, the time of the morning sacrifice.
He died at *the ninth hour*, the time of the evening sacrifice, after crying out, "It is finished!"

⟵──────── 490 years ────────⟶

457 BC	27 AD	31 AD	34 AD		70 AD
Restore/rebuild Jerusalem and the wall in troublous times (Ezra 7:7-13, Nehemiah 4:7)	Baptism of Jesus "anointed" and sealed "The time is fulfilled" 70th Week	Passover Gethsemane Trial "cut off" "midst of the week" "It is finished!"	Final Rejection Stoning of Stephen Acts 7:51-59	Gospel goes to Gentiles	Destruction of Jerusalem

The 490 years (10 jubilees) begin with the decree to restore and build Jerusalem. There are four possible decrees that could qualify for the starting date:

Decree of:	**Issued:**	**Reference:**
Cyrus	538 BC	Ezra 1:1-4
Darius	519 BC	Ezra 5:3-7
Artaxerxes to Ezar	457 BC	Ezra 7:11-16
Artaxerxes to Nehemiah	444 BC	Nehemiah 2:1-8

118   Prophesy Again! **70 Weeks**

The 490 year duration, however, imposes a serious constraint. The 69th week must coincide with the appearance of Messiah the Prince. Only two decrees meet this criteria:

Decree of	Issued	Solar year ending	Lunar year ending
Cyrus	538 BC	48 BC	34 BC
Darius	519 BC	29 BC	15 BC
Artaxerxes to Ezra	457 BC	**34 AD**	20 AD
Artaxerxes to Nehemiah	444 BC	47 AD	**33 AD**

The first two decrees terminate far too early—decades before Christ's birth. The third decree in 457 BC has the best fit for fulfilling the time frame of the Messiah's birth, ministry and sacrificial death. Surprisingly, the 444 BC date can be shown to end about the same time (33 AD) by using 360 day lunar years which are 11 days shorter than a normal solar year. But this appears quite artificial and unnecessary when considering that the 70 year period of Babylonian exile requires no such shoe-horning. Nebuchadnezzar initially besieged Jerusalem in 608 BC. Seventy years later Cyrus returned the favor and conquered Babylon in 538 BC. These two events are exactly separated by 70 solar years. Furthermore, lunar years were adjusted by adding extra months to keep them synchronized with solar years. Thus, long time periods would never become seriously discrepant.

Though the first decree comes on the very heels of the 70 years' end, it is the third decree given in the 7th year of Artaxerxes and recorded in the 7th chapter of Ezra, 80 years later, that marks the start of the seven-seventies *and* the 2300 Day of Atonements. It is the first decree to explicitly address the rebuilding of the city in addition to the temple, "to set up the house of our God, and to repair the desolations thereof, and to give us a wall in Judah and in Jerusalem." Ezra 9:9. Notice the progression of time periods:

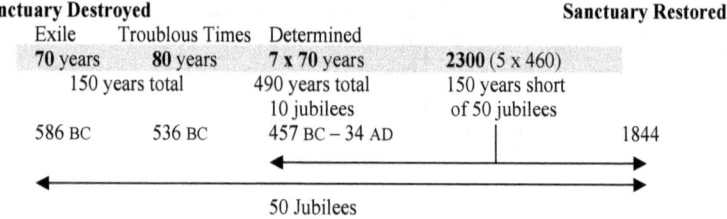

2300 is 150 years short of 50 jubilees (49 x 50 = 2450) which are accounted for in the 70 years of Babylonian exile and 80 years of repeated interruptions in the efforts to rebuild Jerusalem.

Stephen and Christ

The 490 years end with the stoning of Stephen, who parallels Christ in many aspects. Both were persecuted for their good works, both were rejected by their own people, both were tried before the Sanhedrin, both were condemned and killed by the Jewish leadership, both asked God to forgive their executioners. Both were prophets; both spoke with conviction to the leadership of Israel of God's desire for their repentance. Thus, the 70 weeks were determined upon Daniel's people to seal up the vision and the prophecy or the prophet. It is interesting that both Stephen and Christ were anointed with the holy spirit and both had heavenly visions. Christ said, "I see Satan fall as lightning from heaven;" Stephen "being full of the Holy Ghost, looked up steadfastly into heaven, and saw the glory of God and Jesus *standing* on the right hand of God" Acts 7:55. It is at this time, when the Jewish nation, at the end of the second 3½ year period once again rejects the Messiah's invitation, that Jesus stands up when the time of grace is over for the Jewish nation and a signal for the gospel to now go to the world. Likewise, Michael will later stand up to mark the end of probation for the world. Daniel 12:1.

The 3½ year period of time always ends in death.
- **Elijah** prophesied a drought for 3½ years;
  it ended on Mt Carmel and the slaughter of the priests of Baal.
- **Jesus** witnessed to the Jewish nation for 3½ years,
  ending on Passover with the sacrifice of Himself.
- **The disciples** witnessed to the "lost sheep of the house of Israel" for 3½ years
  ending with Stephen's death.
- **The little horn** ravages the saints for 3½ years,
  finally coming to an end with its own deadly wound.
- **The beast** power of the end time will reign for 42 months (3½ years)
  to be slain with the brightness of His coming (2 Thess 5)

```
          3 ½ years        31 AD          3 ½ years         34 AD
   ─────────────────────────▶──────────────────────────────▶
                         Christ dies                    Stephen dies
                       Midst of the week                End of the week
```

"The stone which the builders *rejected*, the same is become the head of the corner: this is the Lord's doing, and it is marvelous in our eyes?...Therefore say I unto you, The kingdom of God shall be taken from you, *and given to a nation bringing forth the fruits thereof.*" Matthew 21:42-43.

Immediately the followers of Jesus are dispersed around the world as the gospel goes to the gentiles. Look at all the places the disciples traveled to take the Good News:

Simon Peter	Parthia [Pontus, Galatia, Cappadocia, Asia, Bithynia], Britain
Andrew (Peter's brother)	Cappadocia, Galatia, Bithynia, Sythia
Simon the Zealot	North Africa [Egypt, Cyrene, Mauritania, Libya], Britain
James son of Alphaeus	Spain, (and possibly Britain and Ireland)
Thomas	Parthia, Media, Persia, Carman, Hyrcani, Bactria [Iran and Afghanistan], Northwest India
Bartholomew	Parthia, Media, Persia, Northwest India
Judas (Thaddeus)	Assyria, Mesopotamia
Philip	Sythia, Upper (Northern) Asia Minor
Matthew	Parthia, Asiatic Ethiopia (Hindu Kush)
John	Gaul? (modern France)
James (brother of John)	beheaded by Herod (Acts 12)
Paul	Southern Asia Minor, British Isles

120   Prophesy Again!   **70 Weeks**

The 70 Weeks Repeated
This pattern is repeated in the lives of the remnant/144,000 at the end.

◄────── 1260 days ──────►

457 BC	27 AD	31 AD	34 AD		70 AD
Restore/rebuild Jerusalem and the wall in troublous times (Ezra, Nehemiah)	Baptism of Jesus "anointed" and sealed	Passover Gethsemane Trial "It is finished"	Final Rejection Stoning of Stephen Christ standing	Gospel goes to Gentiles	Destruction of Jerusalem
Remnant Rebuild wall and their body temples in troublous times	Baptism of Holy Spirit miracles anointed and sealed	Loud Cry Latter Rain witnesses "It is done"	Death Decree Close of Probation for the world Michael stands up	7 Plagues Great Time of Trouble	Destruction of World

The remnant overcomers will build their characters during the difficult period of time leading up to the National Sunday Law. The wall is a symbol of God's Law. The remnant will be the "repairers of the breach" (Isaiah 58) and stand in "the hedge" (Ezekiel 13:5) because they have "gone up into the gaps...to stand in the battle in the day of the Lord." The battle is over the wall. While the remnant warn the world that "the hour of God's judgment has come" (Rev 14:7) their detractors are "saying Peace; and there was no peace" (Ezekiel 13:10).

As the remnant complete their wall, "the prophets...that divine lies" build up their own wall while "others daubed it with untempered mortar." Two different walls; two different laws. The counterfeit looks like the real, but part of it has been torn down (the 4th commandment) and patched back with a cheap, untempered substitute.

Perilous Times	**National** Sunday Law Mark of Beast **Probation** closes for the church	**International** Sunday Law **Probation** closes for the world
First Angel Worship Creator Sabbath His Sign	**Second Angel** Babylon is fallen Come out of Babylon	**Third Angel** Babylon will burn

When the counterfeit wall is imposed as law, the remnant are baptized with the latter rain of the Holy Spirit. They are sealed and begin to witness by giving the Loud Cry, "Babylon is fallen, is fallen! Come out of her! and partake not of her plagues." With establishment of the Mark of the Beast, the abomination of desolation is set up and "with national apostasy, national ruin swiftly follows."

The final generation will repeat the experience of Christ during the 70th week. Jesus was "on schedule" in every step of His earthly journey. At the beginning of the final week He announced the start of His mission by

1. "preaching the gospel of the kingdom of God, And saying,
2. The time is fulfilled,
3. and the kingdom of God is at hand:
4. repent ye,
5. and believe the gospel." Mark 1:14, 15

This 5-point message is repeated in the marching orders delivered by the three angels of Revelation 14:6-12

1. "And I saw another angel fly in the midst of heaven, having the everlasting gospel to preach unto them that dwell on the earth, and to every nation, and kindred, and tongue, and people, 'Saying with a
2. loud voice, Fear God, and give glory to him; for the hour of his judgment is come:
3. and worship him that made heaven, and earth, and the sea, and the fountains of waters.
4. And there followed another angel, saying, Babylon is fallen, is fallen, that great city, because she made all nations drink of the wine of the wrath of her fornication. And the third angel followed them, saying with a loud voice, **If any man worship the beast and his image, and receive [his] mark** in his forehead, or in his hand, the same shall drink of the wine of the wrath of God, which is poured out without mixture into the cup of his indignation; and he shall be tormented with fire and brimstone in the presence of the holy angels, and in the presence of the Lamb: And the smoke of their torment ascendeth up for ever and ever: and they have no rest day nor night, who worship the beast and his image, and whosoever receiveth the mark of his name. Here is the patience of the saints: here [are] they that keep the commandments of God**,**
5. and the faith of Jesus.

The loyal followers of Jesus will also recognize that the time has arrived to begin their witness:

Jesus came "preaching the gospel"	The remnant are given the "gospel to preach"
Jesus said, "the time is fulfilled"	The remnant cry, "the hour… is come"
Jesus said, "the kingdom of God is at hand"	The remnant shout, "worship Him that made!"
Jesus said, "Repent!" (from your fallen ways)	The remnant urge, "keep the commandments" because Babylon is fallen
Jesus invited, "Believe the gospel."	The remnant demonstrate "the faith of Jesus."

The same seven items listed in Daniel 9:24 will also be accomplished at the end:

1. A time period is **determined** upon the remnant, during which God will move to
2. finish the transgression, and
3. make an end of sins, and
4. make reconciliation for iniquity, and
5. bring in everlasting righteousness, and
6. seal up the vision and prophecy, and
7. anoint the most Holy.

Finish the Transgression
As the Jewish nation finished their murderous persecution of God's prophets with the killing of Jesus, so the world will complete their plan to exterminate the saints.

End of Sins
At the same time God, "who began a good work" in His people, "will bring it to completion" Philippians 1:6.

As Christ dwells "in their hearts by faith," they are "rooted and grounded in love...and filled with all the fullness of God...according to the power that works" in them. Ephesians 3:17-21. Sin comes to an end.

They are "preserved blameless unto the coming of our Lord" 1 Thess 5:23. The Great Day of Atonement comes to an end and with it the removal of all confessed and forgiven sin from the sanctuary in heaven and the body temples of the saints on earth. The sins will be placed on the great scapegoat in preparation for his abandonment in the wilderness of planet earth for a thousand years as the two kingdoms (God's and Satan's) perform a parallel demonstration during the 7th millennium.

Reconciliation of Iniquity
Because they are "looking for that blessed hope, and the glorious appearing of the great God and our Saviour Jesus Christ" He redeems them "from all iniquity." Titus 2:13, 14.

Everlasting Righteousness
"Thy righteousness is an everlasting righteousness" Psalm 119:142
His "way [is] everlasting" Psalm 139:24
His "kingdom is an everlasting kingdom" Psalm 145:13
He is "the everlasting Father" Isaiah 9:6
"The earth also is defiled...because they have transgressed the laws, changed the ordinance, broken the everlasting covenant." Isaiah 24:5

Anoint the Most Holy
The final 120th jubilee, the most holy time, will be anointed, to inaugurate the 7th millennium.

> "And he shall confirm the covenant with many for one week: and in the midst of the week he shall cause the sacrifice and the oblation to cease." Daniel 9:27

Popular to Contrary Opinion
The prevailing idea, popularized in mainstream Christianity today, is that there is a future 7 years of tribulation during which an evil despot will take control of the world, initially appear to be a good guy by rebuilding the temple in Jerusalem, but then reveal his true identity as the Antichrist by stopping them after 3½ years. These ideas are purportedly based on the Daniel 9 70-week prophecy as shown here:

49 Years	434 Years	CHURCH AGE	7 Years
7 WEEKS	62 WEEKS	GAP	1 WEEK

This interpretation is based on the appearance of Christ at the end of the 62 weeks to be His triumphal entry into Jerusalem at the beginning of His final Passion Week. Those who place the 70th week in the future in effect deny that Christ made reconciliation for iniquity when He died on the Cross. But if He didn't, then we might as well become Muslims or Zen Buddhists.

Cyrus, "my anointed" Isaiah 45:1 arrived in 538 BC. 49 years earlier, Jeremiah wrote in 587 BC of the rebuilding of Jerusalem and the end of the 70 years (Jer.32:1, 6-9, 13-17, 24-27). But another 434 years after 538 ends in 104 BC. There is nothing important about this date.

Will there also be a matching cessation of sacrifice in the midst of a week at the end? What sacrifice is being offered at this time? In prophetic fulfillment there is both the literal-physical and symbolic-spiritual applications. Most evangelical protestants focus on a literal fulfillment characterized by animal sacrifices conducted in a reconstructed Jewish temple in Jerusalem. This scenario necessitates the involvement of a future "antichrist" who will appear on the scene to stop the sacrifices. To make this work, this interpretation also requires an unfounded separation of the final 70th week from the previous 69 by "stopping the clock," usually at the time of the crucifixion, and imposing a 2,000 year "gap."

But notice, there was no gap between the 69th and 70th year of the Babylonian exile.
Likewise, there should also be no gap between the 69th and 70th week of Daniel 9.
Since there is no gap between the 7 weeks and 62 weeks there should be none between the 69th and 70th.
There is no precedence for such a break in prophetic continuity nor is there any need for one.

The Real Gap
There was a long interlude, nonetheless, within the 70 weeks. It is the 434 years from 408 BC to 27 AD. From Malachi to Messiah, lies the long gap between Old and New Testaments. 400 silent years passed until the *second Moses* arrived to save God's people from the bondage of sin. Between Abraham and Moses was 400 years. God told Abraham, "Know of a surety that thy seed shall be a stranger in a land that is not theirs, and shall serve them; and *they shall afflict them four hundred years*" Gen 15:13. Esther, Antiochus Epiphanes, Herod all lived during this time.

After the first 400 year period God called Moses and led them out of Egypt, "Now the sojourning of the children of Israel, who dwelt in Egypt, was *four hundred and thirty years.*" Exodus 12:40. Then God announces that He will send His Son after 434 years *to free Israel again from the bondage of sin.*

Spiritual Sacrifice
This will be a time, like Christ's initial confirmation of the covenant, to be repeated in the experience of His people at the end. They, too, will confirm the truth of God's promise to dwell in fleshly temples. Even as the "great salvation which at the first began to be spoken by the Lord, and was *confirmed* unto us by them that heard him; God also bearing them witness, both with signs and wonders and with divers miracles, and gifts of the Holy Ghost." Hebrews 2:3,4. Notice: Jesus first confirmed the covenant of salvation for 3½ years, and then "those that heard him" confirmed it for another 3½ years, and miracles, signs and wonders were manifested during both periods to confirm the validity of their witness. This will happen again at the end.

Final Flood

"...and the end thereof shall be with a flood" Daniel 9:27

The physical flood at the end will be a tidal wave of military aggression, cultural turbulence, strife and revolution. The end of the 70 weeks was punctuated by the Jewish revolts that brought the Roman 12th legion under Cestius Gallus to Jerusalem in the fall of 66 AD. When his 6,000 man force was nearly destroyed by rioting Jews, Rome retaliated by sending Vespasian and then (after Vespasian became Emperor following Nero's suicide) his son Titus ("the prince who was to come") to take vengeance on the rebellious city, destroying over 1 millions Jews, obliterating their capitol, and razing the temple leaving it "desolate" Matthew 23:38. Not one stone was left upon another. Matthew 24:2.

The spiritual flood at the end also matches the literal flood in the time of Noah:

> The Flood of Noah started with rain from the windows of heaven.
> The final Flood will begin with the "latter rain" Joel 2:23

> The Flood of Noah resulted in removing the spirit of God from man.
> The final Flood at the end will result in restoring God's Spirit back into man.

> The Flood of Noah came after 120 years of preaching and warning.
> The final Flood of the Spirit will come after 120 jubilees.

The final Flood will flood the world with the glory of God's character:
Numbers 14:21 "All the earth will be filled with the *glory* of the Lord."
Isaiah 40:5 "The *glory* of the Lord shall be revealed, and all flesh shall see it together"
Revelation 18:1 "Another angel comes down from heaven... and the earth was lightened with his *glory*."
Habakkuk 2:14 "For the earth shall be filled with the knowledge of the *glory* of the Lord
             as the waters cover the sea."

The glory of the Lord came down and filled Solomon's temple exactly 490 years (10 jubilees)
after His glory descended on Mt Sinai to deliver the Law on the original day of Pentecost.
1 Kings 6:1 Solomon laid the foundation in the 480th year after the Exodus.
1 Kings 6:38 the temple took 7 years to build. This left three more years of preparation.
1 Kings 7 Solomon commissioned Hiram to cast the entrance pillars, the molten sea and 10 lavers of brass. This could have consumed another three years to complete and outfit the temple for its dedication.
2 Chronicles 7:9 The ceremony was conducted on the 8th and final day of the Feast of Tabernacles.
2 Chronicles 7:5 Solomon sacrifices 120,000 sheep.
2 Chronicles 5:12 120 priests sound their trumpets verse 13 "as one."
The 120 disciples gathered in the upper room and came into "one accord" on the Day of Pentecost.

The disciples also waited 10 days after Christ's ascension for Pentecost. So did the first king of Israel.
Saul also experienced a 10 day wait before his coronation which occurred on the day of Pentecost.
He spent 3 days looking for his father's lost donkeys, half a day later he is anointed "captain over the Lord's inheritance" (1 Samuel 9:20; 10:1). So also Jesus spent 3 ½ days seeking the lost sheep of the house of Israel.

He was then instructed to "tarry" for seven days. At the end, Samuel sacrificed for the feast of Pentecost, the "spirit of the Lord" came upon him, he prophesied, Samuel declared him king, and condemned the people for "rejecting your God" (1 Samuel 10:8-19). This was a model for the final rejection of Israel as they cried out on the day Christ was crowned with thorns, "We have no king but Caesar!" John 19:15.

Cleansing Sons and Daughters
A fascinating lesson can be learned by examining the law of childbirth cleansing.

Leviticus 12:2-4 A woman is "unclean" for 7 days after the **birth of a son** and must remain separate from her husband for 33 more days for a total of **40 days**
Leviticus 12:5 A woman is "unclean" for 14 days after the **birth of a daughter** and must remain separate from her husband for an additional 66 days for a total of **80 days**

Paul contrasts the "flesh" with the "spirit" 1 Cor 15:44
In the Hebrew language, "flesh" is feminine; spirit is masculine.
This parallels the two Adams in 1 Corinthians 15:45.
The first was made a living soul, the second was made a living spirit.

	"Daughters" of Men	**"Sons" of God**	
The Fall		The Incarnation	The End
Feminine mortal flesh		Man child spiritual church	
←	separated from God 80 jubilees	separated from God 40 jubilees →	
	80 periods of cleansing	**40 periods of cleansing**	

Thus, after man fell and became mortal flesh,
God was separated from mankind (the woman-church) for 80 jubilees of separation.
Only then, in the fullness of time, could God visit the woman again.
Jesus was the sacrifice for the woman at the end of her 80 days (jubilees) of separation.
Only then could God impregnate His church with the Spiritual Seed on the day of Pentecost.
This time, the woman became great with a "man child" (Rev 12) who was filled with the Spirit.
The woman-church also received the Spirit on Pentecost.
This time, God would be separated from His bride for only 40 jubilees.
Only then can God return to instill His church with the final outpouring of His Spiritual Seed.

These two periods of purification, 80 and 40, make a total of 120 time periods. This is seen both in the life of Moses, whose life is divided into three 40 year periods, and the parallel history of the world:

Birth of Moses	age 40	age 80	age 120
	Leaves Egypt for Canaan	Exodus at Passover Sinai fire comes down at Pentecost "church in wilderness"	Death Joshua leads Israel into the Promised Land
Creation of Adam	40th jubilee	80th jubilee	120th jubilee
	Abraham Leaves Ur for Canaan	Jesus Crucifixion at Passover	Joshua (Jesus) leads Israel into the Promised Land

Daniel 9 zeros in on the final moments of the 70 weeks, the 10 jubilees of divine forgiveness, that ended with the 80th jubilee when Jesus secured the release of His people from the bondage of sin at Passover by dying in our place. He now awaits the end of the final 40 "days" of purification when he can once again reunite with his virgin bride to conceive a nation of priests in a single day and lead them into the real Promised Land.

9:24	25, 26, 27	Luke 4:18, 19; Isaiah 61
70 weeks determined	desolations are determined	acceptable year of the Lord
finish the transgression	Messiah cut off	gospel to the poor
an end of sins	sacrifices cease	deliverance to the captives
reconcile iniquity	Jerusalem rebuilt/restored	heal the brokenhearted
everlasting righteousness	covenant confirmed	set at liberty the bruised
seal up the vision and prophecy	city and temple destroyed	recover sight to the blind
anoint the most holy	Messiah the Prince comes	Spirit... has anointed Me

"The scenes of the betrayal, rejection, and crucifixion of Christ have been reenacted, and **will again be reenacted on an immense scale**... Those who trample under their unholy feet the law of God have the same spirit as had the men who insulted and betrayed Jesus. Without any compunctions of conscience they will do the deeds of their father the devil." *3 Selected Messages* p. 415, 416.

But our loving heavenly Father "is mindful of what is passing upon the earth. And when a crisis has come, He has revealed Himself and has interposed to hinder the working of Satan's plans. He has often permitted matters with nations, with families, and with individuals to **come to a crisis that His interference might become marked**. Then He has let the fact be known that there was a God in Israel who would sustain and vindicate His people." *Last Day Events* pp 148-153.

The Messiah was born in Bethlehem because Caesar Augustus decreed that all the world should be taxed. Today, again there is talk of a coming "world tax."

THE WORLD TAX TSUNAMI
an article By Joan Veon at NewsWithViews.com
January 29, 2005

DAVOS, SWITZERLAND – "In a keynote speech today at the opening of the Annual Meeting of the World Economic Forum, French President Jacques Chirac called on the world's most powerful business leaders to help raise $50B a year to meet the United Nations Millennium Goals agreed to in 2000."

Actually this is nothing new. The UN first floated the idea of global taxation at the 1995 Social Summit in Copenhagen. Since then, it has become a serious goal that has passed from the UN, to the IMF/World Bank, to the G8, and now, to the World Economic Forum (see weforum.org for more details).

The Ways of a Woman

It all began with a serpent and woman in a garden at a tree.
It ended in a garden at a tree with a serpent and the women.
It will end with a serpent and women and a garden with a tree.

Sin reared its ugly head in the Garden of Eden; its head was crushed in the garden of Gethsemane. Eve was there at the tree in the beginning; Mary and Salome and the other women were at Calvary's tree in the end. Eve was the first spiritual prostitute, seduced by the serpent she then betrayed her husband. "For Adam was formed first, then Eve; and Adam was not deceived, but the woman was deceived." 1 Timothy 2:13.

But Adam shares the blame because he allowed Eve to wander off, to leave his side. They became separated. They were supposed to stick together. "For this cause shall a man... be joined unto his wife, and they two shall be one flesh." Ephesians 5:31.

"This is a great mystery," Paul continues in verse 32, "but I speak concerning Christ and the church." Biblical symbolism equates a women (and especially a wife) with a church. "For the husband is the head of the wife, even as Christ is the head of the church." Ephesians 5:23. God considers us in the most intimate relationship: as His own wife, as one flesh with Him. This was Christ's prayer in the garden, "That they all may be one; as You Father, are in Me, and I in You, that they also may be one in us... I in them, and You in Me." John 17:21, 23. "For your Maker is your husband; the Lord of hosts is his name." Isaiah 54:5.

Ezekiel 16 portrays the nation of Israel as an abandoned newborn "cast out on the open field." Yet God "plighted [His] troth", covered their nakedness, bathed, clothed and crowned them. Dressed in silk and fine linen, decked with gold and silver, they "grew exceedingly beautiful," verse 13. This prophecy tells of Israel's redemption from slavery, their Exodus from Egypt, and the blessings of the Promised Land. God showered all His love and attention on His beautiful bride. But like Eve, Israel wandered away. 2 Thessalonians 2:3.

"You trusted in your beauty and played the harlot," Ezekiel 16:15, just as Lucifer trusted in his beauty and corrupted his wisdom in Ezekiel 28:17. The young woman turns from fidelity to her loving Husband, Jehovah, even aborting her own children. And instead of charging her clients like most whores, this harlot *pays* her customers! "You gave your gifts to all your lovers, bribing them to come to you." Using her "sorceries" (Gr. *pharmakeia*) drugs, hallucinogens, tranquilizers, she deceived the nations. She became a seductress, a temptress, goddess and destroyer. Such is an extreme makeover indeed!

Romans 7:1-4 addresses the legal bonds of holy matrimony. Paul observes that a married woman is bound by law to stay with her husband as long as he lives. If she should leave him, wander off, and become intimately involved with another man while her husband is still alive, she becomes an adulteress. There was no worse sin. The elders of Christ's day hauled a woman "caught in the very act" before Jesus. Throwing her down before Him, they demanded, "Moses said that we should stone great sinners like this!" Yet the penalty for marital infidelity when the woman was the daughter a priest was not stoning, but burning with fire. Leviticus 21:9. The unrepentant harlot priestess at the end of time will also be burned. Revelation 17:16.

128 Prophesy Again! **The Ways of a Woman**

Illicit intercourse is sin, and sin is nothing more than spiritual adultery. First there is seduction, and then sin conceives a child named "death." The tragic truth of this unyielding principle is witnessed every day in the shattered lives of far too many, far too young, far too often. Ironically, they are seeking happiness, but lured by the promise of excitement they experience only pain and bitter agony. Young women are usually the victim of such deception as Hollywood and Madison Avenue offer them glamour and wealth. Like Eve, they believe that indulgence will "open your eyes... and you will be as gods."

In Proverbs 7, Solomon counsels his son to seek Wisdom, "the goodly woman", and avoid the Harlot or the "loose woman." James 3:13-18 describes two kinds of wisdom: one "from above" and the other "earthly." Wisdom from above is "pure, peaceable, gentle, open to reason, full of mercy and good fruits."

Wisdom from below is "devilish, false to the truth" causing "bitter jealousy and selfish ambition." False wisdom is a counterfeit of the true; appealing to reason instead of revelation, sight instead of faith.

Beware! the Wise man cautions. She is "subtle of heart, loud and wayward, her feet do not stay at home... At every corner she lies in wait for her victim, whom she entices with her bed, linens, perfumes. 'Come, let us take our fill of love till morning...For my husband is not at home.' 'He has gone on a long journey, taking a bag of money with him, at full moon he will come.' With much seductive speech...she compels him...as an ox goes to the slaughter." This dummy is no ox, but he cooks his own goose just the same.

On the other hand, Samson *was* an ox. He went to the slaughter by yielding to his "heifer," Delilah, and lost his power, lost his sight, and was finally put to open shame. Judges 13-16. The subtle woman, in league with the subtle Serpent (more subtle than any other creature in the garden), is a lying, homicidal whore, and a tool of "the father of lies" who is himself a "murderer from the beginning." Wherever she goes, death follows.

The results are always the same. For example, Judah fell into adultery with a Canaanite woman, Shua, whose name means "prosperity" and bore him two sons: Er and Onan. Is that where we get the expression, "To Er is human?" Could be. Both sons were ultimately slain for their wickedness. Genesis 38.

Egypt and Sodom are called wayward sisters of Israel in Ezekiel 16. "You are the sister of your sisters, who loathed their husbands and their children." Revelation 11 makes the same connection. "Your younger sister, who lived to the South of you, is Sodom." She "had pride, plenty of food, and prosperous ease, but did not aid the poor and the needy." "They were haughty, and did abominable things before me; therefore I removed them," Jehovah warned.

The woman entices and flatters. She is both religious and glamorous. The United States is a good example of the woman's ways. She sends a powerful message to the rest of the world: we have "the good life," and you can have it too. The world watches American movies and TV shows, they see our beautiful homes and fine cars, and assume that the lives of the rich and famous is the norm. Of course they want to have the same luxuries for themselves. All this female behavior encourages trade and even political revolutions. For example, East Germans defected in masse, collapsing their government because they could look over the Berlin Wall and see the glittering lights and riches of West Germany.

The prophecy of Zechariah 5:5-11 tells the story.

> "This is an ephah that goes forth, and in it are the transgressions of the whole earth. And behold, a talent of lead was lifted up, and **a woman was sitting in the midst of the ephah.** And he said to me, **This is wickedness. And he cast her into the midst of the ephah;** and he cast the talent of lead upon its mouth. Then I lifted up my eyes and looked, and behold, **there came out two women, and the wind was in their wings;** for they had wings like the wings **of a stork; and they lifted up the ephah** between earth and heaven. Then I said to the angel who talked with me, Where are they carrying the ephah? And he said to me, **To build for it a house in the land of Babylon; and it shall be established and set there upon its own base."**

The Harlot of Babylon in Revelation 17 is the same woman. They are both "in the land of Babylon." They are both wicked and filled with the abominations of the earth.

Hope for the Harlot
Yet in spite of all this, God still calls them "the virgin daughter of Jerusalem!" Isaiah 37:22. What an example of God's Amazing Grace! There is hope for the harlot! The Bible proves that it is possible for harlots to heal, for sluts to be saved, for prostitutes to become pure again.

Remember, Rahab, the harlot, chose to align herself with the God of Israel, thus saving herself and her family. Gomer, Hosea's adulterous wife, was brought back from shame and slavery and restored to her home and her husband. Jesus said that harlots would go into heaven before self-righteous Pharisees because they believed. Matthew 21:31. He even said to one "caught in the very act," "Neither do I condemn you. Go, and sin no more." John 8.

Eve, Adam's bride, was created perfect. In Genesis 3:20, after they both had sinned, Adam names her Eve, "the mother of all living." She is a symbol of Christ's perfect Bride, the New Jerusalem above, redeemed from sin, "the mother of us all" Galatians 4:26. Christ, the Last Adam, takes the New Eve as His glorious Bride "without spot or wrinkle" Ephesians 5:27. Revelation 21 pictures the woman of Revelation 12, "Like a bride adorned for her Husband."

The Woman	The Husband	The Path
Eve, the mother of all living	Adam's Wife	Chased from the garden
New Jerusalem, the mother of us all	Christ's Bride	Fled to the wilderness

This female feature can be traced throughout the last half of Revelation.
Beginning with chapter 12, God's Bride, the Virgin appears clothed with the sun, standing on the moon and wearing a crown of 12 stars. But then the Dragon chases her into the wilderness.
Revelation 13 The Dragon continues his war against the woman with threats of boycott and even death.
Revelation 14-16 God counters with serious warnings and a final show down at Armageddon.
Revelation 17-18 focuses on this judgment, returning to the woman in the wilderness. She is now transformed. No longer fleeing from the Beast, she is now riding on it!
Revelation 19, 21 The woman appears at last as a bride coming to the marriage supper of the Lamb.

One is both a woman (the Lamb's bride) and a city (the New Jerusalem).
But there's another feminine actress.
She is both a woman (the Great Harlot) and a city (Babylon the Great and Rome).

One flees from the dragon. The other rides on him. She rides high on world business, world economy, and global commerce. She is the mother of harlots. She has daughters composed of "modern civilization," banking systems, trade unions, merchants and markets, legal systems, educational systems, fostering the pursuit of pleasure for eager shoppers living on the deceptive intoxication of easy credit. "Buy now, be enslaved later."

Tale of Two Rivers

These two women describe two groups at the end of time. Truth is matched with error; Christ is opposed by antichrist; the king of the North confronts the king of the South. Daniel 8 and 10 introduce two similar visions, both experienced on the bank of two different rivers. Notice the many parallels.

Daniel 8: **The Ulai Vision**
This vision reveals the forces opposing the "prince of the Host."
When the Ulai River flows into the sea, it ceases to exist; its work is over.
When Jesus leaves the Most Holy Place, His work is over.
The results: His people are "purified, and made white, and tried." Daniel 12:10.
This river is the story of the redeemed flowing down the pure **River of Life**.
They drink the living water and never thirst again, worshipping the King of Kings.
They have "gotten the victory over the beast...and stand on the **sea of glass**." Rev 15:2.

Daniel 10: **The Hiddekel (Tigris) Vision**
Here we see the initial struggle between the King of the North and the King of the South
When the "great" Hiddekel River flows into the sea, it ceases to exist.
When the King of the North "comes to his end", "none shall help"
This river is the story of the lost flowing down the fouled **River Euphrates** until it dries up.
They drink from the broken cisterns of Babylon, worshipping the King of the North.
Then, "the beast is taken, and with the false prophet is cast into a **lake of fire**." Rev 19:20.

As each river meets its sea or lake, they each cross the line of eternal irreversibility. As long as you are in the river, you can "switch streams in mid-horse" (Rev 5). "Whosoever will, let him take the water of life freely." Rev 22:17. "Ho, everyone that thirsts, let him come and buy milk and wine, freely without price." Isaiah 55.

"Today, if you will hear his voice, harden not your heart." But eventually the river runs out: no further opportunity to change streams. "He that is unjust, let him be unjust still, and he which is filthy, let him be filthy still: and he that is righteous, let him be righteous still: and he that is holy, let him be holy still." Rev 22:11.

"The light that Daniel received from God was given especially for these last days. The visions he saw by the banks of the Ulai and the Hiddekel, the great rivers of Shinar, are now in process of fulfillment, and all the events foretold will soon come to pass." *Testimonies to Ministers*, p. 112,113.

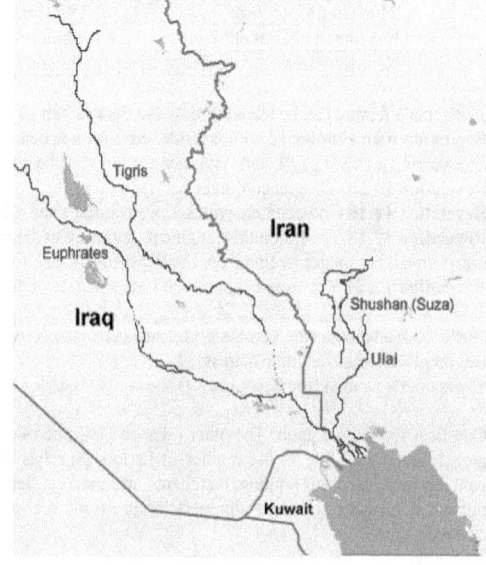

The Woman-Beast Connection

The Biblical prototype of the woman-beast connection is demonstrated by the story of Elijah, the prophet of God, who confronts Israel's apostate king. Ahab abandoned the worship of Jehovah. He did so by the influence of his wife Jezebel, the high priestess of Baal, the state religion. Elijah pronounces 3½ years of famine on the land which ends with a national referendum on who to worship, a contest between two religious powers: Baal, a beastly bull god and Jehovah, the Creator God of Heaven and Earth. The decision ends with consuming fire and drought-ending rain from heaven. Elijah faces a death decree. But instead, the priests of Baal are executed and Jezebel dies.

A Church-controlled State always leads to the legislation of worship.
- Worship Nebuchadnezzar's golden image
  or face the fiery furnace. (Daniel 3)
- Worship Darius or face the den of lions. (Daniel 5)
- Worship the way Rome dictates
  or be burned at the stake. (Daniel 7)
- Worship the Beast along with the rest of the world
  or be put to death. (Revelation 13)

At the end of medieval Babylon's 3½ prophetic years of controlling the kings of Europe from Rome, the Holy Spirit fell as the reformation restored the Word of God and its truths while calling His people "out of her." Crusades are launched against the "heretics" who must flee for their lives. They live for generations under a perpetual death decree. But in the end, the priests were executed on French Revolution guillotines and the High Priest of Babylon was taken to France, died in exile and Babylon fell. The Papal States were dissolved and out of Vatican control for 130 years.

3 ½ Years of Famine on Israel – Jezebel reigns through Ahab the king	Jezebel dies – Priests slain
3 ½ Years of Famine during Dark Ages – Papacy reigns through Emperors	Pope dies – Priests slain
3 ½ Years of Famine & Darkness – Antichrist rides the Beast	Harlot dies – Priests slain

The end time contest between Jezebel's Bull and Jehovah's Lamb, presented in Revelation 13 and 14, follows the same sequence. At that time "all the world" wonders after the Beast and worships it for a similar interval of 3½ years (but this time 1260 literal days) after which the Harlot reigns together with 10 kings for "one hour" (30 days) ending the 1290 days of Daniel 12. Then the Harlot dies and her priests are slain.

1260 days – 42 months – 3½ times: Periods of Witness and Persecution
These numbers belong to the woman. The first pertains to desperate circumstances.
Revelation 12:6 The woman **fled into the wilderness**, where she had a place prepared of God
that they should feed her there 1260 days.
This same number is mentioned in connection with the two witnesses in a similar setting.
Revelation 11:4 The two witnesses shall prophesy 1260 days **clothed in sackcloth**

The equivalent time period of 42 months also describes a time of suppression and duress for God's saints.
Revelation 13:5 Power was given to him to continue [*after* the deadly wound was healed] 42 months
7 to **make war on the saints**

This same number is once again connected with the two witnesses in a parallel setting.
Revelation 11:2 Measure not the court which is outside the temple
for it is given unto the Gentiles; and the holy city shall they **tread under foot** 42 months.

The first two numbers are derived from the last, which consistently relates to times of persecution.
Revelation 12:14 The woman... might **fly into the wilderness**
where she was nourished for a time, and times, and half a time
Daniel 12:7   It shall be for a time, times, and an half; ...**to shatter** the power of **the holy people**.
Daniel 7:25   Saints **given into little horn's hand** for a time, and times, and half a time

Notice the parallel themes of each number's couplet.
The woman is paired with the two witnesses.
The saints are paired with the holy city.
The woman is paired with the holy people and saints.

These time periods are based on the pattern first established at the original fall of Babylon in Daniel 5. Daniel interprets the handwriting on the wall as having three components: mene-mene, tekel, and upharsin. The meaning is: counted-counted, weighed, and divided. This pattern then shows up repeatedly: first in Daniel 7:25 "The saints shall be given into his hand until a time and times and the dividing of time."

tekel,	mene, mene	Upharsin	Daniel 5:25
weighed	counted, counted	divided	Daniel 5:26-28
time,	times,	dividing of time	Daniel 7:25

At the end the 144,000 are counted, they are judged and divided as sheep from the goats (Matt 25). Even the 70-week prophecy follows this pattern to some degree as it is presented in three parts:

7 weeks,   62 weeks,   one week   = 70 weeks   Daniel 9:26

where the final, 70th week is itself *divided* as the Messiah is "cut-off" "in the midst of the week."
A similar expression, found in chapter 12 of both Daniel and Revelation, provides for an exact mathematical formula in calculating the main important time periods of prophecy:

time,	times,	half a time		Daniel 12:7
1	2	½	3 ½ times	Rev 11:9; 12:14
12	24 (12 x 2)	6 (12/2)	42 months	Rev 11:2; 13:5
360	720 (360 x 2)	180 (360/2)	1,260 days	Rev 11:3; 12:6

There is 1 year in a time; 12 months in a time/year; 360 days in a time/year.

At each period of Present Truth, the application of prophecy is manifested in both the physical and spiritual dimensions. At different times in history, the harlot has been Artemis, Ashtoreth, Aphrodite, Minerva, Venus, Isis, Shiva, and Jezebel. In each instance she has been a ruling queen, a goddess and priestess.

Ancient Babylon set the Precedent

Women were a notable feature of the final Babylonian banquet, a trend that repeats throughout prophetic history. Daniel 5:1-4 Belshazzar, the king, held "a great feast...and drank wine before the thousands. He brought the golden vessels that were taken out of the temple of the house of God... and the king, his princes, **his wives, and his concubines,** drank wine in them and praised the gods of gold, and silver, of brass, of iron, of wood, and of stone." The original Babylonian bash was a clear trend-setter.

Spiritual Babylon copies the pattern perfectly

In Revelation 17:2, 4 the Mother of Harlots is arrayed in purple and scarlet and is decked with gold and precious stones and pearls. In her hand she holds a golden cup full of "the wine of abominations and the filthiness of her fornication." The inhabitants of the earth have become drunk with this wine. Daniel 11:38 gives us a further clue. "A god whom his fathers knew not shall he honor with gold, and silver, and with precious stones, and pleasant things." Instead of the humble life of Christ, Babylon flaunts its riches with gaudy display.

Our Lady of Healing at a shrine in Pátzcuaro, Michoacán, Mexico.	Crowned statue of Mary in the Notre Dame du Cap, Cap-de-la-Madeleine, Quebec, Canada. Crowned in 1904 at the orders of Pope Pius X	Our Lady of the Pillar sports a jeweled crown and sun disk at a shrine at Saragossa, Spain.

The woman, arrayed in gold, purple and scarlet, is still a prominent feature of Babylon. Adored, revered, worshiped, this woman is claimed to be the one who first appeared to John in Revelation 12 as the "wonder" in heaven. Paul, however, clearly explains the real meaning of this important Biblical symbol. Speaking of the "body of Christ," the followers of the Lamb, the true and faithful believers in every land, Paul states, "I have betrothed you to one husband, that I may present you as a chaste virgin to Christ." 2 Corinthians 11:1-2. It is the church, the body of Christ, who is the virgin, the pure, chaste woman of Revelation 12.

Another church, however, replaces this women with the "Blessed Mary, Queen of Heaven." Today, we are being deluged with an ever increasing number of reports and sightings and apparitions of "the Blessed Mary." This is today's spiritual manifestation of the woman. She epitomizes the Roman system of substitutes.

In place of a heavenly sanctuary, Rome builds earthly cathedrals; instead of Christ, our High Priest in heaven, Rome substitutes an earthly papal vicar; instead of praying to our "one Mediator, the man Jesus Christ", Rome has installed Mary and a host of saints. She has even been promoted to the level of Co-Redemptrix, an astounding achievement authorized by papal declaration alone.

134 Prophesy Again! **The Ways of a Woman**

November 23, 2005 CBS, ABC and other TV news programs featured pictures of this statue of Mary that was reported to be weeping tears of blood. The statue stands in front of the Vietnamese Catholic Martyrs Church in Sacramento, Calif.	Even 2-dimentional objects like this icon of Mary in a Musetesti, west Romanian church as reported in the Ananova News, January 2003.

In addition to the spiritual application, there is always a physical corollary. Again, historical precedent mirrors the current manifestation. There is no doubt to the reality of Revelation 17 in our world today.

Woman on a Beast

The control of the state by the church is symbolized by a woman riding on a beast. This woman-on-a-beast motif has a long history. Ancient gods frequently idolized fertility (Ashtoreth, Ishtar from which we get the Easter Bunny) and virility (the Egyptian Horus, Phoenician Baal and Greek Zeus—all bull deities). Zeus, father of the Olympian gods, conducted numerous love affairs disguised as a bull-type creature. During one of his amorous escapades he seduced the daughter of King Agenor of Tyre. Deceived by his animal charms (as was Eve with the serpent), Princess Europa was raped and then carried away by Zeus to the island of Crete where she bore him three sons. One of them, Minos, became the famous Minotaur—half man-half bull—of mythology. *(Peri Tes Syries Theoy De Dea Syria*, The Syrian Goddess by Lucian of Samosata 2nd Century C.E.)

Europe has enthusiastically embraced the woman-beast motif as the symbol of her own identity. It's everywhere. Numerous sculptures boast Europa's fling, some less flattering than others.

in Milles Garden

2000 on display in front of the European Council of Ministers Office in Brussels

crowned Europa with scepter and globe

Von Hinten

She's featured on medallions and the new Euro coins…

Early 1990's ECU coin of Gibraltar and the current Greek Euro €2 coin

2003 Euro from Spain

1992 Medallion and Euro €5 coin

1984 Postage Stamp from England

a German Phone Card

and the European Union Flag

Notice the circle of 12 stars on these coins, stamps and flag.
The woman of Revelation 12 also has a crown of 12 stars and Joseph's first dream featured 12 stars.

136 Prophesy Again! **The Ways of a Woman**

Europa as an artistic theme is by no means a modern phenomenon. Yet it survives in our modern press.

This fresco in Pompeii from the first century illustrates the early reality of the myth

Germany's Der Spiegel magazine has adorned its covers with Europa and her bull several times

even Time Magazine in August 1991

It appears that Europe is quite taken with this symbol from Greek mythology in spite of the fact that it celebrates the rape of Europa by the Beast! Revelation 17 plainly states that the woman riding the beast has committed fornication with the kings of the earth. The woman, therefore, cannot be European kingdoms. She is rather an entire ecclesiastical system, supported, empowered, and protected by those kingdoms.

Another religious symbol that Europe has adopted is the Tower of Babel.

This popular poster, modeled on Pieter Brueghel's famous 16th century painting (shown below) features the European circle of 12 stars (inverted in the Satanic goat configuration) flying above a reconstructed Tower of Babel with an army of people carrying bricks as a contribution for the project.

The inverted pentagram is the well-recognized Satanic symbol of the goat's head. The only reason the artist would choose this depiction for Europe's 12 stars is to emphasize the God-defying message that a rebuilding of Babel's tower makes.

Europe's identification with the Tower of Babel is not limited to simply posters. This is the recently completed EU building in Strasburg. The Richard Rogers design was clearly inspired by Brueghel's partially completed Tower of Babel.

The June 2003 Constitution of the United States of Europe (which contains no reference to God) states that Europe is to be "an example for the world of the New World Order." Valery Giscard D'estang says this is intentional "because we are secular".

Isaiah 13 says that Babylon will literally be destroyed at the second coming, therefore it must exist at the present time. How is it here now?

Long Live Babylon!
Babylon endures. The name may change, but its principles of worship persist.
Babylon began at Babel in Shinar, the original one-world, one-language empire of Nimrod.
Babylon re-emerged as the Neo-Babylonian empire under Nebuchadnezzar.
Babylon was conquered by Persia yet its principles survived and were inherited by each new empire.
Babylon lives on in its principles of idolatry, immortality of soul, and sun worship:
- **Solar sunrises** are worshiped through weekly Sunday observance
- **Solar solstices** celebrate Christmas, Santa (anagram for Satan), annual rebirth of the sun god
- **Solar equinoxes** dictate the timing of Easter Sunday sun rise services

Easter bunny eggs honor the fertility goddess Ishtar/Ashtoreth,
Lent commemorates the weeping for Tammuz,
    son of Semirimis, the wife of Nimrod, the first Babylonian..
Medo-Persia added the principle of infallibility (Darius couldn't even change his own law).
Greece contributed the list of deities in their Pantheon (pan-theos: gods everywhere).
Rome introduced the execution of heretics.
This is the legacy of Europe, the Bull on which the woman rides.

A woman is a symbol of the church. Babylon is, therefore, depicted as an adulterous whore. Adulterous, because she "gets in bed" with earthly powers instead of relying on the God of heaven for her support and protection; because she forsakes the true worship of God for other gods: Sunday, Christmas, Easter.

The woman riding the beast has "Babylon the Great" written on her forehead. But she is only a promoter of Babylon. Ultimately, she becomes the victim of a "hostile take over" by her pimp, the devil-incarnate. This will occur at the end when he "fires" her—literally. He will hand her over to the people to be burned. "They shall strip you of your clothes and take your fair jewels, and leave you naked and bare." "They shall stone you and cut you to pieces... and they shall burn your houses." Ezekiel 16. "And the ten horns which thou sawest upon the beast, these shall hate the whore, and shall make her desolate and naked, and shall eat her flesh, and burn her with fire." Revelation 17:16. She has been "used" and now she is discarded, to become the "fall guy"... uh, er, fall girl.

> And here is the mind which hath wisdom.
> The seven heads are seven mountains, on which the woman sitteth. Revelation 17:9

The woman sits on seven mountains. As the Mother of Harlots, she sits on many waters.

> And he saith unto me, The waters which thou sawest, where the whore sitteth, are peoples, and multitudes, and nations, and tongues. Revelation 17:15

There are seven continents. There are seven seas. There are seven wonders of the world. Is it just a coincidence that the Statue of Liberty has seven horns on her head? She is Lady Liberty, the goddess Libertos. Mother of Exiles, she is also upon the waters.

Some have suggested that literal Babylon, modern Iraq, is the Woman of Revelation 17, 18. But the facts don't fit.

Is Baghdad the economic center of the world? Does Iraq have deep water ports along its coast lines from which merchant sailors will bewail?

Does Iraq have the Largest idol of the world in its harbor?
Did Iraq birth and host the United Nations?
Is Iraq the world's policeman?
Is Iraq known for its cattle, goods, fine merchandise, delicacies, and pharmaceuticals (sorceries)?
Is Iraq at rest and dwelling carelessly?
Does Iraq have people gathered from all nations in it?

The Statue of Liberty was designed by French Freemason Frederick August Bertoldi. He boasted that his creation would last as long as the Pyramids of the Nile. When the French Revolution ended with the desecration of Notre Dame cathedral, the "citizens" enthroned a half naked prostitute on the high altar and crowned her as the goddess of reason. She held a torch in her hand symbolizing the light of Lucifer. This became the inspiration of the Statue of Liberty, designed and built by French Freemasons and presented as a gift to American Freemasons, as the largest Luciferian idol in the world.

The woman is the central figure in the end time drama. Prefigured by Vashti and Esther, Rahab and Jezebel, Sarah and Elizabeth, Eve and Mary, they represent the followers of God—in name or in fact, true or false, loyal or apostate, humble or proud, virgins or harlots—who at the end of time are either fleeing from the beast or riding on it back.

The Ways of a Woman
The battle began with a woman in the garden of Eden at a tree with a subtle serpent.
It was won in the garden of Gethsemane and at the tree of Calvary where the taunting Serpent and the weeping women gathered around the cross. But it will finally end with two women, either resisting or yielding to the deceiving Serpent. The women who overcome are given the right to enter into the city, to once again make their home in the garden of Eden restored and drink from the river of life as it flows beneath the tree of life.

Many Antichrists

"It is the last time; and as you have heard that antichrist shall come, even now there are many antichrists; whereby we know that it is the last time. They went out from us, but they were not of us...He is antichrist that denies the Father and the Son." 1 John 2:18, 19, 22

Shortly after the Little Horn "falling away" was established in 538 AD to take the place of Christ with a substitute priesthood, substitute sacrifice and substituted tradition for Scripture, another anti-Christian anti-Jewish power arose. An epileptic Ishmaelite was born in the Arabian Peninsula town of Mecca in 570 AD named Abul Kasem Ibn Abdullah but better known in the Muslim world as Mohammed, the prophet of Allah. His Jewish mother died just two months after his birth. At age six when his father died he was adopted by his uncle, worked as a shepherd during his teen years but remained illiterate throughout his life. When he was 25 years old he married a wealthy widow in Mecca named Kadijah with which he had only one surviving daughter—Fatima.

After years of meditation and solitude in remote and secluded places, Mohammed (now age 40 in 610 AD) reported that he fell into a trance while on Mount Hira and received a call from Gabriel the Archangel. When no further visions came after a long time, Mohammed became despondent, depressed and was about to commit suicide when Gabriel appeared again. Encouraged, Mohammed announced that he was a prophet and reported to receive revelations for the next forty years. These oral recitations were later written in a book called the Koran or Qu'ran which is a mixture of Christianity, Judaism and pagan Arabian religions. It has no organization other than division into 114 chapters. In addition, the Sonna, a commentary on the Qu'ran, is filled with legendary anecdotes and alleged sayings of Mohammed—a collection of tradition—written in the 8th century.

Mohammed took advantage of the thousands of pilgrims (that even in his day flocked to Mecca) to promote his teachings and his claim of prophet. The superstitious Arabian crowds came to worship and kiss the sacred black stone that fell from heaven (a meteorite) housed in the holy Ka'aba. While Mohammed enjoyed debating with the masses, after nine years of struggle and few converts to show for it, his cousin Ali decided to be a bit more persuasive. But his threats of physical violence for their continued disregard of Allah's Prophet only sparked a riot. Mohammed and his band were obliged to flee Mecca on July 15, 622, an event remembered as the Hegira and the beginning of the Islamic calendar.

Ten days later the refugees reached Medina, 250 miles north of Mecca, where he was finally hailed as a prophet. Mohammed spent eight years building up a large following, at first composed of voluntary conscripts. But again this approach was soon abandoned in favor of offering "the unbelievers" three choices: acceptance of Islam, payment of a tribute, and death by the sword. In 630 he returned to Mecca at the head of a conquering army, captured the city, destroyed the 360 idols at the Ka'aba except one—Allah, the moon god.

Two years later, Mohammed took violently ill. His dying words were, "The Lord destroy the Jews and the Christians! Let there not remain any faith but that of Islam throughout the whole of Arabia! Lord, grant me pardon and join me to thy companionship on high!"

Like Judaism, Islam is strictly monotheistic. While accepting Jesus as a prophet on par with Abraham and Moses, it condemns the Christian teaching of the Trinity. Mohammed it their intercessor between Allah, allegedly the same deity as Jehovah, yet recognized as superior with the shout "Allah Akbar!" (Allah is greatest). At "the last day" all will be resurrected to face the judgment when good deeds are balanced against evil ones allowing believers to enter Paradise or fall into hell where they will endure endless torture. The faithful must pray five times a day facing Mecca, keep the month-long daylight "fast" of Ramadan, make at least one pilgrimage to Mecca, give alms, and say, "Allah is one and his prophet is Mohammed."

Pilgrims circling the Ka'aba the required three times as a meritorious act to gain paradise.

Kissing the Ka'ab's Black Stone

The greatest meritorious act is the propagation of Islam by Jihaad (holy war) against "infidels" where plunder and slaughter is legalized.

Polygamy is extolled, the dignity of women is destroyed. Four wives is the legal limit (Sura 4:3), but Mohammed exempted himself with 14-22, depending on whether they are classified as wives and/or concubines (Sura 33:36-40).

The career path for Mohammed and Joseph Smith was similar in that both claimed to receive instruction from an angel, both claimed to be prophets, and both promoted polygamy. Mohammed even took his stepson's wife (prohibited in Sura 4:31), the youngest of his many wives (and his favorite) whose name was Ayesha when she was only nine years old and he was 53.

Comparison between the two major world religions, Catholicism and Mohammedism, is quite amazing. These two women represent just over 2 billion, 1/3 of the earth's current population.

Similarities:

Catholicism	Islam
St. Peter, the "first pope"	Mohammed, Allah's prophet
Adoration of the virgin Mary	Adoration of the virgin Mary
Apparitions of Mary at Fatima, Portugal 1917	Fatima was Mohammed's daughter
Features sun burst and moon "monstrance"	Features star and crescent moon
Fights heretics by waging crusades (holy wars)	Fights unbelieving infidels by waging jihad
Coercive methods of evangelism	Coercive methods of evangelism
Salvation comes through faith and good works	Salvation comes through faith and good works
Scriptures (Bible) and Tradition (Fathers)	Scriptures (Quran) and Tradition (Hadiths)
Self-flagellation and penance brings merit	Self-flagellation and martyrdom brings merit
Recitation of the Apostles Creed "I believe in the Father, in His Son, Jesus Christ, and the Holy Spirit"	Recitation of the Islamic Creed "There is only one God, Allah, and Mohammed is his prophet"
Recitation of Ave Maria's and Pater Noster prays counted with rosary beads	Pray five times a day, repetitious counted with strings of beads
Fasting during month of Lent, Fridays, etc.	Fasting during month of Ramadan
Alms giving offered as an indulgence for sin	Alms giving is 4th pillar of Islam
Promotes pilgrimages to Rome	Promotes pilgrimages to Mecca
Human saints intercede before God	Mohammed intercedes for believers at judgment
Believe in Purgatory, Hell, Paradise at death	Believe in Purgatory, Hell, Paradise at death
Sexual-abuse cases are notorious	Mohammed married 9 year old child
Pope claims to be the vicar of Christ on earth	Mohammed claims to be Allah's greatest prophet
Autocratic form of Church government	Autocratic form of Church government
Aspires to world domination	Aspires to world domination

Their clerics attire themselves in a similar manner, wearing long robes:

Tunica alba   **Cassock**   **Stole**   **Mullahs**   **Imam**
Catholic vestments   Islamic vestments

142 Prophesy Again! **Two Women**

Nuns in their typical habit attire. Islamic women in their burka's.

Catholics engaged in self-flagellation in the Philippines. Islamic flagellation in Pakistan.

Jonathan Edwards, the first President of Princeton University and one of the most respected American theologian, wrote during the 18th century in his book *A History of the Work of Redemption*:

> "The two great works of the devil which he wrought against the Kingdom of Christ are . . . his Anti-Christian (Romish or Papal) and Mahometan (Muslim or Islamic) kingdoms, which have been, and still are, two kingdoms of great extent and strength. Both together swallow up the Ancient Roman Empire; the (Papal) kingdom of the Antichrist swallowing up the Western Empire; and Satan's Mahometan kingdom the Eastern Empire."

Islam teaches that Jesus is not the Son of God, He did not die for our sins, was not divine, is not the Saviour (Sura 4:157; 5:19, 75; 9:30). They mistakenly believe the Christian Trinity is the Father, Mother Mary, and the Son Jesus (Sura 5:73-75, 116). They teach that Mohammed is the "Helper" of John 14:16 instead of the Holy Spirit.

Shooting for the Stars: Shared Symbols

The moon, as a religious symbol and object of worship, has a very long and ancient history.

The Egyptian moon god Khonsu is shown here with a lunar crescent over his upper chest.

Khonsu was also shown at times with a falcon's head. Here, the large moon disk and crescent are shown in exaggerated size above the god's head.

Allah, the god of Islam, comes from al Lat, the moon. Allah is the moon god of Muhammad.

Canaanite moon worship showing lunar disk with crescent cupped below it.

Nabonidus, last king of Babylon, shown on this stele with a crescent moon dated 550 BC.

Star and lunar crescent was a favorite motif on many Roman coins, this one is from the reign of Hadrian.

144 Prophesy Again!   **Two Women**

The flags of Islamic nations depict the moon and star in various configurations. It is seen in the seals and crests of their governments and the crescent adorns the top of all mosques.

Arabic art incorporates the 8-pointed star (composed of two intersecting squares) in much of its work.

| 8-point Star from Iran | 8-point Star from Jordan | 8-point Star from Australia |

Shriners and Freemasons have also adopted the lunar-star symbol on rings, belt buckles, fez hats, etc.

the inverted arrangement used by secret societies betrays their Satanic roots.

And interesting side note about the fez: it comes from the city of Fez in Morocco, where Muslim fighters allegedly dipped their hats in the blood of Christians, 50,000 of which they slaughtered in their invasion of Spain in 711 AD.

Shriner's temple dome in Milwaukee, Michigan (right):

Catholicism used the lunar crescent long before Islam came into existence.

146 Prophesy Again! **Two Women**

This painting by Jose Mota 1720 and detail below shows the lunar crescent beneath Mary's feet.

Albrect Durer engraved the Madonna and child borne by a large lunar crest (right).

The mother-son cult has a long tradition.
Maya and Buddha, Isis and Horus, Mary and Jesus, Devaki and Krishna.

Allah was one of many gods worshiped by the pre-Islamic Arabian tribes. The Koran mentions three daughters of Allah in Sura 53:19-20: "Have ye seen Lat, and 'Uzza, and another, the third, Manat?" The following two verses state that these goddesses were daughters of Allah the Moon god. Lat was the sun god; Uzza was the planet Venus; Manat was the god of good fortune. Other gods are also mentioned in the Koran such as another Moon god Wadd, Suw'a, Yaghuth, and Nasr (Sura 71:23).

The only mention of the word "allah" in the Hebrew scriptures is its use in describing an oak tree. Strongs entry #427 appears in Joshua 24:26 and Ezekiel 6:13 where it is a location for idol worship along with "every green tree, and every thick oak, the place where they did offer sweet savour to all their idols."

147

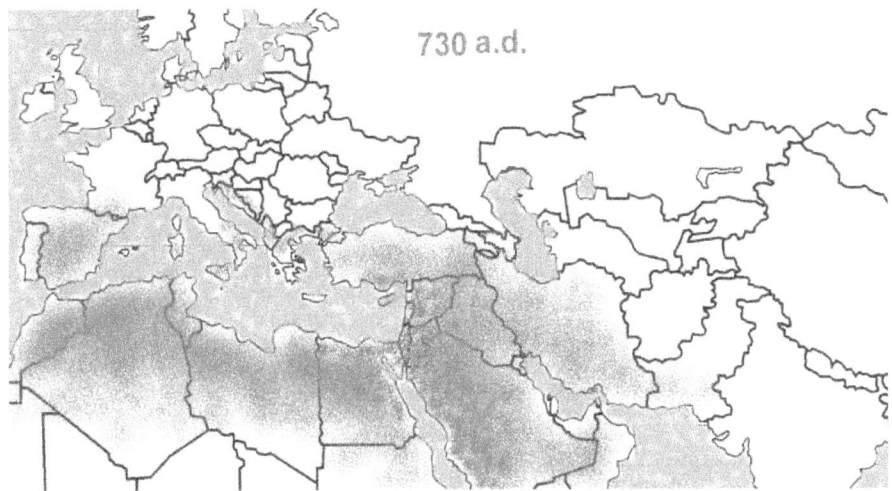

730 a.d.

Mar. 13, 2006 22:26
Mubarak and Pope Benedict XVI hold talks in Rome
By ASSOCIATED PRESS

VATICAN CITY Pope Benedict XVI and Egyptian President Hosni Mubarak held talks at the Vatican Monday evening about Iran, Iraq and the prospects for lasting peace in the Middle East, the Holy See said. "There was a deep exchange of ideas about the situation in Iraq and also a look at the issues regarding" Iran. Egypt's semiofficial Middle East News Agency said without detail that Benedict and Mubarak discussed "recent regional developments" as well as dialogue between civilizations and respect for religion.

March 17, 2006, 7:56PM
Russian Patriarch Communicates With Pope
© 2006 The Associated Press

VATICAN CITY — The leader of the Russian Orthodox Church has told Pope Benedict XVI he hopes for a "rapid resolution" of ongoing problems that divide the Catholic and Orthodox churches, according to a letter released Friday by the Vatican.

Patriarch Alexy II also said in the Feb. 22 letter to the pope that he was convinced defending Christian values in contemporary society should be a priority for both churches.

"I hope that the rapid resolution of outstanding problems between our two Churches will also contribute to this end," Alexy wrote in thanking the pope for a letter he sent to mark the patriarch's birthday.

He Shall Come To His End

The historicist position of Daniel Chapter 11 focuses on the papacy and the French Revolution. Yet, the inspired pen records, "We have no time to lose, troublous times are *before* us. Soon the scenes of the trouble spoken of in the Prophecies *will* take place. The prophecy of the eleventh of Daniel has *nearly* reached its complete fulfillment. Much of the history that has taken place in fulfillment of this prophecy will be *repeated*." Letter 103, 1904 page 5.

"In the **thirtieth verse** a power is spoken of that

> 'shall be grieved, and return, and have indignation against the holy covenant: so shall he do; he shall even return, and have intelligence with them that forsake the holy covenant. And arms shall stand on his part, and they shall **pollute the sanctuary of strength, and shall take away the daily** *sacrifice,* **and they shall place the abomination that maketh desolate**. And such as do wickedly against the covenant shall he corrupt by flatteries: but the people that do know their God shall be strong, and do *exploits*. And they that understand among the people shall instruct many: yet they shall fall by the sword, and by flame, by captivity, and by spoil, *many* days. Now when they shall fall, they shall be holpen with a little help: but many shall cleave to them with flatteries. And *some* of them of understanding shall fall, to try them, and to purge, and to make them white, *even* to the time of the end: because *it is* yet for a time appointed. And the king shall do according to his will; and he shall exalt himself, and magnify himself above every god, and shall speak marvelous things against the God of gods, and shall prosper till the indignation be accomplished: for that that is determined shall be done.' Daniel 11:30-36.

"Scenes similar to those described in these words **will take place**. We see evidence that Satan is fast obtaining the control of human minds who have not the fear of God before them. Let all read and understand the prophecies of this book, for **we are now entering upon the time of trouble** spoken of:

> 'And at that time shall Michael stand up, the great prince which standeth for the children of thy people: and there shall be a time of trouble, such as never was since there was a nation *even* to that same time: and at that time thy people shall be delivered, every one that shall be found written in the book. And many of them that sleep in the dust of the c earth shall awake, some to everlasting life, and some to shame *and* everlasting contempt. And they that be wise shall shine as the brightness of the firmament; and they that turn many to righteousness as the stars for ever and ever. But thou, O Daniel, shut up the words, and seal the book, *even* to the time of the end: many shall run to and fro, and knowledge shall be increased.' Daniel 12: 1-4." *Manuscript Releases,* number 13, p. 394

Following, we inject a possible secondary fulfillment. Since we already know that chapter 11 involves a war scenario, let's isolate the powers of the struggle. One power is the King of the North. A second power is the King of the South. A third power involves the ships of Chittim. There are several countries and locations which are named independently. In being consistent with Adventist theology, we need to discuss the truths we hold to be true, recognizing that with all prophetic symbols there is both a physical and spiritual aspect.

King of the North
First, the spiritual identity of the true King of the North is Christ. Therefore, the counterfeit king of the North must be the enemies of God and His people. During the time of Daniel and thereafter this power was at different times both spiritual as well as literal. During Daniel's time Babylon was a real place. It was a literal enemy of Israel. This power tried to exterminate God's followers. It was done through many methods— trying to change their allegiance through re-education (psyops, brainwashing), altering their diets, and ultimately by forcing the worship of a golden image.

During each of the three times that Nebuchadnezzar invaded Israel, he took back the brightest and best to convert to his theology. Eventually physical Babylon came to her end. Yet Babylon, which means confusion, continues to exert its presence in the world. Satan has consistently used nations and governments to instill confusion on the world.

After the fall of Babylon, Rome became the enemy from the North. The Seventh-day Adventist Church correctly teaches that spiritual Rome was and is the little horn power as discussed throughout the old and new testaments. And the reading of chapter 11 shows us that there is an enemy of the North. It begins as a literal entity. In Modern times the physical enemy of physical Israel, we believe, is Iran.

Someone might be asking, Do you believe like the evangelicals that Israel is once again to be favored by God and become the land of peace after the final war? Of Course Not. The Bible is perfectly clear that Israel lost her most favored status in 34 AD. However, she is a real country today, which constantly struggles for survival. We will discuss this in more detail later.

King of the South
A second power mentioned is the King of the South and his daughter. The most common interpretation for these symbols has been those countries around Israel who did not follow the true God of Israel. Today, that would be all the Arab countries including, but not limited to, Jordan, Lebanon, Syria and Egypt. Historically these countries never have appreciated their Hebrew neighbors. This of course has intensified since 1948 when Israel once again became a legal nation. Most of this region has not recognized the legal status of Israel. Islam, which is the religion of all these countries today, has made a concerted effort to destroy Israel and "wipe it off the face of the map."

Chittim, Kittim and Javan
This brings us to the "Ships of Chittim." If you examine the location of ancient Chittim on a map you discover that it is the island nation of Cyprus today. Chittim or Cyprus is very important to the United States. Why? Because it is where the Sixth fleet naval operations is located. Here the largest assembly of American ships resides outside the United States. There is only one nation which has repeatedly stated they would stand by Israel to provide protection. That country is the U.S.A.

Chapter 11 also infers that the little horn power will become involved. How do we know this? Verse 36 is eerily similar to Daniel 7:25.
- In both instances great words are spoken against the true God of the Universe.
- In both instances he exalts himself.
- In both instances He prospers as God's People are involved.
- In both instances he does according to his will.
- In both instances he comes to his end.

A further similarity from the preceding verses of chapter 11 shows us that this little horn powers seeks to pollute the sanctuary. He seeks to do wickedly against the covenant. And he attempts to corrupt through flatteries.

Lets now clarify what we believe will happen. Today everyone is hoping for peace in the Middle East. We believe that when it concerns Israel and the Middle East we are sitting on a powder keg. We believe that with tensions rising as high as they are that someone will blink first and cause sensational problems. Paul tells us in 1st Thessalonians 5:3 the following," For when they shall say 'Peace and safety' then sudden destruction shall come." There is going to be a war where the Arab nations will attempt once again to destroy Israel.

When these tensions begin, the United States will have no choice but to defend Israel. This will cause nations around the world to choose sides. Then Daniel 11:45 will be fulfilled, in a complete and unambiguous way. Examine this text closely. Daniel writes,

> "And he shall plant the tabernacles of his palace between the seas in the glorious holy mountain; yet he shall come to his end, and none shall help him."

James White argued that this text dealt with the little horn power of Papal Rome. Uriah Smith argued that this text must be applied to Muslim Turkey. Their differences caused a great deal of discussion. Amazingly enough, the inspired pen was nearly quiet on this text. Because of this silence God has allowed us to use our own minds to exact meaning from this scripture. However, in doing so we must stand on the shoulders of those who have come before us. We must be consistent with the truths God has abundantly blessed us with. Moreover, it must ring true and credible. It is our conviction that the following interpretation does just that.

Verse 45 describes the fate of the king of the North. In the political realm, the north-south conflict in Daniel 11 parallels the east-west collision of Daniel 8. The American he-goat attacks the ram with great fury, even as the king of the North comes against the king of the South like a whirlwind. Ominously, while the ram is stomped into the ground, the goat's horn is broken and divided. This is consistent with the plight of verse 45 where no one comes to his aid.

Relocating Headquarters
But all symbols have both a political and religious element. The "he" discussed in the first part of verse 45 is also the persecuting little horn power or the king of the North." It says that this little horn power will change his headquarter from Rome to Jerusalem in an effort to secure peace. When war breaks out between the Middle East powers and the U.S., what power can alone offer any prospects for peace? The only possible solution would be the little horn power of Rome. The leader of the Vatican or the Pope is already looked upon around the world as a leader of peace. It does not matter what individual holds this chair, it is the power itself.

Daniel tells us this little horn power plants his tabernacles in the glorious holy mountain. The next question to be addressed is what does the word 'tabernacle' imply? The obvious answer is worship. This little horn's central place of worship will shift to Jerusalem. Jerusalem is the only place of interest between the seas. Further, Daniel 9:16 states that Jerusalem is God's "holy mountain." We know from historical accounts that as far back as the early 1990's that there were secret high level conversations between the Vatican and Israel. We also know that in the early 1990's the Vatican established relations with the P.L.O. and several other Arab nations.

The little horn power and her Arab partners share a number of similarities. This little horn power also holds a great deal of influence with Israel and the United States. So that there is no confusion, we are saying that the little horn power or the pope will soon move his world headquarters to Jerusalem. This will take place after war erupts between the U.S-Israel alliance and those who would try to destroy her. But it does not end there.

Pope Concedes to Christ
According to Gilbert Bagnani in an essay of church and state entitled "Rome and the Papacy, an essay on the relations between church and state" (1929),

> "The Lateran treaty thus closes a period in the history of the papacy, but at the same time it opens another. No man can know the measure by which God will preserve the independence of His church. We can only await the future with confidence, certain that the divine providence will preserve the spiritual authority of Rome until the awful day **when Christ Himself will take the place of the vicar**."

In other words the Pope will turn over authority to "Christ." We believe that this is one of the last deceptions which will take place on this earth. Let us explain how we believe it will unfold.

For millennia Satan has tried to usurp Christ's power. He did it in heaven first, and has been continuing it here on this earth. Satan has constantly tried to impose his form of worship on this planet. But more than this, he has dreamed of receiving the worship of God himself. He wanted Christ to bow down and worship him. He has succeeded in getting mankind to venerate, adore and essentially worship "his holiness" the pope. But this vicarious fulfillment is not enough. Satan longs to be worshiped as God.

As the controversy between Christ and Satan draws to its final conclusion, all individuals on earth must decide who will attain their allegiance. And while Satan uses lies and deception to secure our devotion, Christ only uses truth and love to win our loyalty. Jesus Himself said "For there shall arise false christs and false prophets, and shall show great signs and wonders; insomuch that, if it were possible, they shall deceive the very elect. Behold, I have told you before. Wherefore if they shall say unto you, Behold, he is in the dessert; go not forth; behold, he is in the secret chambers; believe it not. For as the lightning cometh out of the east, and shineth even unto the west; so shall also the coming of the Son of Man be." Matthew 24.

The apostle Paul states in 2 Corinthians 11:14, "Satan himself is transformed into an angel of light" Over one hundred years ago my favorite author commenting on this great deception wrote in the book *Great Controversy* page 624 the following,

> "As the crowning act in the great drama of deception, Satan himself will personate Christ. The Church has long looked to the Saviors advent as the consummation of her hopes. Now the great deceiver will make it appear that Christ has come. In different parts of the earth, Satan will manifest himself among men as a majestic being of dazzling brightness, resembling the description of the Son of God given by John in Revelation. The glory that surrounds him is unsurpassed by anything that mortal eyes have yet beheld. The shout of triumph rings out upon the air, 'Christ has come! Christ has come!' The people prostate themselves in adoration before him, while he lifts up his hands, and pronounces a blessing upon them, as Christ blessed His disciples when He was upon the earth. His voice is soft and subdued, yet full of melody. In gentle, compassionate tones He presents some of the same gracious, heavenly truths which the Saviour uttered; he heals the diseases of the people, and then, in his assumed character of Christ, he claims to have changed the Sabbath to Sunday, and commands all to hallow the day which he has blessed. He declares that those who persist in keeping holy the seventh day are blaspheming his name by refusing to listen to his angels....This is the strong, almost overmastering delusion. The multitude from the least to the greatest, give heed to these sorceries, saying this is the power of God."

Of course Bible students know according to 1 Thessalonians 4:15-17 and Matthew 26:64 as well as other texts that when Jesus returns at the Second Coming His feet shall not touch the earth. My favorite author continuing in the previous book page 625 further reveals that "Satan is not permitted to counterfeit the manner of Christ's advent...this coming; there is no possibility of counterfeiting. It will be universally known—witnessed by the whole world."

He Shall Come To His End

As Satan tries to pull off this delusion, Daniel 11 says. "Yet he shall come to his end, and none shall help him." In Daniel 12 verse one the prophet continues to tell us that Michael (Jesus, see Jude 9, Revelation 12:7) stands up and the seven last plagues begin to fall to counteract this great act of deception. The last scenes of earth's history will draw to a close. Though the world is still in for difficult times God remains with His people through the power and promise of His Holy Spirit. God does not forget His people during this time. Isn't it wonderful to know that in times like these we can take hope in the words of the apostle Paul in Hebrews 13:5, "For he hath said, I will never leave thee nor forsake thee."

We will now take a verse by verse examination of Daniel 11.
Much of the material in the following section is adapted from the work of Jeff Pippenger.

Daniel 11

Historical Interpretation
11:1-13 Persian and Greek Empires
11:14 "Robbers of your people" Roman occupation and taxation is clearly identified.
11:20 Caesar Augustus "Raiser of taxes" brings Joseph and Mary to Bethlehem.
11:22 Rome breaks "the prince of the covenant" crucifying Christ on the cross.
11:24 Pagan Rome rules the world "even for a time" = 360 years (Papal Rome for 3 ½ times)
Rome's appearance as a world empire was the battle of Actium, September 2, 31 BC
360 years later, 330 AD Constantine moved empire from Rome to Constantinople
This move signaled the downfall of the empire: pagan Rome declines while papal Rome ascends.

Verses 30-36 describe the transition from pagan to papal Rome and parallel verse 40-45
11:30 "ships of Chittim" come against Rome (Vandals from Carthage) Rome is "grieved"
Dan 7:23,24 "another kingdom arises" after Rome, "shall subdue three kings"
"indignation" Papacy discards Bible "the holy covenant"
"intelligence" Bishop of Rome made head of the church
"arms stand" Clovis, king of the Francs, first Catholic nation to defend the papacy
This earned for him the title of "Most Christian Majesty, Eldest Son of the Church"
Clovis converted to Catholicism and was baptized in 496 AD
France dedicated its finances and army to defend Papal Rome
and defeat the 3 Arian horns: Heruli, Goths, Vandals.
508 AD first Arian horn attacked, 'daily' desolation of paganism started to be taken away.
538 AD last Arian horn removed, Papacy ascended the world throne as the desolating abomination.

11:32-35 Dark Ages persecution of 1260 years from 538 to 1798.
11:36-39 Papal "king shall do according to his will", "exalt himself, and magnify himself above every god"
"speak marvelous things, against the God of gods." This behavior is described in 2 Thess 2:3,4
where "a falling away" is foretold and the "man of sin revealed, the son of perdition" appears who
"opposes and exalts himself above all that is called God, or that is worshipped"
"he sits as God in the temple of God, showing himself that he is God."

11:40-45 A spiritual war, Papacy vs Atheism, is the basis of a physical conflict, the French Revolution.
"King of the south shall push at him" "king of the north shall come against him…with many ships."
1798 Deadly Wound of Rev 13: Pope taken captive by French general under Napoleon's command
France was the atheistic king of the South. Papacy loses civil powers, political kingdom taken away.

At **the time of the end**, 1798, France controlled Egypt (Napoleon's army discovered Rosetta Stone there)
France was the king of the south (spiritual Egypt) "that great city" Rev 11:8 (Paris)
Papacy was the king of the north (spiritual Babylon) "that great city" Rev 17:4-6,18; (Rome)

But at **the end of time**, Communism and then Islam is the king of the south.
While Russia was atheistic, Iran is fiercely religious in its adherence to a false prophet.
America-Britain, cooperating with the papacy and defending Israel, is now king of the north.

Pagan Rome was a desolation and an abomination. Papal Rome is also the "abomination of desolation"
Daniel 9 speaks of "desolations" and "abominations" plural. Both Romes are abominations. When Clovis
eliminated the pagan abominations, the papacy was free to promote its own abominations (baptized
paganism). Daniel 11 verses 31 to 39 detail the first rise of the papacy which is a model for the second rise
beginning in verse 40.

154 Prophesy Again! **He Shall Come To His End**

First Rise of the Papacy

vs 30		ships of Chittim shall come against him	Vandals from Carthage "vandalize" Rome
		he shall be grieved and return	Papacy emerges to remove 3 Aryan powers
		and have indignation against the holy covenant	Papacy discards the Bible
		and have intelligence with those who forsake	Bishop of Rome made head of the church
vs 31		arms shall stand on his part	Clovis dedicates his armies to the papacy
		they shall **pollute the sanctuary of strength**,	pagans abandon their religion
		and shall **take away the daily**, and	submit to Catholicism, diverts prayers
		place the abomination that makes desolate.	538 last of Arian powers defeated
vs 32-35		do wickedly against the covenant	Dark Ages persecution of true Christians
		they shall fall by the sword, flame, captivity	Papal crusades against heretics
		even **to the time of the end**	1260 years end in 1798
vs 36		the king shall do according to his will;	"man of sin is revealed, son of perdition"
		exalt and magnify himself above every god	"opposes and exalts himself above all"
		speak marvelous things against the God of gods	"as God sits in God's temple" 2Thes 2:3-4
vs 37		Neither shall he regard the God of his fathers	Vicar of Christ
		nor the desire of women	Celibacy
vs 38		He honors the God of forces:	Popes launch crusades
		and a god whom his fathers knew not	Mary
		with gold, and silver, and with precious stones,	Mary worship, shrines, statues, processions
vs 39		a strange god he shall... increase with glory:	
		and shall divide the land for gain	Pope divided New World to Spain/Portugal

Second Rise of the Papacy

vs 40		**at the time of the end**	in 1798 (deadly wound) lost civil power
		the king of the south shall push at him	France (spiritual Egypt) attacks Papal States
			Atheism moves from France to Russia
			French Revolution to Bolshevik Revolution
		king of the north shall come against him	Papacy (spiritual Babylon) attacks Russia
		with chariots, and with horsemen,	with US military might (cold war arms race)
		and with many ships; like a whirlwind	and with economic pressures
		enter into the countries, and shall overflow	Soviet Union (the countries) topples 1989
vs 41		enter also into the glorious land,	United States of America embraces Rome
		many countries shall be overthrown:	Latin America, Balkins, Africa, Viet Nam
		but these shall escape: Edom, Moab, Ammon	Previous enemies join God's people
vs 42		land of Egypt shall not escape	The entire world "wonders after the beast"
vs 43		power over the treasures of gold and of silver	Control of World economy
		all the precious things of Egypt	Control of Middle Eastern oil resources
		Libyans and the Ethiopians shall be at his steps	Libya renounces terrorism

Now, notice how verse 40 parallels verse 30:
    pagan Rome "grieved" as king of the south (Vandals) push at him during the Punic Wars
    papal Rome "grieved" as king of the south (Islam) pushes at him "to the time of the end"
"at the time of the end"
    papal Rome "grieved" as king of the south (France) pushes at him during the French Revolution
"at the end of time"
    papal Rome "grieved" as king of the south (Communism) pushes at him during the Cold War
    papal Rome "grieved" as king of the south (Islam) pushes at him during the Gulf Wars

History is Repeated

France, the great city (Paris), spiritually is Sodom (immoral) and Egypt (atheistic)
Clovis and six other European nations came to the support of the papacy at her inception
    fighting against the forces of paganism/atheism (3 barbarian nations)
United States comes to the support of the papacy at her restoration
    fighting against the forces of paganism/atheism (3 barriers to world domination)

These 3 barriers are three walls:

vs 40 Fall of the **king of the south** (Iron Curtain of Soviet Union, symbolized by the **Berlin Wall**)
    Atheism conquered after 200 years of spiritual-political warfare.
    Papacy battled from French Revolution 1789 to fall of Communism 1989.
    Communism stole all the Catholic countries: Cuba, Romania, Hungary, Yugoslavia, etc
    With the Holy Alliance between Regan and John Paul II in 1989 this wall is now history.
vs 41 Control of the **glorious land** (United States, **wall of separation** between church and state)
    Protestantism is nearly conquered (this battle began with the Protestant Reformation)
    Ecumenism is aiming at uniting all churches under the Pope...this is currently underway.
vs 42, 3 Domination of **other countries** (the entire world, **wall of national sovereignty**)
    Democracy conquered (this battle began with the American and French Revolutions)
    Papal goals are aligned with the One World globalization aims of the UN

A "glorious land" was promised to ancient Israel where they could prosper and witness to the world.
The "glorious land" was also given to modern Israel as an asylum for prosperity and missionary activity.
The Papacy has issued many encyclicals denouncing democracy and nationalism.
For example, Pius IX's 1864 *Quanta Cura* and *Syllabus of Errors* which condemns the rights of citizens.
The Papacy supports the "divine right of kings" just as it claims the divine right of "Petrine succession."
It will finally "enter also into the glorious land"—the United States.

Many countries will be overthrown as they "clasp hands" with the Papacy and agree to its authority.
But others will escape "out of his hand" as refugees from Babylon as the Loud Cry is made: "Come out!"
The "other sheep" not of the fold, hear His voice. John 10:16; Rev 18:4; Isa 56:8; Isa 11:14-16; Zeph 8:23
They come out of Babylon, as "Lot went out of Sodom" Luke 17:29 just before the fire falls on the city.

Three tribes come out—close relatives to God's chosen line, associated with unlawful relationships:
Edom (Esau, Jacob's brother, was the "profane fornicator" Heb 12:16) "offended and revenged" Ez 25:12
Moab and **Ammon** (sons of Lot's incest with his daughters) "reproached and reviled" Zeph 2:8
Nehemiah: Sanballat (Moabite), Tobiah (Ammonite), Geshem (Arabian Edomite) resisted God's people.
In 2 Chronicles 20 Edom, Moab, Ammon joined forces to attack Israel. Today, they are doing the same.
They were enemies of God's people, practicing false worship. But the Edomites were different.
Edomites could join Israel after 3 generations; Moabites and Ammonites were excluded "forever" Deut 23.

They represent the "three parts" of the great city of Babylon Rev 16:13,19: dragon, beast, false prophet.
They are **Spiritualism, Catholicism, Protestantism.**

Prophesy Again! He Shall Come To His End

vs 44	tidings out of the east and out of the north shall trouble him:	Christ's coming announced
	go forth with great fury to destroy	Persecution
vs 45	plant the tabernacles of his palace between the seas	Middle East or America?
	in/and the **glorious holy mountain**	God's Church
	he comes to his end and none shall help him.	

Tidings out of the east and north trouble the King of the north
East is the direction of Christ's coming:
Rev 7:2   An angel "messenger" ascending from the east with the seal of God
Isa 41:2, 25   The Righteous Man is raised up...from the north but comes from the rising of the sun (east).
North is the location of God's dwelling.
Psalm 48:2   Mount Zion, on the sides of the north is the city of the great King.
Isa 14:13   Lucifer/Satan has longed to take control of heaven and "sit...in the sides of the north"
North is also the direction of God's judgments:
Ezekiel 26:7   Nebuchadnezzar, king of Babylon...comes from the north.
Ezekiel 9   "Six men came from...toward the north" to slay all except those with the mark of God.

King of the North (Papacy) goes forth with great fury to destroy
Jer 30:5-7   All faces turn into "paleness" That day is great, none is like it: the time of Jacob's trouble.
Dan 12:1   A time of trouble, such as never was

Between the seas and the holy mountain
Rev 17:15   Waters...are peoples, multitudes, nations, tongues.
Isaiah 56:7   God will bring strangers who keep the Sabbath to His "holy mountain" house of prayer
Isaiah 11:9   New earth is God's "holy mountain" The rest there will be "glorious"
Isaiah 2:2,3   In the last days the mountain of the Lord's house is established in the top of the mountains.
Isaiah 66:20   God's holy mountain is Jerusalem
Ezekiel 28:14 Lucifer was once "upon the holy mountain of God"
Dan 9:16   God's city Jerusalem is God's holy mountain
Joel 3:17   Jerusalem will be holy when God dwells in Zion, His holy mountain
Zech 8:3   Jerusalem will be called a city of truth, the holy mountain when God returns to dwell in Zion

The Papacy places itself between the people (sea) and God's holy mountain house of prayer.

> "These were the first of the heirs of St. Peter, the Popes of Rome, some of them loved, some feared, some venerated, some murdered. One of the proudest and most powerful, Innocent III (1198-261), started calling himself **The Vicar of Christ** because he said he was "set **midway between God and man**" and given "the whole world to govern." *The Oxford Dictionary of Popes*, quoted in *TIME*, July 14, 1986

This was foretold in the prophecy of Zechariah 5 where the prophet is shown a vision of a woman sitting in a ephah basket covered with a lid of lead, carried by two other women with wings like storks, lifting the basket-riding-woman up "between the earth and the heaven" on her way to "the land of Shinar" (Babylon) where they would build her a house.

"Satan...has planted his satanic throne between the human worshiper and the Divine Father" *Manuscript Releases*, vol 7, p. 215.

"The Sabbath is the Lord's test, and no man, be he king, priest, or ruler, is authorized to come between God and man." *Testimonies*, vol. 9, p. 234.

The Fall of Communism

The fall of Communism in the Soviet Union clearly fulfills verse 40. Look at these headlines:

"Gorby's Bow to **the Roman Legions**" – title of article in *U.S. News & World Report*, December 11, 1989.
"When the Holy Roman Emperor Henry IV decided to seek pardon of Pope Gregory VII in 1077, he stood barefoot for three days in the snow outside the papal quarters in Canossa, Italy. Gorbachev's concordat with the church was no less significant in its way." *Time*, December 11, 1989.
"In 1935 Josef Stalin, absolute ruler of the Soviet Union, was given some unsolicited advice. Make a propitiatory gesture to the Vatican, he was told. Pushed too far, his country's Catholics might become counter-revolutionary." Stalin sneered, "'The Pope. And how many divisions has he?' The answer then was that he has none. The answer now is that he *needs* none." John Paul II "helped bring about 'The **greatest policy change since the Russian Revolution**.'" *Life*, December 1989.
"The **rush to freedom** in Eastern Europe is a sweet victory for John Paul II." *Life*, December 1989
"Freedom in his Polish homeland...swept like brush fire across Eastern Europe...The end of **the 20th century's most dramatic spiritual war**, a conflict in which the seemingly irresistible force of Communism battered against the immovable object of Christianity." *Time*, December 4, 1989.
"The **chain reaction of liberty**...has swept through Eastern Europe." *Time*, December 4, 1989.
"The **tide of freedom** washing over Eastern Europe" *Life*, December 1989.
"Days of the **Whirlwind**" – Title of article in *Newsweek*, December 25, 1989.

"Holy Alliance"   *Time* magazine cover title, February 24, 1992 discussed the United States-Vatican connection. Both survived assassination attempts only 6 weeks apart in 1981, both declaring God intervened to save them. On Monday, June 7, 1982 they met and agreed to conduct a clandestine campaign to dissolve the communist empire. It was "one of the great secret alliances of all time" Richard Allen, Reagan's National Security Adviser. Reagan "saw the collapse coming and he pushed it—hard."

Five part plan:
1. **US Defense** buildup using the Strategic Defense Initiative-Star Wars to bankrupt the Soviets.
2. Covert **reform movements** in Hungary, Czechoslovakia and Poland
3. **Financial aid** to Warsaw Pact nations that protect human rights and adopt free-market reforms.
4. **Economic isolation** of Soviet Union by withholding Western and Japanese technology.
5. Voice of America and Radio Free Europe **propaganda**.

"The Pope and President exploited the forces of history to their own ends."
Time, February 4, 1992, pp 29-30.

The Islamic Eschatological World View

Islam is anxiously looking for **Mahdi**, the 12th Imam Messiah, who they expect will soon appear as a young man with black hair, a high forehead, a hooked nose, bearing the full name of Islam's prophet, Muhammad ibn Abd-Allah. He will be descended from Muhammad's daughter, Fatima, appear as a sunrise in the West riding a white horse leading a great army as a conquering hero, after there is a war and a plague, at the same time that Daajal appears in the East with a bright star. One prophecy states that Mahdi will come when there is a solar and lunar eclipse during Ramadan, and a great fire in the sky in Iraq. Another claims that Allah will raise Mahdi to power in one day. At the same time, Jesus will return from heaven to a mosque in Damascus, confess that he deceived his followers with his false claim to be the son of God. He will defeat and kill the Daajal, destroy Gog and Magog (destructive powers from the north), Christians, and then enforce Islamic law, rule for a while and then die.

Al-Harith ibn Hirath will come with an army of his own to establish the government of Mahdi and cause all to serve him in a new utopian world of peace which the Mahdi will rule for 7, 9 or 19 years distributing great wealth to all who serve him.

Shi'I Muslim prophecies predict the coming of the 12th Imam

In the 19th century, an Iranian named Baha'u'llah claimed to be the prophecy's fulfillment and founded the Baha'I Faith. It maintains Muhammad as Allah's prophet, the sacredness of the Quran, but promotes its main teaching "the Oneness of Mankind" which includes sexual equality and the elimination of prejudice.

Iran's President Ahmadinejad sincerely believes that the 12th Imam will only come when the world is in global turmoil. This explains why he eagerly welcomes a military confrontation with America.

The basic features of the Islamic prophecies are referenced in Biblical prophecy as well:
Daniel 11:22 a king sweeps away an overwhelming army arrayed against him.
Verse 24 invading other nations.   Verse 25, heading a large army.
Verse 31 his armed forces serve him.   Verse 38 honoring a god of fortresses.
Verse 39 he attacks the mightiest of fortresses (America).
Verse 40 he heads a huge military force against the king of the South.
Daniel 8:24, 11:39, etc his power is not his own but that of a "foreign god" (Allah)
Daniel 9:27 mentions a covenant with many for one seven year period.
Ezekiel 38 military attack on Israel when peace and security have come to the world.
Daniel 11:23 agreements of peace followed by deceit.
Daniel 11:24 distributing plunder, loot and wealth to his followers.
Verse 39 distribute lands as rewards making them rulers over many people.
Revelation 13:11-18 a false prophet (Mohammed?) forces everyone to worship the beast.
One prophecy states that Mahdi will come when there is a solar and lunar eclipse during Ramadan.
Nov 8, 2003 was one such lunar eclipse in the Middle East and Nov 23 a solar eclipse in Antarctica.
Oct 3, 2005 was an Annular solar eclipse over North Africa and a partial lunar eclipse occurred Oct 17.

There have been a number of would be aspiring Mahdi.
In the 19th century, an Iranian named Baha'u'llah claimed to be the prophecy's fulfillment and founded the Baha'I Faith. It maintains Muhammad as Allah's prophet, the sacredness of the Quran, but promotes its main teaching "the Oneness of Mankind" which includes sexual equality and the elimination of prejudice.

The late Ayatollah Khomeni was favored as a likely candidate for a while.
Saddam Hussein believed he was destined to fill the role.
There is some indication that Iran's current President Ahmadinejad senses that he has come to power at a moment of destiny. If nothing else, he is serious about his belief in the imminent return of the 12th Imam. At the end of his haranguing tirade at the UN General Assembly in September, 2005, he suddenly delved into a mystical soliloquy:

"From the beginning of time, humanity has longed for the day when justice, peace, equality and compassion envelop the world. All of us can contribute to the establishment of such a world. When that day comes, the ultimate promise of all divine religions will be fulfilled with the emergence of a perfect human being who is heir to all prophets and pious men. He will lead the world to justice and absolute peace. O mighty Lord, I pray to you to hasten the emergence of your last repository, the promised one, that perfect and pure human being, the one that will fill this world with justice and peace."

Bible Prophecies of Islam

The Bible has prophecies that address what today is Islam. Ezekiel 35-48 is a prophecy about Islam and its future. Mount Sier, Edom, Idumea is addressed. These are the modern territories of Jordan, Arabia where the Muslim descendants of Ishmael and Esau live today. The first few verses of chapter 35 set the tone:

> 3 ..."O mount Seir, I am against thee, and I will stretch out mine hand against thee, and I will make thee most desolate.
> 5 Because thous hast had a perpetual hatred, and hast shed the blood of the children of Israel by force of the sword in the time of their calamity, in the time that their iniquity had an end:
> 6 Therefore, as I live, saith the Lord GOD, I will prepare thee unto blood, and blood shall pursue thee...
> 10 Because thous has said, These two nations [Judah and Israel] and these two countries shall be mine, and we will possess it; whereas the LORD was there:
> 11 Therefore, as I live, saith the Lord GOD, I will even do according to thine anger, and according to thine envy.. and I will make myself known among them, when I have judged thee.
> 12 ...I have heard all thy blasphemies which thou hast spoken against the mountains of Israel saying, They are laid desolate, they are given us to consume.
> 15 As thou didst rejoice at the inheritance of the house of Israel, because it was desolate, so will I do unto thee: thou shalt be desolate, O mount Seir, and all Idumea, even all of it...

Idumea is the ancient land of Edom lying to the east of Israel. It is occupied today by Muslims whose hatred for Israel is universal. Following the attacks of September 11, 2001, the United Muslim Association explained why it happened:

> "Since Sept. 11, Americans want to know what is behind such anti-American sentiment in the Muslim world...[It is] Our support for...Israel [which] has been responsible for the killing and maiming of thousands of Lebanese, Palestinians and Iranians...Through our $3 billion-a-year aid to Israel...we have supported Israel's unjust and illegal occupation of Palestinian lands." Tampa Tribune, November 17, 2001.

Meanwhile, on October 26, 2001, Sheikh Raid Sallah, head of the Islamic movement in Israel, said at a rally in the Tamra, Israel:

> "Oh, peoples of the West...we say to you: We are the masters of the world and we are the repository of all good, because we are the 'best people, delivered for mankind' (Koran, 3:111). We do not hesitate, Oh Bush and Blair: We invite you to Islam. Enter Islam, you and your peoples."

Here is the clear admission of Islamic ambition: global domination. But, because of their hatred for Israel, Ezekiel 35 reveals their fate:

> 4 I will lay thy cities waste, and thou shalt be desolate...
> 7 Thus will I make mount Seir most desolate...
> 8 And I will fill his mountains with his slain men: in thy hills, and in thy valleys, and in all thy rivers, shall they fall that re slain with the sword.

Other prophecies seem to suggest the militant qualities of radical Islamic powers:

He Shall Come To His End

Daniel 11:22 a king sweeps away an overwhelming army arrayed against him.
Verse 24 invading other nations.
Verse 25, heading a large army.
Verse 31 his armed forces serve him.
Verse 38 honoring a god of fortresses.
Verse 39 he attacks the mightiest of fortresses.
Verse 40 he heads a huge military force against the king of the South.

Daniel 8:24, 11:39, etc his power is not his own but that of a "foreign god."
Daniel 9:27 mentions a covenant with many for one seven year period.
 (spiritually in Christ, but physically too)
Ezekiel 38 military attack on Israel, peace and security have come to the world.
Daniel 11:23 agreements of peace followed by deceit.
Daniel 11:24 distributing plunder, loot and wealth to his followers.
Verse 39 distribute lands as rewards making them rulers over many people.
Revelation 13:11-18 speaks of a false prophet forces everyone to worship the beast.

Muslims believe that the city of Rome is the next object of conquest.
Constantinople (now Istanbul) was first.

There are also 10 Islamic OPEC nations:
 Algeria,
 Indonesia,
 Iran,
 Iraq,
 Kuwait,
 Libya,
 Nigeria,
 Qatar,
 Saudi Arabia,
 the United Arab Emirates'

Dome of the Rock on Temple Mount, Jerusalem

> Patrick Devenny, Henry M. Jackson National Security Fellow at the Center for Security Policy in Washington, D.C.
> *The American Spectator*, 2005

Of Prophets and Profits

The book of Revelation describes a great Global Enterprise that controls the world at the end of time. It captures the attention of the entire planet; all wonder and are astonished at its power and capabilities.

Two major characteristics identify this End Time power:
Religion and Money
- worldwide Worship and world wide Commerce
- global Ecumenical unity and global Economics
- a Universal Church, and a World Bank.

We now live in that time—another time of prophetic fulfillment—when these two main themes of Religious and Economic force are the prominent agents of human destiny. For many centuries Protestants have identified the worldwide universal church that champions global ecumenical unity as the Papacy of medieval times. Today it is fast regaining its former prestige and influence. But efforts to identify the global *economic* power at the end are usually given only superficial attention. Yet the prophecies make significant reference to the role that money, finance, and trade play at the end of time.

In addition to the book of Revelation (chapters 13, 17 and 18) the Beast is also featured in Daniel chapters 7, 8, 9 and 11, Isaiah 47 and Jeremiah 50. Taken together, these references paint a picture of a dominant end-time superpower with global religious influence that ("causes all the world to worship the beast") and boasts of its physician security (in a land of "unwalled villages"), its military might ("who is able to make war" with it?), and its economic strength ("causes them that dwell on earth...that they should not buy or sell").

America Flew the Coup
As predicted, the United States of America has emerged at the end of the 20th Century as the world's sole remaining Superpower. This "land between the seas" that was "once desolate" but "now inhabited" by people who were "gathered out of the nations into the midst of the land." This land is "abundant in treasures" so that "her merchants" and "great men of the earth" have "grown rich by the abundance of her delicacies." This land is "given to pleasures" and "entertainment...craftsmen...[and] weddings are heard in her." The location of this land is further identified as it arises "from the earth" (the New World) in contrast to previous powers that arose "from the sea" representing the populated areas of the Old World.

Now, combine with this the sequence of powers emerging from the remnants of the Roman Empire, the European nations, as depicted in Daniel 7—not in their initial fulfillment as ancient kingdoms of Western Civilization—but in their final secondary fulfillment as Empires of the modern age. At the "time of the end" (when the papal power of the middle ages was receiving its deadly wound in the late 1700's) a "lamb-like" power was appearing on the world scene. It was revolting from the British crown (the superpower of its day) in order to create a haven for civil, economic, and religious freedom. America succeeded in leaving the royal nest and taking flight on its own (even as the eagles wings were plucked from the lion in Daniel 7 and the woman fled to the wilderness in Revelation 12 on eagles wings).

For over a hundred years, this new nation remained politically isolated and economically independent from the rest of the world. We explored our frontiers and expanded our resources without any outside help and untouched by external foes. Then the U.S. changed its foreign policy and began forging a previously unthinkable alliance with its old nemesis. This reversal—from enemy to imitator—was an extreme makeover into the image of its mother monarchy. The resulting Anglo-American system, constructed to fight the menace of Communism, is sadly today itself a menace. Despite the claims of congressional leaders, business leaders, church leaders and mass media that the goal of the American-dominated New World Order is the expansion of democracy, the defense of freedom and the promotion of global prosperity, just the opposite is true.

The real goal of the Anglo-American Empire is the expansion of consumerism, the defense of corporate profits, and the promotion of "free trade"—free of any restrictions for a relatively small privileged class of investors, bankers, and multinational corporations who *are free* to pursue pure profit at the expense of the poor and unfortunate billions who barely eek out an existence in the Third World. America's New World Order is not new and its policies are quite un-American. In fact, its morals are very un-Christian. It is not even based on democracy, but pure Economics.

While most Christians fear an evil Antichrist from the East who will form a "One World Government" in the near future, they naively applaud the advantages and benefits of our booming "free-market" capitalism as a heavenly blessing with which the Church can grow and prosper. Big Business, Big Oil, Big Tobacco have been joined by Big Christianity to form today's massively wealthy and hugely influential political machine in furthering the aims of Globalization. Instead of misdirecting our fears toward a future Antichrist that is yet to unleash his demonic forces, we should open our eyes to the very real and present World Empire of oppression and injustice. The Beast has already set up shop; Antichrist is already here, alive and well; together they are even now steering the world to perdition. Sadly, many uninformed Church-going, Bible-toting, conservative, religious citizens pray and vote for the military-industrial-financial complex that perpetrates this rape and plunder.

The Gospel of Greed
In 1776, when the United States was declaring independence from Great Britain, British economist Adam Smith authored his "free trade" bible, *The Wealth of Nations*. The timing was not coincidental. The American Revolution was fought, in part, because of Britain's self-serving economic policies. Remember the tea tax? Smith argued that powerful, invisible forces would miraculously guide and expand a nation's economy, stabilize market prices and inevitably lead to a perfect society free from want and poverty—if only people were simply allowed to freely pursue their own self-interests without any outside interference (like colonial governments imposing import tariffs on foreign goods as a means of protecting local producers).

Adam Smith preached his *laissez-faire* (leave it alone) economic theory as a Gospel of Greed. Profits, he promised, are the key to a just society and all human happiness. This delusional fantasy was absolutely contradictory to the inspired position taken by the Apostle Paul who emphatically stated that "the love of money is the root of all evil." 1 Timothy 6:10. The truth of this is proven by the fact that Smith's system of enriching the rich at the expense of the poor actually created an opposing system.

Karl Marx, Engels and Lenin all drew their inspiration from the abuses perpetrated by the British Empire and its Adam Smith-inspired "greed-is good" unrestricted capitalism to advocate the totally restricted system of Communism. In 1844 a young German named Karl Marx observed the plight of poor workers in the sweatshops of the Empire and stated, "The worker becomes all the poorer the more wealth he produces" (*Economic and Philosophic Manuscripts*). Four years later after visiting German immigrant workers in London, he wrote the *Communist Manifesto*. Immediately a wave of revolutions spread across Europe as monarchy's toppled and Marxism exploded. Marx spent the rest of his life in England. It was there that he met Charles Darwin, whose theory of Biological Evolution inspired Marx to formulate his own theory of Social Evolution.

It was from England that Charles Darwin inoculated the world with his theory that given enough time primitive organisms can advance through the magic of Natural Selection in ever higher forms, thus removing God from His role as the Creator of all things. From this, Marx, developed his own theory: given enough time people will eventually rise up in rebellion against greedy Capitalistic Imperialism and form a more advanced system that will restore equality for the "common" good of all. So much for theory.

These two totalitarian systems (Imperialism and Communism) are both evil extremes that exploit the masses—economically and religiously. One is a brutal system of power, profit, and luxury for a small aristocracy, based on the philosophy that "might makes right." Imperialism's small ruling class humiliates, dominates, and plunders the large working class while promoting the state religion of the Anglican Church or the Catholic Church or an Islamic Mosque—it all depends on the Imperial power.

The other system, Communism, is just as brutal and also favoring a small class of bureaucrats, in charge of *enforcing* the distribution of "wealth" (basic necessities) and promoting an atheistic philosophy of life that forbids freedom of religion, freedom of assembly, free press and free enterprise. Because it is an over-reaction to one extreme at the far right of the political-economic-religious spectrum, it moved to the far left and inevitably produces the same results (for the many and the few) but for different reasons.

Religious freedom was first attacked by the British Empire right at home when Henry VIII commandeered the Church of England putting himself in charge! Its pattern of religious suppression continued in Ireland against the Catholics, in India against the Hindu, in Burma against the Buddhists, in Egypt against the Muslims, in Palestine against the Jews and in every country it colonized. It was to escape religious intolerance that the Puritans fled England; it was to guarantee religious liberty that America determined to provide its citizens with Political, Economic *and* Religious freedom.

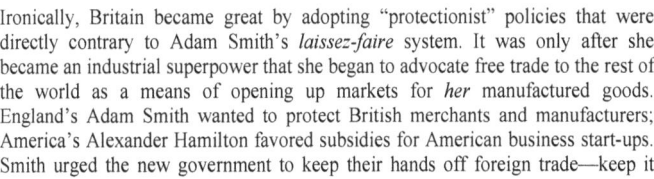

Communism, like Imperialism, suppresses Political and Religious freedom. For 70 years Russia was the world's leading atheistic power, a legacy of the French Revolution against an aristocratic monarchy and corrupt Church. Ironically, Russia is now thirsting for the Word of God and ripe for the Gospel and evangelism while today England is the dominant atheistic influence in Europe. That's the fruit of the Gospel of Greed.

Ironically, Britain became great by adopting "protectionist" policies that were directly contrary to Adam Smith's *laissez-faire* system. It was only after she became an industrial superpower that she began to advocate free trade to the rest of the world as a means of opening up markets for *her* manufactured goods. England's Adam Smith wanted to protect British merchants and manufacturers; America's Alexander Hamilton favored subsidies for American business start-ups. Smith urged the new government to keep their hands off foreign trade—keep it "free"; Hamilton recommended a federal policy of high tariffs on British imports, a National Bank and Mint so that the new American economy could not only be strong but also *financially* independent from Britain.

The General Welfare

It was, after all, the Declaration of Independence which endorsed the Biblical truth that mankind is one continuous brotherhood, created in the image of God and equally endowed with a divine purpose and potential. Furthermore, the preamble of the United States Constitution explicitly states the fundamental principle of the original American Economic system: "We the People of the United States, in Order to form a more perfect Union, establish Justice, insure domestic Tranquility, provide for the common defense, *promote the general Welfare*..." Our general welfare, not some other country's.

Hamilton's system was remarkably successful until the end of the nineteenth century when the British-allied financial ruling class of Morgan and Rockefeller were finally able to replace it with Adam Smith's "free trade" policies. These American aristocrats of the Northeast were descendents of pro-British Tory merchant dynasties, fat cat middle men who bought and sold, but rarely consumed or produced, and naturally were constantly pushing for "free-trade" in America (cheap foreign imports that provide handsome profits). Also sympathetic with the tactics and aligned economically with the ambitions of the British Empire were the Southern plantation owners who profited handsomely from the British Babylon of their day by offering an abundance of raw materials harvested by cheap slave labor.

The issue came to a crisis during Abraham Lincoln's presidency. His economic advisor, Henry Carey, observed that slavery was a critical requirement for free trade. "We see the slave trade prevail to so great an extent in all countries subject to the British system... It is the most gigantic system of slavery the world has yet seen... By adopting the 'free trade,' or British system, we place ourselves side by side with the men who have ruined Ireland and India, and are now poisoning and enslaving the Chinese people." Lincoln summarized the situation in his own unique common-sense way: "I don't know much about the tariff, but I know this much: When we buy manufactured goods abroad we get the goods and the foreigner gets the money. When we buy the manufactured goods at home, we get both the goods *and* the money."

America Goes Free

For over a hundred years, America remained isolated politically and protected economically. Business historian Thomas McCraw, of the Harvard Business School, tells the story: "For 150 years after the Revolution [there was] a pronounced tendency toward protectionism, mostly through the device of the tariff." But after we became the dominant economic force on the planet, the US also "began preaching *laissez-faire* to the rest of the world. American support for worldwide free trade is quite a recent phenomenon." (James Fallows, *How the World Works*.) This was exactly the same career path taken by Britain years before.

The theories of Adam Smith can be justly blamed for the economic catastrophe that exists in the Third World today because it has been steadily forced upon those nations since the end of World War II. Britain used "free trade" to destroy any competition that might have existed in her colonies: Ireland, India, Egypt, Ghana, etc, etc. Free trade reduced them to poor dependencies that could only export cheap raw materials and nothing more. Meanwhile the successful American System of national economy was adopted by Germany, Japan and Russia who also grew strong by resisting the intoxicating wine of Britain. When American foreign policy reversed itself under the influence of the Houses of Morgan and Rockefeller in the late 1800's, however, our previous allies became our enemies in the World Wars and Cold War that followed.

The Great Rapprochement
Historians call America's switch from enemy of the British Empire to imitator of it the "Great Rapprochement." There was nothing great about it. It was actually a betrayal of our fundamental values. The book of Revelation calls it the "Image to the Beast." Doing just what the Beast did, a carbon-copy image of the original.

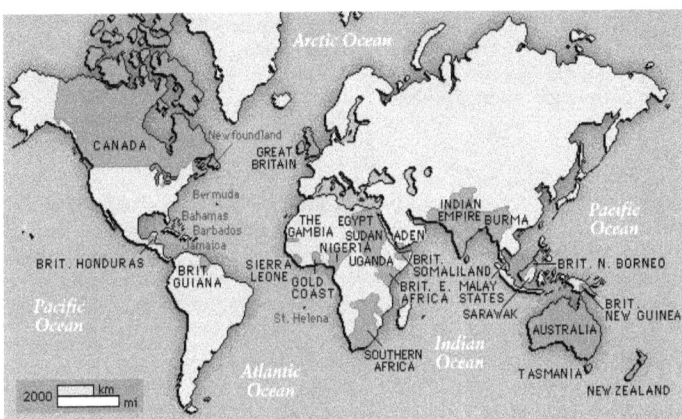

The British Empire at the time of the American Revolution was the world's richest superpower, covering over a quarter of the planet's land area, ruling the seven seas and controlling a fifth of the world's population. But within this huge Empire only a tiny white minority actually exercised their God-given rights to "Life, Liberty and the Pursuit of Happiness." The rest were enslaved economically or subdued violently. As Lincoln observed, "the foreigner got the money." To the poor developing Third World countries Britain was that foreigner.

The wealthy elite ruling families of America's northeast wanted their chance to share in the booty of the Empire. If only they could convince the American government to follows Britain's example. Christopher Hitchens in *Blood, Class, and Nostalgia – Anglo-American Ironies* notes that the East Coast Establishment has always been just an American branch of the British Empire. Success in their struggle for "free trade" came with the installment of Theodore Roosevelt as President of the United States. Relations with the mother country were restored and American foreign policy strategists began to learn the British way of doing things.

The British Lion Roars
When pro-British President Woodrow Wilson entered office he slashed the tariff, created the Federal Reserve in 1913 which enabled American financing to fund the planned British war against Germany.
(The Federal Reserve is a misnomer. It is neither "Federal" nor does it have any "Reserves." It operates completely independent of governmental control, adjusting only the prime lending rate of interest paid by the great privately owned banks of New York: Citicorp, Chase-Manhatten, etc.) Wilson then took the US into World War I in 1917 to secure a British victory. These measures enabled Britain to make its greatest one-time expansion ever while the US entered the Great Depression following the British engineered bust of the "Roaring 20's"

166 Prophesy Again!   **Prophets and Profits**

The key players in this project were Sir Montagu Norman, governor of the Bank of England from 1920-1944 and Benjamin Strong, governor of the New York Federal Reserve Bank from 1914-1929. Their roles are detailed by historian Webster Tarpley in his essay *British Financial Warfare: How the City of London Created the Great Depression*.

Sir Montagu Norman   Benjamin Strong

Norman wished to insure the primacy of the gold-based British Sterling pound in the world market, but it had become "grotesquely overvalued" because "the British were running a balance of payments deficit" as a result "of their excess of imports over exports," Tarpley explains. Exactly the same situation prevails today in the US. At the time America was a producer and Britain had developed into a consumer economy. Today those roles are reversed. Then, British gold was flowing towards New York, where now most of the world's gold is accumulating.

Sir Montagu Norman's solution to stop this golden hemorrhage was to get the US "to launch a policy of easy money, low interest rates, and a weak dollar—in short, a policy of inflation." This was now possible because, with the development of the Federal Reserve System, the money bosses were independent of the US government's political control. Benjamin Strong cooperated and soon the country was enjoying the wonderful financial "bubble" of the "Roaring" 1920's. We saw the same thing happen in the late 1990's Dot Com bubble.

The newly available credit could now be used to furnish American loans to a Germany recovering from the devastations of WWI and for speculative stock purchases that ran the Dow up to a glorious high. The stage was set for an inevitable American economic collapse. And when it came on Black Friday, October 13, 1929, the Wall Street giants (John D. Rockefeller, J.P. Morgan, Joseph P. Kennedy, Bernard Baruch, Henry Morganthau, Douglas Dillon) were "wise" enough to bail out of the stock market just before the Crash ending up even richer at the expense of the majority who lost everything.

John D. Rockefeller   J.P. Morgan   Bernard Baruch   Joseph P. Kennedy   Henry Morgenthau

The Nature of the Beast
America's roots and relationships are inexorably bound to Great Britain. Both have been superpowers. Both share a common heritage, language and Judeo-Christian culture.
The linkage is shown in the prophecies of Daniel 7 and Revelation 13, the beasts from the sea.

Revelation 13 lists them in reverse order (10 horns, leopard, bear, lion)
from the sequence provided in Daniel 7 (lion, bear, leopard, 10 horns). There are two reasons for this.
One is that Daniel and John were writing from two different historical perspectives.
Daniel was looking forward into the future from his position at the time of the Babylonian empire.
John was looking back into past history from his position at the time of the Roman Empire.

The other explanation is that for those who will be living at the end of time, the reversed order will be appreciated by identifying these beasts in the contemporary world powers existing just prior to the second coming of Christ.

Daniel 7 →				Revelation 13 →			
Lion	**Bear**	**Leopard**	**10 horns**	**10 horns**	**Leopard** body	**Bear** feet	**Lion** mouth
Babylon	Persia	Greece	Rome	Papacy	Germany	Russia	Anglo-America
				Wounded-Healed	WWI WWII	cold war	war on terrorism

The 10 Horns
Revelation 13 begins by describing the beast coming up out of the sea as a seven-headed creature with 10 horns. As Greece fragmented into 4 horns (Daniel 8), so Rome fragmented into 10 horns. This initial characteristic identifies the power corresponding to the fourth beast of Daniel 7 which also had 10 horns. Historically, this dreadful beast is the Roman Empire. In the setting of Revelation 13:7, when "power was given him over all kindreds, tongues and nations," is speaks of the Holy Roman Empire which received its power when Rome broke up to form the initial ten European nations in the 5th century.

With the rise of the Little Horn, 3 Arian horns were uprooted, leaving **7 Nicene Christian Nations:**

1 Herules	(Scandinavian now extinct) Arian	
2 Ostrogoths	(eastern Goths, Balkan tribe now extinct) Arian	
3 Lombards	Italy	
4 Vandals	(Carthage North Africa, now extinct) Arian	
5 Sueves	Portugal	
6 Visigoths	Spain (western Goths)	Arianism persists today as:
7 Franks	France	**Unitarians, Jehovah Witnesses, Mormons**
8 Burgundians	Switzerland	
9 Allemans	Germany	
10 Anglo-Saxons	England	

Revelation 13 picks up where Daniel 7 left off. The European nations are freeing themselves from the domination of the little papal horn as it is ending its 1260 year rule, weakening and finally receiving a deadly wound as the Word of God is placed in the hands of the laity fueling the Protestant Reformation in the 16th century. It is after the wounded head is healed that the three beastly powers begin to make their mark on the world stage. The prophecy specifies a certain order: "the body of a leopard, feet like a bear, and the mouth of a lion." France, the first nation to defend the papacy, was also the last to bring it to its knees.

The Revelation 12 dragon has 10 horns, but only 7 crowns (one for each head)
The 10 horns, therefore, would most logically be located only on one of the seven heads: Rome.

Let's now explore the emergence of the Revelation 13 beast.

168   Prophesy Again!   **Prophets and Profits**

The Body of a Leopard – The German Panther
The next superpower to oppress the Jewish people, was the German Third Reich (the First Reich began with Charlemagne 800 AD and lasted for 1000 years; the Second Reich was the German Empire ruled by Kaiser Wilhelm from 1871-1918). Lead by Adolph Hitler's ambition to create an Aryan Super Race, Germany attempted the systematic extermination of millions of Jews in the Holocaust.

Interestingly, the alternate name for Leopard (Panther) is most commonly used in India from where the Sanskrit term Aryan is derived. Germany favored the Panther in naming its tanks, cruisers, gunboats and armored Panzer divisions.

PZ IV Panzerkampfwagen
Over 8,000 were produced between 1938 and 1945
It sported a 12-cylinder 700 horsepower engine that propelled it to nearly 30 mph and with excellent suspension possessed "unusually good cross-country mobility."

The leopard-panther is not only a swift predator, this one has four wings! This symbol of speed characterized both Daniel's Greece under Alexander the Great and Revelation's Germany. Both Prussian military strategists in WWI and the Nazis in WWII were notorious for their deployment of the Blitzkrieg "lighting" warfare. Responsible for the first two world wars, Germany promoted the use of aircraft and was the first in history to use missiles in modern warfare.

The Panther's four heads parallel the he-goat's four horn division. The original fulfillment was in Alexander the Great's succession by his four generals. The final fulfillment at "the time of the end" is the occupation of defeated Germany after Hitler's fall by four military commanders under the Quadripartite Agreement. The Allies (UK, US, France, Russia) divided Germany into four zones supervised and managed by a general from each of these four nations.

Both Greece and Germany:
- lead by charismatic leaders
- conquered surrounding nations with remarkable speed
    Alexander ruled 12 years from 334-323 BC
    Hitler ruled 12 years 1933-1945
- ended with the death of their Leader
- succeeded by a transitional government "headed" by four military leaders

1870 German states unite to fight France gaining Alsace-Lorraine. Chancellor Bismark took advantage of the nationalism following the war to unite the southern German states with Prussia: unification of Germany under Kaiser Wilhelm crowned as Emperor of the New German Empire on 18 January 1871 in Versailles.

East and West Germany unification in 1992

Present Truth for our time continues the symbols of Daniel 7 with the Bear.

The Feet of a Bear – The Russian Bear
Daniel 7:5 And behold another beast, a second, like to a **bear**, and it raised up itself on one side, And it had three ribs in its mouth between its teeth: and they said to it, "Arise, devour much flesh."

In stark contrast to the human-hearted lion, a cruel devouring bear appears. Russia is commonly illustrated as a bear in political cartoons. The Russian Bear has been featured on the covers of *Time* May 21, 1984, and October 27, 1980, *USA Today* front page September 9, 1988 and the *Economist* magazine on January 25, 1997.

Bears are omnivorous predators; they will eat anything. Their affect on Jerusalem was through the many Russian *pogroms* which purged and persecuted native Russian Jews with some of the worst anti-Semitic hatred of modern history. The Bolshevik Revolution also began in 1917 and in the same month (November) as the British liberation of Jerusalem! The bear was to "devour much flesh" a clear reference to Joseph Stalin's mass execution of 50 million people, making the Soviet Empire's 70 year reign the cruelest in history.

The bear rose up on one side with three ribs in its mouth. During the Imperial Czarist rule the Bear devoured three Trans-Caucasian states (Armenia, Georgia, and Azerbaijan). Then Communist Russia rose up, the first "leftist" government in world history, and "gobbled up" the three Baltic countries of Estonia, Latvia and Lithuania at the beginning of WWII striking a deal with Hitler that gave him Finland and Poland.

Both Persia and Russia:
- ordered Jewish exterminations under Harman and Stalin
- murdered the royal family when they conquer their predecessors
    Darius and Cyrus killed Belshaz**zar** and his family
    Lenin and Trotsky killed the C**zar** and his family

The Mouth of a Lion – The Eagle Has Landed

The dominant world power at "the time of the end," the empire upon which "the sun never set", the United Kingdom that ruled the seven seas, was Britannia, Queen of the Oceans. Great Britain, since before the time of Richard the Lionhearted, has featured in its royal Coat of Arms a rampant Lion standing on its hind feet. Num 23:22-24 Jacob and Israel is called "a people rises like a lioness, and lifts itself up like a lion."

William the Conqueror   Henry II   Queen Elizabeth II   The American Eagle

170 Prophesy Again! **Prophets and Profits**

Great Britain reached its zenith as a global superpower during the reign of Queen Victoria in the 19th century. The British colonies in America adopted the Bald Eagle as their national symbol and "broke away" from its lion parent gaining independence from the United Kingdom to establish the United States in 1776. British Babylon was the first modern Empire but America would soon copy it and become a "spittin' image" of its mother as the second half of Revelation 13 predicts.

It is interesting to note that Ancient, Medieval and Modern Babylon share common identifying characteristics: Each is the superpower of its day, they combine religion and government, and affect the city of Jerusalem.

Ancient Babylon ruled the world in 600 BC, Nebuchadnezzar enforced public worship on pain of death in a fiery furnace, and destroyed the city of Jerusalem in 586 BC.
Medieval Spiritual Babylon crowned the kings of Europe, commanded armies, enforced church doctrine on pain of death, and launched a long series of crusades to recapture Jerusalem from the Muslims.
Modern Political Babylon colonialized poor nations, enslaving them through financial markets, trade controls, and economic sanctions. It formed its own State religion, the Anglican Church of England controlled by the monarchy. The British army liberated Jerusalem from the Muslims by force in 1917 under the command of General George Allenby. Britain's Balfour Declaration set the stage for establishing the modern Jewish state of Israel.

But America is predicted to partner with Modern Babylon as shown in the second half of Revelation 13. It has already done this economically and militarily during the last half of the 20th Century. It will soon more fully align itself religiously.

It was in this setting that Franklin Delano Roosevelt was elected 32nd President in 1933. A distant cousin to Teddy Roosevelt, FDR was well-connected. His uncle was a founding member of the Federal Reserve Board. He should have aligned with the Eastern Establishment, but from the very beginning he set himself in a face-off against Wall Street, London and the House of Morgan. The first thing he did was to sign a bill making it illegal for private citizens to own gold. All gold had to be turned into the US Treasury. This immediately strengthened the dollar. Then he created old-age pensions, unemployment insurance, labor regulations, and the Works Progress Administration, initiated Social Security, backed the first Federal minimum wage law, created the Federal National Mortgage Administration (Fannie Mae) and the Securities and Exchange Commission to protect private stock market investors, created the FDIC to protect small banks from runs and panics, and developed public electricity by creating the Tennessee Valley Authority—all policies aimed at improving the General Welfare, taking the economy back for the people and away from the private interests of Big Business.

America stood directly opposed to the British system which was facing its own problems. When WWII began Prime Minister Winston Churchill found his nation broke, isolated from her colonies, and Germany poised to invade. The entire British Empire was at the mercy of America to save it. So FDR scheduled a meeting with Churchill on August 13, 1941 at a naval rendezvous in Argentia, Newfoundland to discuss American assistance in the war. FDR made it clear that American support was conditional on a revision in Britain's trade policies that he had drafted in a document known as the Atlantic Charter.

FDR's son, Elliot Roosevelt, recorded the following discussion in his book, *As He Saw it:*

> "Those Empire trade agreements... [FDR began] It is because of them that the people of India and Africa, of all the colonial Near East and Far East, are still as backward as they are."
> Churchill's neck reddened and he crouched forward. "Mr. President, England does not propose for a moment to lose its favored position among the British Dominions. The trade that has made England great shall continue..."
> "You see," said Father [FDR] slowly,..."I am firmly of the belief that if we are to arrive at a stable peace, it must involve the development of backward countries...It can't be done obviously by eighteenth-century methods."
> "Who's talking about eighteenth-century methods?"
> "A policy which takes raw materials out of a colonial country, but which returns nothing to the people of that country...Twentieth-century methods involve bringing industry to these colonies,...increasing the standard of living, by educating them, by bringing them sanitation—by making sure that they get a return for the raw wealth of their community."
> "You mentioned India," [Churchill] growled.
> "Yes, I can't believe that we can fight a war against fascist slavery, and at the same time not work to free people all over the world from a backward colonial policy."
> "What about the Philippines?"
> "I am glad you mentioned them.. They get their independence, you know, in 1946. And they've gotten modern sanitation, modern education, their rate of illiteracy has gone steadily down..."
> "There can be no tampering with the Empire's economic agreements."
> "They're artificial..."
> They are the foundation of our greatness."
> "The peace," said Father firmly, "cannot include any continued despotism."

The British delegation objected most to the charter's third clause:

> ...respect the right of ALL peoples to choose the form of government under which they will live;
> ...to see sovereign rights and self government restored to those who have been forcibly deprived of them.

Churchill finally signed the Atlantic Charter and when it was released to the media oppressed peoples in colonies around the world cheered! But Roosevelt remained cautious. He feared that only vigilance in dismantling colonialism could prevent another war.

> "The colonial system means war. Exploit the resources of an India, a Burma, a Java; take all the wealth out of these countries, but never put anything back...things like education, decent standards of living, minimum health requirements—all you're doing is storing up the kind of trouble that leads to war."
> "I'm talking about another war. I'm talking about what will happen to our world, if after this war we allow millions of people to slide back into the same semi-slavery! Don't think for a moment, Elliott, that Americans would be dying in the Pacific tonight, if it hadn't been for the shortsighted greed of the French and the British and the Dutch. Shall we allow them to do it all, all over again? Your son will be about the right age, fifteen or twenty years from now."

This advice to his son was exactly fulfilled in Vietnam. FDR's anti-Imperialist views are the key to understanding his Presidency. He has been described as "a loner," "cunning," and even "devious." He had good reason to be careful. Confiding in his son, Elliott, he once explained:

> "Some of those career diplomats over there [in the State Department] aren't in accord with what they know I think. They should be working for Winston. As a matter of fact, a lot of the time, they are...Any number of 'em are convinced that the way for America to conduct its foreign policy is to find out what the British are doing and then copy that!...It's like the British Foreign office."

172   Prophesy Again!   **Prophets and Profits**

Right in the middle of WWII FDR found himself resisting French, British and Dutch efforts to start a new theater of operations in Southeast Asia—all because they were anxious that their precious colonies (Dutch Indonesia, British Malaysia and Burma, and French Vietnam) might be lost to independence. FDR argued with Churchill about this at Casablanca. "Sure, the British want to recapture Burma. It's the first time they've shown any real interest in the Pacific war, and why? For their colonial empire!...Burma—that affects India, and French Indo-China, and Indonesia—they're all interrelated. If one gets its freedom, the others will get ideas...De Gaulle isn't any more interested in seeing a colonial empire disappear than Churchill is." In *The Empire Strikes Back*, John Newsinger confirms this: "Once Japan was in retreat the European powers were determined to reclaim their empires. With France and Holland still too weak after suffering the effects of German occupation, it fell to the British Labour government to restore French rule in Vietnam and Dutch rule in Indonesia as well as reoccupying Britain's own colonies." But they met fierce resistance.

The worst was in Vietnam. During WWII, American ally Ho Chi Minh led his forces against the Japanese finally securing Hanoi by August 19, 1945. Two weeks later he declared independence for the nation of Vietnam quoting from the American Declaration of Independence and ending with a passionate condemnation of the French colonial masters. Ho Chi Minh then looked to the US for support as they had previously supplied his forces with arms and equipment to fight the Japanese. Instead, Truman stood by as the British reconquered Vietnam and handed it back over to the French "but only after the liberal use of artillery, the deliberate burning of areas held by the rebels and the rearming and use of surrendered Japanese troops...in an effort to keep down British casualties." Britain saved Vietnam for the French but in so doing sparked a war of national liberation that lasted for the next 30 years. World War II was a crushing defeat not just for the imperialism of Nazi Germany, but for that of the British Empire as well. The contagion of independence spread quickly through her colonies:

   1947 India, Pakistan
   1948 Burma, Sri Lanka
   1956 Egypt took over the Suez, Sudan became independent
   1957 Ghana in West Africa
   1960's   Malta, Cyprus, Kuwait, South Yemen, Malaysia, Singapore, Samoa, Surinam, Guyana, Lesotho,
            Swaziland, Kenya, Tanzania, Uganda, Malawi, Sierra Leone and Gambia
   1970's Bahrain, Oman, Qatar, United Arab Emirates and Fiji

The Lamb Becomes a Dragon

After FDR, America's role in the world changed dramatically—from being a liberator to being a dominator and oppressor—in perhaps the greatest and most damaging betrayal of American values and human hopes the world has ever seen. The lamb-like beast of Revelation 13 began to "speak as a dragon" and caused "fire to come down in the sight of men" verses 11, 13.

President Truman placed the United States on the road to Empire through the influence of his Wall Street advisors: Kennan, Acheson, Bohlen, Lovett, Harriman and McCloy. (*The Wise Men – Six Friends and the World They Made*,

Walter Isaacson).

- He presided over the dropping of the atom bomb on Hiroshima and Nagasaki. The Cold War was born.
- Next Truman signed the National Security Act of 1947 (written by Clark Clifford, a Wall Street banker and lawyer) and created the CIA placing the US on a permanent war footing (under the direction of Sir William Stephenson, head of *British* Intelligence in the US).
- While FDR had supported Chiang Kai-Sheck and the nationalist party that later became Taiwan, Britain favored Mao Tse Tung because he promised not to threaten her Hong Kong holdings. Obediently, Truman stood by and let Mao's Communists take over mainland China.
- The "Truman Doctrine" was created for the Puppet President allowing America to engage in preventive actions and intervention into the affairs of any other nation that was "going Communist".
- Truman orchestrated the breakup of Korea into North and South, escalating the Korean Conflict into outright war and then fired General MacArthur for trying to actually win it.

Covert Neo-Imperialism
With the demise of overt Imperialism, the Anglo-American powers switched to a policy of covert neo-Imperialism. Although centuries of colonial rule appeared to reach their end and the Third World nations became "Independent," the looting of natural resources, tax collection, suppression of popular revolts and general oppression of the impoverished masses eventually resumed under the hands of the newly empowered Third World leaders, a new generation of indigenous elite that acted as partners in crime with their superpower masters. Together they resisted Reform, then Democracy itself as Dictators were installed to allegedly "keep the peace" and create "stability" while actually increasing *Profit*.

The disenfranchised peoples of the "developing nations" looked to America for help since she was the self-proclaimed "Defender of Democracy." The United States, by her very example and rhetoric, actually encouraged revolution. But instead of turning to the poor as political patriots America embraced the rich as business partners. How could the people achieve freedom? Communism offered the only hope.

America had divorced its historic mission and decided to become just another Empire. Not surprisingly, an explosion of newly independent countries around the world adopted Communism: Cuba, Angola, China, Korea, Vietnam... And the sleeping Empire saw in Communism, the most powerful anti-Imperialist force in the world, the perfect excuse to breath new life into Imperialism—all in the name of "fighting the Red menace."

174 Prophesy Again! **Prophets and Profits**

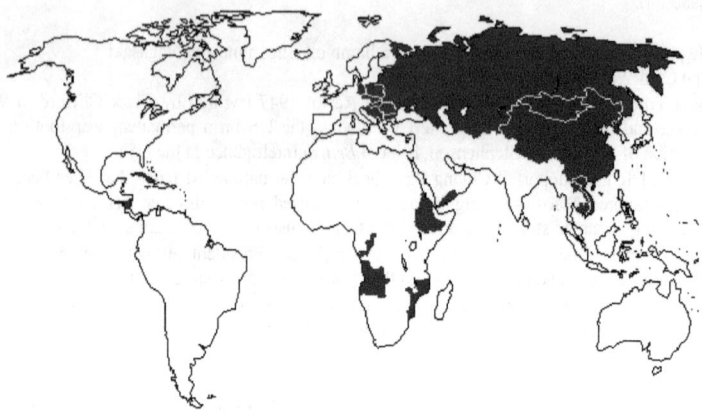

We know this era of Imperial Empire building as the "Cold War," but former CIA director John Stockwell rightly identifies is as the "Third World War." Communism was simply a smoke screen to hide the real war fought against the real enemy: Third World Nationalism.

> It is a war that has been fought by the United States against the Third World. Others call it the Cold War and focus on the anti-Communist and anti-Soviet rationales, but the dead are not Soviets; they are people of the Third World... Altogether, perhaps twenty million people died in the Cold War. As wars go, it has been the second or third most destructive of human life in all of history, after World War I and World War II. The six million people the CIA has helped to kill are *people* of the Mitumba Mountains of the Congo, the jungles of Southeast Asia, and the hills of northern Nicaragua. They are people without ICBMs or armies or navies, incapable of doing physical damage to the United States. The 22,000 killed in Nicaragua, for example, are not Russians; they are not Cuban soldiers or advisors; they are not even mostly Sandinistas. A majority are rag-poor peasants, including large numbers of women and children.
> *(The Praetorian Guard – The U.S. Role in the New World Order*, John Stockwell, 1991)

The change from America as a Republic to America as an Empire, from the defender of freedom to its most powerful opponent, was not an accident. Churchill's emissary to General Eisenhower during World War II, Harold Macmillan (who later became the British Prime Minister), admitted to Eisenhower that Britain well knew that its inevitable fall would be followed by America's rise and then remarked that it was the responsibility of the UK to play the role of Greece to the new American Rome, just as the ancient Roman Republic was initially influenced by the positive qualities of classical Greek culture, philosophy and Democracy. (Notice the standing lion on Time's cover).

"American rediscovery of the intoxications of a 'natural' aristocracy, of an 'expansionist' credo, of an affection for the marks and baubles of caste—all this was conveyed from England as directly as the chests of tea that had once ended up in Boston Harbor."

"In the titanic battle against Hitler, [England was] forced to acknowledge that the proportions of the relationship had changed, and that Britain could now survive only as junior partner. But along the way, huge alterations had been made in the American system. The United States found itself committed in far-off places with which it had no common history." *Blood, Class, and Nostalgia – Anglo-American Ironies*, British author Christopher Hitchens

Birth of the Empire
The origins of the Anglo-American Empire began in the 18th century with the formation of the first modern multinational corporation, the British East India Company centered in London its financial nexus of merchant bankers like Lehman, Rothschild, and Baring. Across the pond and 200 years later, political and economic power concentrated in Americans like Morgan (banking), Rockefeller (oil), Harriman (railroads), Carnegie (steel), Ford (automobiles) and DuPont (arms) who centered their operations in New York City

Society of the Elect
Common goals and ambitions at the dawn of the 20th century brought these two systems together with the shared desire to dominate the world and make a lot of money in the process. This union was spearheaded by Cecil Rhodes who dreamed of forming a secret organization "copied from the Jesuits" that would bring an end to all wars, perpetuate one language throughout the world, gradually absorbing its wealth.

He invited William T. Stead, Lord Alfred Milner, and Lord Esher to establish with him the "Society of the Elect" on February 5, 1891. His long range vision included the selection and education of the best and brightest in the philosophies and methods of the Empire and become supporters of its imperial agenda. To further this he founded the Rhodes Scholarships as his most notable legacy.

Cecil Rhodes

After Rhodes passed off the scene, Lord Alfred Milner took over and the name informally became the Milner Group. In 1919 at the Versaille peace talks following WWI, the Group joined with Lionel Curtis and Sir Abe Bailey and a group of American experts from J.P. Morgan affiliated universities to organize the Royal Institute of International Affairs. The RIIA set up headquarters in London at Chatham House and officially merged with the CFR (Council on Foreign Relations) its American counterpart in 1921 through the efforts of Wall Street lawyer Elihu Root. Root (also Secretary of War under McKinley, Secretary of State under Theodore Roosevelt —the president who in 1897 said "I should welcome almost any war, for I think this country needs one.") well understood the benefits of Imperial behavior. The RIIA and the CFR are indeed closely related, for the two are really one.

Council on Foreign Relations
The CFR, while attacked by the far right John Birch Society as pro-Communist, discounts such ravings as simply "conspiranoia." If true, the CFR should then advocate the *total* governmental control of national economies as Communism would proscribe. In reality, its consistent aim since WWII as the most important US foreign policy engine (controlled by American—predominantly New York-based—corporate and financial interests) is to emasculate Nation-States down to a limited role as simply protector and promoter of

176 Prophesy Again! **Prophets and Profits**

the general welfare. The CFR promotes the Empire by using *laissez faire* Capitalism as its weapon, not Communism.

America's Imperial Capitalist Achievements

The following summaries illustrate a few examples of how successful America has been in improving profitability for her corporate sponsors as prophesied in Revelation 18.

Guatemala

Guatemala won independence from Spain in 1821, but the masses were still suppressed by a series of dictators. In the 1930's the Boston-based United Fruit Company (UFCO) enjoyed friendly support by then President Jorge Ubico who gave them a large plantation, reduced taxes, duty-free import status, low wage allowances. UFCO then took over International Railways of Central America and assumed complete control of international commerce. In 1944 the military ousted Ubico and allowed the nation's first democratically-elected president Juan Jose Arevalo who raised average wages 80%. Jacobo Arbenz became the next elected President in 1951 with plans for Guatemala to become economically independent and increase the standard of living by using science and technology in agriculture. But his land reform policies were ambushed by American-owned UFCO. They owned all telephone facilities, the only Atlantic harbor, all railroad track in the country, had close ties with the Dulles brothers, the State Department, congressmen, and Eisenhower's personal secretary.

In 1953 Guatemala expropriated the uncultivated portion of UFCO's massive land holdings (over 2/3 of their 300,000 acres) paying them at the severely undervalued worth as stated in their property tax documents. When UFCO cried "Thief!" World Bank President John J. McCloy denied a load request from Arevalo and later oversaw a CFR plan to remove Arbenz. He was rewarded for his efforts with the directorship of United Fruit. The propaganda mill took over depicting Guatemala as a "bastion of communism," "an outpost for terrorism," "a Soviet Republic", "a base" for the Russians to seize the Panama Canal. The US allied with Nicaraguan dictator Anastasio Somoza as well as Honduras's dictator, both of whom shared America's interest in stopping the spread of democracy that would threaten their own regimes. In 1954 the CIA and UFCO financed and armed a military coup that installed a cooperating dictator, Castillo Armas, who promptly returned UFCO's "stolen" land.

Congo

Third largest nation in Africa, Congo got independence from Belgium on June 30, 1960. Democratic elections put Patrice Lumumba into office. Two months later Belgium, Britain, and the US squashed the young Democracy for good in order to control the fortune in natural resources, richest in Africa, that it possessed: 50% of the world's uranium (purchased almost entirely by the US), 75% of the cobalt, 70% of the world's industrial diamonds and the leading producer of rubber, plus gold, silver and copper mines, vast cotton, oil, palm, cocoa plantations, cattle ranches, and sawmills. Eisenhower and the National Security Council immediately ruled that Lumumba was "dangerous to the peace and safety of the world" because he determined to not settle for just political liberation but economic independence as well. To keep his favored position, ruler of the Katanga province, Moise Tshombe, proclaimed independence from the Congo instigated by the European companies that were based there. Belgian, British, Rhodesian and South African troops immediately moved into Katanga to support the secession. The UN condemned Katanga's rebellion. Lumumba plead for US help in regaining control. When the US turned him down he desperately turned to the Soviets who quickly sent trucks and planes. Just as Egypt's Nassar was pushed into the arms of the Russians after the World Bank refused to help finance the Aswan Dam.

But now the West could label Lumumba as "Communist" and with financial incentives from the CIA the country's President illegally dismissed Prime Minister Lumumba. He went straight to the Congolese legislature who voted him back in. But the Pentagon succeeded again through the CIA to encourage General Joseph Mobutu to use military force to usurp Lumumba's position. But Lumumba was a "dangerous" loose canon. The CIA dispatched Dr. Sidney Gottlieb in September to the Congo with a diplomatic pouch containing "lethal biological material" intended for Lumumba's assassination. He was finally captured in December, handed over to Tshombe who promptly executed him just three days before John F. Kennedy took office. Just in time because the Empire knew that JFK clearly understood the forces at work in Africa. At a speech in LA four years earlier he said, "the Afro-Asian revolution of nationalism, the revolt against colonialism...has reaped a bitter harvest today – and it is by rights and by necessity a major foreign policy campaign issue that has nothing to do with anti-communism." Once in office Kennedy privately informed the Russians that he would negotiate a truce in the Congo. Ambassador Timerlake learned of it and phoned Allen Dulles and Pentagon Chief Lyman Lemnitzer alerting them to Kennedy's break with policy as a "sell-out" to the Russians. JFK called on the UN to bring all foreign armies under control, to neutralize the country and make it off-grounds to any East-West competition, and to free all political prisoners. Kennedy supported the UN action to remove Tshombe "Africa's most unpopular African" from power. The breakaway Katanga province was brought back into the Congo Republic. But when JFK died four years later, Mobutu brought Tshombe back into the government making himself the sole military dictator of his new nation, Zaire, changing his own name as well to Mobutu Sese Seko, the Anglo-American favorite in Africa where he ruled at the expense of his people with total authority and in opulent luxury until 1997.

Osei Boateng in *New African* magazine. *Killing Hope*, William Blum.

Brazil

The largest nation in the South American continent, one of the world's richest in natural resources, Brazil was also one of the Empire's prize possessions and long-time colony of Portugal. When João Goulart became President in 1961 he dared to end the foreign exploitation of his country by promoting land reform, pursuing nationalization and industrialization in tapping the nation's enormous potential. JFK encouraged him with the Alliance for Progress foreign aid initiatives that came directly from the government, sidestepping the profit-driven initiatives of the World Bank, IMF and Wall Street. Kennedy received immediate criticism for this audacious act from the Rockefeller brothers, the *Wall Street Journal, Fortune* magazine and McCloy's CFR journal *Foreign Affairs*. David Rockefeller complained that Kennedy's shift in foreign economic aid policy enabled underdeveloped countries to fund publicly owned enterprises that competed with privately owned (i.e., American controlled) companies and encouraged political independence from Washington. (A Reappraisal of Alliance for Progress, 1963 in *Thy Will Be Done – The Conquest of the Amazon: Nelson Rockefeller and Evangelism in the Age of Oil*, Gerard Colby, 1995). Goulart wanted to nationalize communications then held by Rockefeller's ITT; he wanted to expropriate Rockefeller's Hanna Mining Company, the United State's largest iron ore producer. Coincidentally, JFK was shot in November, 1963 and Goulart was then removed by a CIA-backed right-wing military coup four months later. The Rockefeller family's extensive and diverse Brazilian holdings (oil, mining, electricity, communications, cattle ranching, agriculture, banking and investment, most of which were under the umbrella of Nelson's massive International Basic Economy Corporation, the IBEC) were now no longer at risk. Goulart's fall was celebrated in America as a "rescue from communism" yet the disinterest of Khrushchev to provide financial aid during Goulart's presidency suddenly changed to the tune of $120 million a year once the military dictatorship of General Costa e Silva took power—dictatorial power heavily sponsored by the Soviet block well into the 1980's. The outcry against communist influence was silent during these years because the Soviets did not threaten American corporate profits now safe in the hands of their pet dictators.

Indonesia

When Indonesia gained independence from the Netherlands in 1949, Achmad Sukarno began to forge a middle path between the Eastern Soviet and Western Imperial rule. He convened the Conference of Asian and African Nations in 1955 and created the Nonaligned Movement in 1961 composed of Sukarno (Indonesia), Nehru (India), Nasser (Egypt), Tito (Yugoslavia) and Kwame Nkrumah (Ghana). Their attempt to create a new international Third World economic order, however, was just no match for the Anglo-American Empire. When the world market price of natural rubber suddenly dropped in the 1950's, the World Bank seized the opportunity to offer Sukarno hefty loans provided he would denationalize the previously foreign-owned companies. Before a mass rally in Jakarta, President Sukarno yelled at the US ambassador, "Go to hell with your aid!" With Sukarno unwilling to play ball, the "communist threat" card was pulled out to justify a CIA sponsored military takeover under General Suharto that claimed to rescue the day from the PKI communist party uprising which was eliminated along with anyone else on the CIA-provided list of "dangerous persons." Indonesia was engulfed for several years in a horrendous bloodbath of up to a million victims, suspected communists, ethnic Chinese and other undesirables were arrested, tortured and killed. Finally, in November 1967 Time-Life Corporation convened a 3-day meeting in Geneva for the corporate takeover of Indonesia by the major oil companies, banks, General Motors, Imperial Chemical Industries, British Leyland, British-American Tobacco, American Express, Siemens, Goodyear, International Paper Corporation and US steel.

A contract was crafted by Harvard economist Dave Cole (who had just finished re-writing South Korea's banking regulations) following Washington's directions. Indonesia offered an abundance of cheap labor, a treasure house of resources and a vast potential market. Henry Kissinger-affiliated Freeport Company got a mountain of copper in West Papua, Americans and Europeans got its nickel, Alcoa got most of Indonesia's bauxite, a group of American, Japanese and French companies got Sumatra's tropical forests—and all this plunder was made tax-free for five years. Then the World Bank stepped in to roll out the big loans. "Indonesia," said one official, "is the best thing that's happened to Uncle Sam since World War Two." Sukarno had kept the country relatively debt free, but after 30 years under Suharto Indonesia now has a debt of over $260 billion. "There is no debt like it on earth. It can never be repaid. It is a bottomless hole." (*The New Rulers of the World*, John Pilger). Revelation speaks of a "bottomless pit." Yet in spite of this, General Suharto was able to flee the country in 1998 with a "retirement bonus" of $17 billion.

Ghana

The Gold Coast, British colony for 80 years, Dutch colony before that and Portuguese before that, was the home of the slave trade. After World War II, when the contagion of Independence was sweeping Africa, the people rose up in demonstrations and civil disobedience which was met with brutal and violent British repression. On February 28, 1948 a large group of former servicemen marched, unarmed and defenseless to present a petition to His Majesty's Governor, Sir Gerald Creasy. Government troops attacked and killed 63 of the formerly loyal soldiers. After five days of rioting and looting, the Governor read the Riot Act of March 1 to them, declared a state of emergency, censored the press (precedent established with the Book and Newspaper Registration Ordinance of 1887 made the press in Gold Coast under the supervision of the Colonial Secretary), rounded up the resistance leadership and exiled them to the north. Among them was Kwame Nkrumah, who had received degrees at Lincoln and Pennsylvania Universities in the US, and returned to his homeland to lead in the fight for freedom. When a study of the situation published its recommendations at the end of 1949 that fell short of full independence, Nkrumah led a protest movement of labor strikes; he was arrested and put in jail. When released 13 months later, he had won the national elections. Finally, March 6, 1957 the Gold Coast, now known as Ghana, was granted political independence from Great Britain with Nkrumah as it first Prime Minister. He co-founded the Organization of African Unity, built factories and industries, a new harbor, new roads, expanded the Civil Service, constructed the Akosombo Dam and forming the largest man-made lake in the world which produces enough electricity to export to neighboring countries, nationalized private companies, created jobs, increased wages, established Ghana's Black Star shipping line, built new hospitals, schools and three universities. All this was bound to raise the ire of the Empire.

Economic pressures were soon in coming. World cocoa prices (the main income for Ghan) suddenly plummeted in the early 1960's. Unemployment rose, food prices skyrocketed. When America, once again, failed to help, Nkrumah resorted to Russian and Chinese assistance. This very predictably served to justify corrective measures. By 1965 the CIA office in Accra, the capitol city, swarmed with 40 operators who were busy advising and supporting dissident Ghanaian army officers. The inevitable military-led coup finally took place in February, 1966. Overnight, the state-owned industries were returned to private hands, emergency food assistance arrived (even though it had been turned down only four months earlier). The channels of aid, previously clogged, now opened wide. Amazingly, only one month after the coup the international price of cocoa rose 14%. (*Neo-Colonialism – The Last Stage of Imperialism*, Kwame Nkrumah; *The Daily Telegraph*, London, 1972. *National Reconciliation Commission*, Volume 4, Chapter 3, Section 3.1.1, October, 2004.)

Cambodia
After a long history of French colonial rule, Cambodia received its independence, Prince Norodom Sihanouk abdicated the throne to be elected Prime Minister of the new republic in 1955. The same year he was paid a visit by John Foster Dulles, US Secretary of State, who tried to pressure Sihanouk into accepting the protection of the South-East Asia Treaty Organization. The PM refused because he considered SEATO "an aggressive military alliance" aimed at neighboring countries with alien ideologies with which Cambodia had no quarrel. Soon after the "acidy, arrogant" John Foster left, his brother, CIA Director Allen Welsh Dulles, arrived with a stack of "dubious" documents "proving" that Cambodia was about to fall victim to "communist aggression" and that the only way to save the country was to accept SEATO's protection. Sihanouk was not convinced and remained firm in having no part of SEATO. (*My War With the CIA: the memoirs of Prince Norodom Sihanouk*, 1973) In a Mafia-styled response, the Empire began destabilizing Cambodia economically by funding and training hostile Khmer factions. In 1958 while Sihanouk was receiving a 21-gun salute by Eisenhower in Washington, a member of his delegation was planning a plot against him with American officials in New York. The conspirators were exposed once back home and executed for treason, but Sihanouk became increasingly suspicious of American aid. On November 20, 1964 two days before JFK's assassination, the Cambodian National Congress voted to "end all aid granted by the United States" the first time that any country had voluntarily repudiated American aid. Sihanouk saw how this restricted aid (which couldn't be used for state institutions, only *private* enterprise) had corrupted Cambodian officials and business men making them "necessarily obedient to the demands of the lavish bestower of foreign funds." Robert McNamara and Walt Rostow in the LBJ administration focused on South Vietnam as a strategic beachhead against Communism and began the troop buildup that escalated into high gear in late 1969 under Nixon's new National Security Advisor Henry Kissinger. Henry was Harvard trained by his personal tutor William Yandel Elliot, an Oxford Rhodes Scholar and admirer of British Round Table strategist H.G. Wells and his 1928 Empire bible, *The Open Conspiracy: Blueprint For a World Revolution* (New York: Doubleday, Doran and Company). Kissinger was invited into John J. McCloy's Council on Foreign Relations in 1955 and developed the policy that the US must convince the Soviets of its willingness to engage in limited nuclear war as a tool for detante. Kissinger found a position under the National Security Affairs assistant but was promptly fired during the Berlin crisis when JFK heard that Henry was advocating the use of limited nuclear weapons. But LBJ sent him as a delegate to the North-South Vietnam Paris peace talks in 1968. Soured by Hubert Humphrey's campaign position on peace, Kissinger decided to sabotage the talks by sharing confidential details with the Nixon team who then urged the South to walk out and wait until after elections for a better deal from the Republicans. When Kissinger took the reigns of power the following year he worked to consolidate American control over the Third World. While appeasing Russia and China with peace overtures, arms control agreements, technology transfers, financial assistance and trade (most often through the Rockefeller's Chase Manhattan Bank), he promoted US interventions against neutral or communist-leaning states. His first target was Cambodia with the onslaught in March of 14 months of large-

180   Prophesy Again!   **Prophets and Profits**

scale sustained attacks across the Cambodian border flying over 3,600 B-52 "carpet combing" raids as our military chased the Vietcong deeper into the country. Prince Sihanouk was displaced in 1970 by General Lon Nol who was "cooperative with U.S. officials." But now intensely loyal pro-Sihanouk troops fought Nol's troops which were fighting the Vietcong and North Vietnamese who were struggling against the Khmer Serei and Khmer Krom forces which were faced off against the powerful Cambodian communist movement, the Khmer Rouge led by the infamous Pol Pot. American troops then jumped into the fray to assist General Nol and suddenly encountered Communists coming from all directions. The invasion was strongly protested by the US peace movement demonstrators. Four members of Kissinger's department resigned in protest. The end result was a Communist victory with the fall of Phnom Penh to the Khmer Rouge on April 17, 1975 and the start of the Pol Pot's massive and self-destructive genocide of 1-4 million Cambodians.

Iran

In 1950 the privately held Anglo-Iranian Oil Company made a profit of £170 million but Iran only received 12%, the rest went to Britain. When Dr. Mohammed Mossadeq attempted to nationalize AIOC, the British government accused Iraq of turning "communist" started operation "Boot" to oust Mossadeq, and appealed for American assistance with the lure of "big business interests that lay behind the anti-communist rhetoric." Secretary of State, John Foster Dulles, and his brother Allen, CIA Directory of Plans, took over. A CIA executed and funded coup against Mossadeq restored the Shah's power on August 19. AIOC changed its name to British Petroleum, US oil firms took 60% of the booty. (*MI6 – Inside the Secret World of Her Majesty's Secret Intelligence Service*, Stephen Dorril) The Rockefellers participation in planning the coup was rewarded by Shah Pahlavi with huge deposits in Chase Manhattan and contracts for a new Palace to a Rockefeller firm. (Syndicated columnist Jack Anderson, December, 1979)

Iraq

For nearly thirty years Iraq had been led by Prime Minister Nuri Said, the most pro-British Arab leader in all the Middle East. When the British Mandate over Iraq expired in 1932, it was Said who sponsored a British-Iraqi treaty to extend British military presence and influence. In 1936 he advised the Grand Mufti of Palestine to end the anti-British rebellion. In 1948 he refused to allow the Iraqi army in Palestine to aid Egyptian forces under Israeli attack insuring the Jewish victory. In 1956 he even supported the British-French-Israeli invasion of Egypt following Nasser's takeover of the Suez Canal. His luck ran out on July 14, 1958 when a military coup toppled the monarchy. King Faisal II was executed, Nuri Said hid in the home of a friend and then tried to escape dressed as a woman. But a mob recognized him, killed him on the spot, tearing him to bits and repeatedly running over whatever was left until there was nothing left to bury.

The new President, General Abdel Karim Kassem made Iraq dangerous because he successfully pressured the British-controlled Iraq Petroleum Company (IPC) into increasing the countries share of the oil profits, closed the British military bases, encouraged trade unions, built new cities for workers, distributed land to peasants, reduced rents, created a People's Militia and signed arms deals with the USSR. April 28, 1959, CIA Director Allen Dulles warned before the Senate Foreign Relations Committee, "Iraq is today the most dangerous spot on earth." While Dulles feared an Iraqi-Egyptian alliance to strengthen the Arab block, Britain believed the old Babylon vs Egypt mentality would prevail. This proved true and Nassar decided to rub out Kassem by sending a young Baath Party hit man named Saddam Hussein to do the job. Saddam was wounded in the failed attempt and fled to Cairo in 1959. Next Kassem laid claim to Kuwait as rightfully Iraq's before being yanked away by the British after World War I. Now Anglo-American oil profits in Iraq and Kuwait were at stake. The CIA went to work by recruiting Colonel Saleh Mahdi Ammash, who had served in the Iraqi embassy in Washington, D.C. Together with Baath Party dissidents, including Saddam Hussein, the coup was launched February 8, 1963. Kassem surrendered, underwent a sham tribunal and then executed with a shot in the head. Baath Party members were given a list of communist suspects in the country and the purges began that eliminated from 5,000 to 30,000 people of all rank and file, professionals, young and old, tortured in separate detention centers by Ba'athist hit squads that performed like "Hitlerian shock troops." The plan worked. Shell, BP, Bectel, Mobil and other British and American companies were allowed to re-enter Iraq to develop its oilfields. American contractors got contracts to build the Basra dry-dock facilities. Such were the many CIA-Iraqi economic benefits. But careful monitoring was still required. When Abdel Salam Aref was appointed President to appease the people, he was soon eliminated when he began to strengthen ties with Egypt. Another CIA-backed coup was ordered and the Baath Party was installed in 1968 and firmly supported by the US an British governments.

Then there was Chile in 1973, Nicaragua in 1981. And how about Granada, Iraq, Afganistan? Their stories are much the same, products of Imperial foreign policy. But why didn't the Empire invade Rwanda? or Sudan? There were plenty of blatant human rights injustice, a reason cited in previous interventions. Does the lack of strategic (lucrative) resources have anything to do with it? One can only wonder.

Corporate Foreign Relations
The value that the CFR holds in the eyes of Corporate America can be seen by the degree of financial support Big Business makes to the Council. By 1972, 157 companies were contributing hundreds of thousands of dollars each year to the CFR. The ROI (Return On Investment) must have been many times that. Without a doubt, the CFR is well worth it. The list of firms with four or more members as Directors or Partners in the CFR reads like the Fortune 500: U.S. Steel, Mobil Oil, Exxon, IBM, ITT, GE, DuPont, Chase Manhattan Bank, J.P. Morgan and Co., Chemical Bank, Bank of New York, Equitable Life, New York Life, Metropolitan Life, Morgan Stanley, Lehman Brothers. These are truly multinational entities. Exon makes 39%, ITT 38%, and Mobil, IBM each earn more than 50% of their profits overseas. Chase Manhattan has subsidiaries in over 100 countries, J.P. Morgan in 32, DuPont in 29, and GE in 24 countries world wide. U.S. Steel owns major portions of manganese mines in Gabon, copper mines in South Africa, nickel in Indonesia, Iron in Canada and steel making facilities in Spain, Nicaragua, Italy, France, Brazil, India and Germany.

The CFR virtually created the International Money Fund (IMF) and the World Bank. It dispatched a memorandum on November 28, 1941 to FDR and the State Department recommending the establishment of an "international investment agency which would stimulate world trade and prosperity by facilitating investment in developmental programs the world over." This was later refined to a two institution recommendation:

"one an international exchange stabilization board and one an international bank." These became reality in 1944. Cecil Rhodes' dream of "gradually absorbing the wealth of the world" was taking shape.

World Currency
The dominance of the US Dollar began in 1928 when the seven major world oil suppliers met in Achnacarry, Scotland to form the first oil cartel. Long before OPEC, the 'Seven Sisters' (Exxon, Mobil, Gulf Oil, Texaco, Chevron, Royal Dutch Shell and British Petroleum) agreed to fix the world oil price and end competition and price wars among themselves, which had been so destructive to the profit margins of the banks that owned them. J.H. Bamberg, *The History of the British Petroleum Company, Volume 2: The Anglo-Iranian Years, 1928-1954* (Cambridge: Cambridge University Press, 1994).

182 Prophesy Again! **Prophets and Profits**

On April 20, 1933, as Adolph Hitler was taking control of Germany and America was trying to dig its way out of the Great Depression, FDR signed the Emergency Banking Act making it illegal for private citizens to own gold—they had to turn it all over to the US Treasury. (U.S. Statutes at Large: 73rd Congress, 1933 p. 1-7). This boosted the nation's central gold reserves. At the end of WWII America survived as the only undamaged major power while the rest of the world lay in economic shambles. Furthermore, the United States ended up with 80% of the world's gold reserves, some $30 billion. It was the perfect opportunity to apply the Golden Rule: he who has the most gold makes the rules.

So, in 1944 the United Nations Monetary and Financial Conference was convened at Bretton Woods, New Hampshire where 700 delegates from 44 countries constructed a new global economic system. The first order of business was to determine the value of money in the post WWII era. Since America had the highest amount of gold-based reserves, the US dollar was named the world's international reserve currency, fixed to the gold standard at $35/ounce. At the same time, the World Bank, the International Monetary Fund (IMF), and the World Trade Organization (WTO) was conceived with the stated purpose "to promote foreign trade." All three were then placed under the control of the independent US Federal Reserve.

The Bretton Woods system was hailed as being "without precedent in the history of international economic relations." It was based on a monopoly of the Big Five American oil companies which used their dominant position to double the price of oil over the next two years. This oil cartel supplied half of western Europe that was struggling to recover from the war under the provisions of the Marshall Plan (which conveniently restricted its aid from being used to rebuild European oil refineries).

America profited handsomely from this arrangement over the next two decades, until Europe and the Third World were able to rebuilt enough to become self-sufficient and less dependent upon American dollars. With oil reserves running dry in the West, the Middle East found itself in the position of control. After years of Arab world political struggles, Saudi Arabia emerged as the dominant force in the newly formed OPEC oil cartel. It was the largest producer with the largest known reserves and was the only member that did not have a fixed production quota, making it a "swing" producer that could create a glut or shortage of crude at will. Thus, beginning in the early 1960's, OPEC took over the role of setting world oil prices. Fortunately, it remained fairly steady at about $1.90/barrel for the next 20 years.

Gold Standard Gone

The only problem with the provisions of the Bretton Woods System was the allowance for any foreign country holding US dollars to convert them to gold at any time! By 1968 America had spent nearly $500 billion on the Viet Nam war alone (paid primarily with paper Green-backs that we could print as needed, circulate through the economy and enable the purchase of foreign electronics, cameras, watches, automobiles, clothes, etc.). Dollars began building up in foreign countries as the US became the biggest debtor in history. In June 1968, French President Charles deGaulle, realizing that the gold window may not stay open much longer, decided to cash in all his dollars for gold before they started dropping in value as it already had for the Sterling. Other nations began to follow the French lead and by 1971 the Fort Knox gold reserves had become seriously depleted, dropping to only $10 billion. On August 15, Nixon boldly announced the end of the gold standard, putting the world on a direct Dollar-standard and allowing the currency to "float" in the international monetary market. Dollars were in essence now just paper IOU's. The world supply of gold was finite, but the number of dollars that could be printed was infinite. Within weeks the US dollar began to fall around the world, dropping to 40% of its worth within six months. Consequently, the price of oil rose 50% to $3.01/barrel during the same period.

After America went off the gold standard in 1971, everyone else followed suit (except for Switzerland) and by 1973 the rest of the world was trading paper just like the US. With world currencies now "floating" against each other, international currency exchanges became traders, playing different currencies against each other. Worldwide currency transactions doubled in the five years between 1979 to 1984 to a hefty $150 billion a day changing hands—almost 40 times the average daily volume of the New York Stock Exchange! In 1996 the daily exchange volume topped $1 trillion.

It was evident to everyone that Nixon was no financier. So the financiers stepped in. The annual Bilderberg meeting in 1973 (first held at the Bilderberg Hotel near Arnheim, Holland in 1954 by Prince Bernhard) assembled (this time in Saltsjoebaden, Sweden) 84 of the worlds top corporate executives and politicians. CFR member Walter Levy suggested that the Empire's global economy plan would actually benefit from even further oil price hikes. His plan was to orchestrate a massive international increase in the price of oil which would effectively put a damper on the world's "out of control" industrial growth and tilt the balance of power back into the hands of the financial centers. (*Mit der Olwaffe zur Weltmacht*, W.F. Engdahl, 2002).

His three-step plan required
(1) a global oil embargo that would create a world-wide fuel shortage, which in turn would
(2) force a dramatic increase in the price of oil, which since 1945 was priced in dollars. This would
(3) impose an equally dramatic increase in the world demand for US dollars to pay for all the oil that was now so necessary. Henry Kissinger, Nixon's intelligence "czar," engineered step one by facilitating an invasion of Israel by Egypt and Syria on Yom Kippur, October 6, 1973 and then managed the Arab oil embargo that ensued through his infamous "shuttle diplomacy." Within 10 days OPEC acted according to plan by raising the price of oil to $5.11/barrel and by the end of the year to $11.65/barrel!

Petro-Dollar Profits

What made this so profitable for the Empire's banking centers was the OPEC agreement to accept only US Dollars as payment for OPEC-produced oil in return for promised US protection (sale of arms) to Saudi Arabia. This arrangement was struck in June 1974 by Secretary of State Henry Kissinger when he established the U.S.-Saudi Arabian Joint Commission on Economic Cooperation. The global demand for "petro-dollars" was now tremendously increased and the Empire's domination of the global economy was assured. Developing nations had to have oil, to get the oil they had to have dollars, to get the dollars they had to sell their natural resources, their industries, their land to private outside corporations (privatization) or borrow dollars from the World Bank and the IMF.

Prophesy Again! Prophets and Profits

The Empire manipulated political events to create a 400% increase in oil prices, then turned to the victimized countries and "offered" to lend them petro-dollars at highly inflated interest rates! Henry Kissinger called this money laundering scheme "recycling petrodollars."

The Third World nations were "over a barrel." They had to make a choice:
(1) stop developing, betray the hopes of their people and use the money they had borrowed from the World Bank for industrializing their countries to buy oil or
(2) borrow money from the IMF (as a sort of second mortgage) to buy the oil and service their World Bank debts to keep developing.

Either way they were digging a deeper hole of debt. Thus it was that the international banking cartel of London and New York came to control the entire world's economic destiny.

Today this influx has resulted in foreign petro-dollars being invested in 48% of the US Treasury bond market, 24% of the US corporate bond market and 20% of all US corporations amounting to over $8 trillion in total US assets. This provided the United States with enormous power to manipulate the world economy, set rules and prevail in international markets. US currency now accounts for 2/3 of all exchange reserves, over 4/5 of all foreign exchange transactions and half of all world exports. This is Dollar Imperialism.

The Thatcher Revolution and Reaganomics

Once the sinister alliance between OPEC and the Iron Triangle was forged, the Empire decided to make US Dollars also harder to get. The leader, as usual, was Britain. By the late 1970's with oil reaching $40/barrel and the cost of living soaring, Margaret Thatcher was elected Prime Minister in May, 1979 on a platform of "squeezing inflation out of the economy." The "Iron Lady" (and soon Ronald Reagan) placed the blame on government deficit spending, high taxes, labor unions and industrial regulation (rather than on the outlandish increase in the cost of oil).

The Thatcher Revolution and "trickle-down supply-side Reaganomics" both claimed that
- cutting the supply of money to the economy (an unprecedented 42% increase in the cost of loans),
- savagely cutting government spending (eliminate social welfare programs in order to lower taxes),
- deregulating industry (remove safeguards from banking) and
- breaking the power of organized labor (fire striking air controllers as an example to others)

would solve the problem. It did. Overnight, inflation was whipped and depression hit. Businesses went bankrupt unable to pay their staggering loan payments, families stopped buying new homes, long-term investments in power plants, subways, and infrastructure ground to a halt, unemployment doubled in 18 months.

Then it was Fed Chairman Paul Volcker's turn to declare war on "global inflation" (plummeting dollar value) by jacking up the Fed's interest rates up to an astonishing 20%! This unilateral move now made dollars even more expensive to borrow, and once you got them they would buy even less oil. Big Oil and Big Banking on the banks of the Thames and Hudson were having a hay day in lucrative loans to Latin America and real estate speculation in Hong Kong while scalping the rest of the world. The trickle-down benefits to the workers and producers of goods and services was nothing compared to the flood of money filling the banks and bank accounts of the real winners.

The Debt Crisis

The party finally ended with a "debt crisis" in the Third World nations. They began threatening to default on their World Bank and IMF loans that were now burned by impossibly high interest rates. Mexican President Lopez Portillo lead the charge. Mexico had been enjoying a booming economy as a major oil producing nation. With their profits Portillo had begun an ambitious building program to improve the backward nation by constructing new roads, ports, petrochemical plants, agricultural complexes, even a nuclear power program. Then the interest rates went up. The Empire conducted a very successful mass-media campaign to warn Western investors of the risks facing Mexico. There was a run on the Mexican peso, dropping its value 30% as capital flowed out of the country. Unemployment, inflation went up as the price of Mexico's raw materials and living standard went down. On August 20, 1982 Mexico announced to the New York Federal Reserve that it was unable to pay the $82 billion it owed in foreign debt. Ten days later the President nationalized all banks in Mexico. On September 30 George Schultz, then Secretary of State and friend of Milton Friedman, advised the UN General Assembly that the IMF should be authorized to step to police defaulting nations in their debt repayment and restructure their economies to make their exports more attractive to the West (i.e., drop their prices and tariffs) so that the resulting "Free Market" would allow the wealthier countries to "buy them out of debt."

The following day, October 1, 1982 President Portillo took his turn, blasting the US plan as stifling to some countries and suicidal to the rest. "We cannot paralyze our economies or plunge our people into greater misery in order to pay a debt on which servicing has tripled without our participation or responsibility, and on terms that are imposed on us... Our efforts to grow in order to conquer hunger, disease, ignorance and dependency have not caused the international crisis."

But time ran out for Portillo. Two months later, new elections replaced him with a meek and cooperative new President that caved into IMF pressure with a "pistol to his head" to sign the refinancing papers so generously provided by Citicorp and Chase Manhattan of New York. Signing these new loans obligated the victim contrary to certain "conditionalities:" cutting imports, slashing government budgets, raising taxes and devaluing their currency. Of course, all this advice on restructuring came with a tidy "service" fee that was tacked on to their already hefty principal. The benefit of playing this game was a slide in the 12:1 peso to dollar exchange rate in 1982 to a wild free-fall by 1989 of 2300:1. This was a virtual replay of the economic measures imposed on Germany following World War I. The subsequent financial stresses then bred an Adolf Hitler.

The same draconian austerity was repeated in Argentina, Brazil, Peru, Venezuela, Zambia, Zaire, Egypt and most of Asia. A reversed capital rip-tide drained 190 debtor countries between 1980 and 1986 of $326 billion in interest alone which combined with their outstanding principal of $332 billion produced a whopping $658 billion jackpot for the creditor banks who, thanks to the wonders of compound interest and floating interest rates, saw their accounts receivable blossom into more than $880 billion!

The Greatest Peacetime Recovery

The 1980's proved to be the most profitable decade in history for the US, allowing the Reagan Administration to finance the largest peacetime deficits in world history while claiming credit for achieving the longest peacetime "recovery." American banks were bloated with a massive cash influx, the padded the GNP and Wall Street, but not Main Street. In May, 1986, the Joint Economic Committee of the U.S. Congress presented a study entitled "Impact of the Latin American Debt Crisis on the US Economy." It listed the devastating loss of US jobs and exports as our Neighbors to the South went broke and stopped importing our goods. The report concluded: "The Reagan Administration's management of the debt crisis has in effect, rewarded the institutions that played a major role in precipitating the crisis and penalized those sectors of the US economy that played no role in causing the debt crisis." Almost verbatim of what Portillo said at the UN.

But the banks were booming, flush with big bucks. And what do you do with extra cash reserves? You loan it out so you can make interest and more profits! Third World countries, cash poor but resource rich, were ripe for development that could be financed with huge loans. So the poor nations got the loans and the rich nations got the interest. It was a wonderful arrangement for the Empire with an endless opportunity for exploitation. But to keep the cycle going, America has agreed to be the "importer of last resort." In doing so, we have switched from being the greatest manufacturer in the world to the greatest consumer.

The process follows four simple steps:
1. **Privatization.** Incentivize developing nations to sell off their national assets (at a discount price to foreign "investors") by offering political leaders a 10% commission (paid to their Swiss bank accounts). The 1995 sell-off of Russian industries stripped the country, cutting its national output in half and sending it into depression and starvation.

2. **Deregulation.** Removing real estate and banking controls allows outside investors to speculate in land and currency then bail at a profit at the first signs of trouble. This "Hot Money" cycle can drain a nation's reserves in hours. Then the IMF steps in and demands the nation raise its interest rates to 30, 50, 80%. Property values are demolished, industrial production suffocates and national treasuries bleed to death.

3. **Market-Based "Volume Pricing."** For example, the World Bank instructed South Africa to privatize their water utilities, lower the price to high-volume (i.e. rich) consumers and raise it for low-volume (poor) customers. By the way, this reverse Robin Hood practice is promoted by an institution that is 51% owned by the US Treasury. Because step three is guaranteed to incite riots and demonstrations, the IMF plan includes provision for rubber bullets, tanks and teargas. But this "economic arson" has its bright side: foreign corporations can pick off the countries remaining assets at fire sale prices.

4. **Free Trade.** The World Bank and IMF call this "poverty reduction strategy." It's the same tactics used by the British against China in the Opium Wars of the 19th century only today its the Europeans and Americans who are kicking down the barriers to sales, not only in Asia, but Latin America and Africa while barricading our own agricultural markets against Third World invasion.

Amazingly, we never learn. "Free Trade" is anything but free. GATT and NAFTA are merely profit tools for the world's financial capital, New York. The "Free Market" is free only in the sense that the Beast is free of any competition from other governments in its mastery of the global economy. Money, not the will of the people, is in today's political climate the supreme arbiter of mankind's destiny. The ultimate irony is that it is the globalization of *Capitalism* that is proving to be a more dangerous anti-State force than Communism in its potential for creating a One World Government. For the Third World, Globalization has been an economic version of the Black Death. Latin America's per capita GDP growth plunged from 75% in 1960-1980 to only 6% today. In Sub-Saharan Africa, the growth during the same periods went from 36% to – 15%!

The world revolves around the US Dollar, the currency that holds the whole system together. It is, after all, the primacy of the dollar that allows America to be the main consumer market for the over-production of goods that the world system is churning out. In turn, corporate demand constantly urges Americans to buy more and more of their goods (great for manufacturers) with money they don't have but easily obtainable from ever increasing mortgages and credit card debt (great for the banking industry).

And as this applies to personal debt, so it holds true for national debt as well. Persistent trade deficits (buying more foreign cars than domestic ones and foreign oil to run them) means increasing foreign indebtedness. Before 1989 the US was a creditor nation, making more on its foreign investments than it had to pay in interest. Ten years later, at the peak of the dot.com bubble, the foreign debt had reached $1.4 trillion. Five years later it was over $4 trillion. Declining wages, loss of high-income employment from offshore job migrations and outsourcing limits our capacity to sustain mass consumption and economic dominance. A very rich nation can manage these conflicting financial pressures for quite a long time. But not forever. Eventually the United States will no longer be able to afford its role as buyer of last resort.

The Petro-Euro Threat

The situation becomes especially precarious with the rise of the new Euro. Currently OPEC only accepts dollars for oil. But the Euro's competition and threat to the dollar in the oil market lies at the 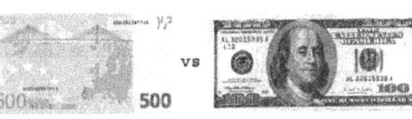 heart of the US conquest and occupation of Iraq all denials to that accusation notwithstanding. If OPEC ever agrees to accept anything other than US Dollars for oil, the American *and* global economies will implode. When 11 European countries formed a monetary union around the Euro on January 1, 1999, the test case for this issue was inevitable. In November, 2000 the French finally convinced Saddam Hussein to drop the dollar, defy the United States, and begin taking Euros for his UN-supervised oil-for-food program. He then converted his $10 billion reserve fund at the Un to Euros which were deposited in the leading French bank, BNP Paribas. This breech of the petro-dollar standard could not be tolerated. As the French recognized in an April 4, 2003 Reseau voltaire.net article, *Suprematie du dollar: Le Talon d'Achille des USA,* "The diminishing dollar is America's Achilles heel.

When rumors of a widespread switch to Euros was being contemplated by Russia, Iran, Indonesia and Venezuela, plans to remove Hussein were immediately drawn. "Regime change" in Iraq was a strategic move in saving the dollar from collapsing under a global shift to Petro-euros. (*Iraq and the Hidden Euro-Dollar Wars*, William Engdahl, 2004 at globalresearch.ca).

After September 11, 2001, when the Patriot Act made the seizure of Arab assets a real possibility, a further blow was inflicted by moving billions of dollars out of New York to Arab banks before their accounts were frozen to prevent funds from possibly going to terrorists. Only a few weeks later, US troops took over Afghanistan and established 19 military bases in Uzbekistan, Tajikistan, Kyrgyzstan, Turkmenistan—all potential oil producers and all surrounding Iran.

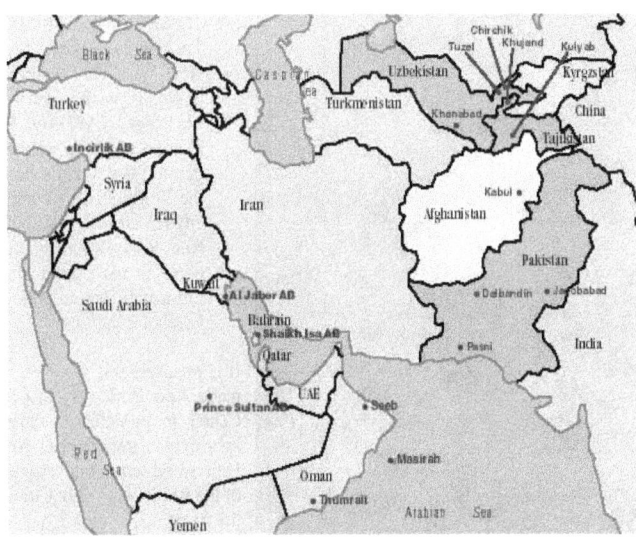

188 Prophesy Again! **Prophets and Profits**

The economic benefits of invading and occupying Iraq and Afghanistan are several:
1. Safeguard the US economy by restoring Iraqi oil back to US dollar pricing.
2. Secure the second largest oil reserve under direct US control.
3. Persuade other oil producers to not flirt with the Euro and abandon the petrodollar system.
4. Afghanistan is a strategic route for oil and gas pipelines to Pakistan and India.
5. The UN's oil for food program could be scrapped and replaced with a new US-designed Iraqi Assistance Fund fueled with US dollars.
6. European bidding on Iraq's reconstruction could be denied and instead awarded to predominantly large US corporations like Halliburton, Exxon Mobil, Bechtel, etc.
7. Military contracts certainly benefit industrial giants like Boeing, Lockheed-Martin, Raytheon, etc.

Now that Iran has recently abandoned the dollar for oil payments and switched to the Euro it, too, has become a US target for military intervention on the basis of its Nuclear threat. It is conveniently squeezed between US occupied Iraq and Afghanistan. "Just as Britain in decline after 1870 resorted to increasingly desperate imperial wars in South Africa and elsewhere, so the United States is using its military might to try to advance what it no longer can by economic means." (*Iraq and the hidden euro-dollar wars*, F. William Engdahl, globalresearch.ca, 2004). We are not engaged so much in a "War on Terrorism" as a "War on the Euro."

Capitol of the World
Just like the World Bank and the IMF, the United Nations was also a recommendation of the CFR. It was officially created in 1945 at an international congress in San Francisco attended by 74 CFR members in the American delegation. The following year John D. Rockefeller Jr generously (perhaps eagerly) donated the 18 acres in Manhattan on which the UN headquarters now stands. It is no accident that the nerve center for the global community is located conveniently and efficiently in the very capitol of the American Empire: New York City, the most powerful and wealthiest city in the world.

- New York City is the **financial capitol** of the world, home to the wealthiest and most influential banks that control the Federal Reserve and the US Treasury, the IMF, the World Bank and the World Trade Organization.
- New York City is the **commercial capitol** of the world, home to Wall Street, the New York Stock Exchange, NASDAQ, AMEX. It serves the world's greatest consumer nation with massive port facilities that are the world's busiest and wealthiest. Though the World Trade Center complex was destroyed the city remains the undisputed capitol of world trade.
- New York City is the **political capitol** of the world, home to the United Nations and the world's most influential foreign policy think-tank, the Council on Foreign Relations.

It is precisely this focus on money, profit and greed that made New York City in general, and the World Trade Center in particular, a target of such significant and apocalyptic importance. Apocalyptic, not just in the Hollywood sense, but particularly in the Biblical meaning of the word. New York City is Revelation's final Babylon the Great.

The most striking depiction of this truth is found in the 18th chapter of Revelation where the allusions to a great economic power are unmistakable:

"Babylon the great is fallen...
For all nations have drunk of the wine of the wrath of her fornication, and the kings of the earth have committed fornication with her, and the merchants of the earth are waxed rich through the abundance of her delicacies... How much she has glorified herself and lived deliciously... And the kings of the earth, who have committed fornication and lived deliciously with her, shall bewail her, and lament for her, when they shall see the smoke of her burning... And the merchants of the earth shall weep and mourn over her: for no man buys their merchandise any more: The merchandise of gold, and silver, and precious stones, and of pearls, and fine linen, and purple, and silk, and scarlet, and all scented wood, and ivory, and most precious wood, and of brass, and iron, and marble, and cinnamon, and odors, and ointments, and frankincense, and wine, and oil, and fine flour, and wheat, and beasts, and sheep, and horses, and chariots, and slaves, and souls of men... And every shipmaster, and all the company in ships, and sailors, and as many as trade by sea, stood afar off, and cried when they saw the smoke of her burning, saying, "What city is like this great city!" Selected verses 2-19.

Yet this account is describing a crisis that is yet future. At the moment, Babylon is not fallen. It has and is still seducing all nations and the kings of the earth with her self-serving economic policies.

The merchant corporations of the earth have and are still waxing rich through very profitable but immoral and illicit relationships with that Great City. Babylon's shipping trade has been and still is extremely lucrative, serving the rich "by reason of her costliness." Babylon is still a great city without peer in the world market.

A prelude to that final collapse, when the market will ultimately fall, when the Great City will really crash and burn was indelibly burned into the collective consciousness of the world on September 11, 2001. The horrific scene of twin towers, burning, collapsing, falling, sending gigantic plumes of smoke and dust high above the Manhattan skyline, engulfing the city as the entire world stared in disbelief, in shock, in wonder, in fear—was only a "shot across the bow," an introductory sample of Revelation's final fulfillment for Babylon and her prophetic destiny.

This warning is also an appeal.

> If my people, which are called by my name, shall humble themselves, and pray, and seek my face, and turn from their wicked ways; then will I hear from heaven, and will forgive their sin, and will heal their land. 2 Chronicles 7:14

Have Americans humbled themselves? They don't appear to have. We sing that we are "Proud to be an American where, at least, [I think] I'm free." We flaunt Gay Pride marches and the Power of Pride bumper stickers. American is the most proud of all nations. She seems to have forgotten what pride did for Lucifer. She should remember that "Pride goeth before destruction, and an haughty spirit before a fall" Proverbs 16:18

Prophesy Again! **Prophets and Profits**

Have Americans turned from their wicked ways? They don't appear to have. Thousands of abortions are still being performed every day. Sodomy is still practiced, promoted, and glorified on TV, theater screens, and Broadway productions. Witchcraft and the occult is still big business and now targeting the children that are not slaughtered with everything Harry Potter. If the surviving children become unruly, they are simply drugged into submission.

> Behold, I am against thee, O thou most proud, saith the Lord GOD of hosts: for thy day is come, the time that I will visit thee. And the most proud shall stumble and fall, and none shall raise him up: and I will kindle a fire in his cities, and it shall devour all round about him. Jeremiah 50:31, 31.

Role Reversal and Repeating History

Remembering that prophetic symbols can have both spiritual and physical, good and evil applications, we must consider yet another perspective in the role of the United States at the end of time. America is currently waging an alleged "war on terror" (the politically correct designation for the conflict) which is actually a clash of ideologies founded on differing religious principles. Where Christian Crusaders faced Muslim Arabs a thousand years ago, today the Christian West is facing down the same Muslim world again, only this time it is not armed with swords.

President Ahmadinejad of Iran sent President Bush an 18 page letter, condemning the nation that professes to follow Jesus Christ with acts of aggression and the use of froce. He concluded with an appeal for America to convert to Islam, accept Allah and join his pursuit of gobal peace and justice. This, in itself, was an echo of the Islamic Revolution's founder, Ayatollah Ruhollah Khomeini when he sent a very similar letter to the President of the Soviet Union, Mikail Gorbachev in 1989.

While in Iran Ayatollah Ahamd Jannati is clling Ahmadinejad's letter "an inspiration from God" and "a sign of the Imam Mahdi's return, the gesture is remarkably similar in both substance and circumstance to one issued by another Islamic ruler nearly 1,400 years ago.

The superpower of the day was then the Persian Empire led by Yazdgird III, the King of Kings, the Light of Aryans and King of Persia. He, too, was the recipient of a letter inviting the ruler to surrender to the will of Allah. It came from the second Islamic Caliph, Umar Ibn Al Khattab who told the Persian monarch that

> "Your troops are defeated on all fronts and your nation is bound to collapse. I offer you a way to rescue yourself. Start praying to Allah, a single union God, the only God who created everything in the universe."

Yazdgird's response is particularly cogent for today.

> "You suggest we worship a united and single God without knowing that for thousands of years Persians have worshiped the mono God... We established the tradition of hospitality and good deeds in the world... You behead God's children, even the prisoners of war, rape women, attack the caravans, mass burder, kidnap people's wives and steal their property! Your hearts are made of stone; we condemn all these evils which you do. How can you teach us Godly Ways when you commit these actions?"

> "Is it Allah who commands you to murder, pillage and to destroy? Is it you the followers of Allah who do this in his name? Or is it both?"

History records the result of this dialog: the Islamic conquest of Persia. Will history repeat itself this time?

The parallels between Ancient Persia and Modern America are strikingly similar.

Both were at one time the most powerful government in the world.
Both were tolerant empire-builders, ruled by law, absorbing other cultures into their own.
Both were Zionists. Ancient Persia ordered the release of the Jews from Babylonian captivity and even financed the establishment of their restored national homeland. America continues to support Modern Israel and publicly announces its intent to defend her financially and militarilly.

For ancient Persia the struggle was between Zoroastrianism and Mohammedism.
For modern America the conflict is very much a Christian-Islam struggle.

"Blessed Is He That Waits"

For the last two thousand years, each generation has prayed that their generation would be the one which would usher in the second coming of Jesus. Though each generation has been disappointed, nonetheless each generation has seen present truth revealed to them. Jesus is quoted in gospel accounts of both Matthew and Mark as stating that no man knows the day nor the hour of His second Coming. The Bible however, gives us plenty of Signs to identify the nearness of Jesus' appearing in the clouds. The whole purpose of this endeavor has been to show the reader that this time is near.

In our last chapter we spoke of how scripture supports the belief that The Roman Catholic Church will soon move its headquarters to Jerusalem. Further, that the dragon will usurp the beast power. Satan Himself will arrive upon the scene saying He is Christ. Daniel 12, however, shows us that Michael stands up and responds to this imitator. The inspired Word tells us that this ushers in a "time of Trouble" that this world has never seen before. In essence we know it is speaking of the seven last plagues.

While many commentators have spoken on the first few verses of this chapter, we have noticed an absence of definitive relevance to verses five through thirteen. Before we wade into those waters, however, let's peruse part of a letter Ellen White wrote to Elders Prescott and Daniells in July of 1903.

> "Let us study the 12th chapter of Daniel.
> It is a warning we all shall need to understand before the time of the end."

We believe that the inspired author was sounding the trumpet that the Mark of the Beast of Revelation 13 would and could be seen in Daniel 12. By looking at the flow chart provided you can seen that there are three time periods mentioned in these verses. There is a striking similarity between these and the three mentioned in Daniel's 9th chapter.

In Daniel 9 there is the seven weeks of rebuilding the city walls and streets. Next is the sixty-two weeks following which Messiah the Prince arrives upon the scene. Last is the time when He dies in the midst of the week. But all of this 70 Week prophecy speaks of when Probation is closing on the most favored nation clause for the Jewish nation.

Likewise we see the period of 1335 days in Daniel 12. As part of the 1335 days are two shorter time periods. One is 1260 days the other is 1290 days. However, as seen in the chapter, verse four tells us that the closer we get to the end the more our knowledge shall be increased. This is promised by Christ Himself in verse 7. The trigger point for all of this is in verse 11 where the abomination of the desolation is mentioned.

Abomination of Desolation
This is the same language, the same phrase used by Jesus Himself in Matthew 24:15. What does it all mean? Throughout scripture an abomination against God was when Israel or God's people attempted to establish or replace something that God required for worship with something *they* substituted. If we were to boil it down to the lowest common denominator, it would be that mankind is trying to replace righteousness by Faith in Jesus Christ and His atoning sacrifice with a counterfeit. That Counterfeit would be righteousness by the works we perform. It was seen in the story of Cain and Abel. It was seen in the tower of Babel. It is seen in the mark of the Beast.

What mark will the beast power try to impose that will cause the world to shudder? Let us share two statements from the inspired pen.

"The Sabbath will be the great test of loyalty; for it is the point of truth especially controverted. When the final test shall be brought to bear upon men, then the line of distinction will be drawn between those who serve God and those who serve Him not." *Great Controversy* p. 605.

"Satan will excite indignation against the humble minority who conscientiously refuse to accept popular customs and traditions...legislators will yield to the demand for a Sunday law." 5T 450, 451.

In order to make things crystal clear lets show another time line.

Abomination	1260 days	1290 days	1335 days
of Desolation	Scattering	Set up	Blessing

From the abomination that maketh desolate to the scattering of God's people in chapter 7 is 1260 days. From the abomination until someone is set up in verse 11 is 1290 days. Finally, from the abomination until the blessing to "he that waiteth" in verse 12 is 1335 days.

Now remember, as we discussed in an earlier chapter, prophetic time as we know it (as far as the day for a year principle) ended in 1844. If this is the case, and if prophetic time has ended, and if the little horn power is going to control the world yet again, then these time periods, we believe, are literal time.

This is not to say that the historical interpretation of the Daniel 12 time periods is not valid. Clovis *did* indeed rise up to defend the little horn in 508 AD and the sweet prospect of Christ's second coming *did* give rise to a blessed hope during the Advent Movement of 1843 exactly 1335 years later. Yet we must be alert to the possibility of present truth in our day. Only as current events fall in line with the possible time frames will anyone be able to say for certain this is will be another fulfillment. Watch and be ready is the key.

We believe we are buoyed in this testimony by the words of the inspired pen which wrote the following in 5T page 11: "We are living in the time of the end. The fast fulfilling signs of the times declare that the coming of Christ is near at hand....The agencies of evil are combining their forces, and consolidating. They are strengthening for the last great crisis. Great changes are soon to take place in our world, and the final movements will be rapid ones." Thus going back to our chart again we see chapter 12 unfolding this way:

Abomination	Little Horn rules	Satan sets up empire	Blessing for waiting
of Desolation	3½ yrs of hard times	death decree made	God responds
Sunday Law	1260	1290	1335

We as Adventists have stated historically that the little horn power would become ugly once again. We as Adventists have preached that Satan would personate Christ. We have preached that Jesus would respond to this imposter. We have even preached how God works for His People. But we have never made the connection between the blessing of Daniel 12 with the abominations that take place between Satan personating Christ and attacking Christ's people. We believe, in fact, that the inspired authors do that for us.

Notice first Joel 2:11. "And the Lord shall utter his voice before his army: for his camp is very great :for he is strong that executeth his word: for the day of the Lord is great and very terrible; and who can abide it?" Ellen White in *Great Controversy* p. 310 makes it abundantly clear that this is talking about the solemn events transpiring at the close of probation. What has to do more with the close of Probation for the world than the blessed hope, the second Coming of Jesus Christ? Jesus said He would bring His reward with Him in Revelation 22:12. Therefore, the blessing of Daniel 12 to those who wait (as verified here in Joel and Revelation) is the day and the hour of Christ's second Coming announced to His People.

This thought is further evidenced by the inspired pen again in *Great Controversy* page 640. Notice:

> "The voice of God is heard from heaven, declaring the day and hour of Jesus' coming, and delivering the everlasting covenant to His People. Like peals of loudest thunder His words roll through the earth. The Israel of God stand listening, with their eyes fixed upwards. Their countenances are lighted up with His glory, and shine as the face of Moses when he came down from Sinai. The wicked cannot look upon them. And when the BLESSING is pronounced on those who have honored God by keeping His Sabbath holy, there is a mighty shout of victory." Emphasis supplied.

Thus, in summary, the world is facing the time very soon when this little horn power as seen throughout the pages of Daniel will once again rear its ugly head. As John the Revelator writes its "deadly wound will be healed." Further, this power will have two allies which will make up a counterfeit trinity. Those powers include the dragon (which is the devil) and the false prophet (the image of the beast) which is the U.S.A. Together in tandem they will bring difficulties upon the whole world. With each action there will be a reaction. God will not sit by and idly do nothing. Jehovah still sits upon the throne and nothing takes place without His blessing.

In conclusion, God is pleading with each of us today to put His word in our hearts. To live for Him. For as the prophet Micah wrote long ago, "Wherewith shall I come before the Lord, and bow myself before the high God? Shall I come before him with burnt offerings, with calves of a year old? Will the Lord be pleased with thousands of rams, or with ten thousands rivers of oil? Shall I give my firstborn for my transgression, the fruit of my body for the sin of my soul? He hath shewed thee, O man, what is good; and what does the Lord require of thee, but to do justly and to love mercy, and to walk humbly with thy God?"

Signs in the Heavens

1991 appears to have been a defining moment in history. It began and ended with earth shaking events. January 16, the US announced the commencement of Desert Storm, beginning what has clearly become a Crusade for the West and a Jihad for the East. The first Gulf war was declared and commanded by a President Bush which became a dynastic precedent, establishing a family tradition focused on the Persian Gulf. On December 21st, the Soviet flag came down and the Russian flag was raised over the Kremlin as the Soviet Union was officially disbanded. On Christmas day, Soviet leader Mikhail Gorbachev resigned. Natural disasters were equally memorable. The April 30th cyclone in Bangladesh killed 139,000 and Mt. Pinatubo, Luzon, Philippines erupted June 15th, causing the US military to abandon Clark Air Force Base. (*The World Almanac and Book of Facts*, 2005, p. 206, 491).

This beginning has even greater significance and confirmation in heavenly signs. Like the sign prophesied by Jacob in Genesis 49 signaling the Messiah's first Advent, the Second Advent also is heralded by "a star departing from between the feet" of the "lion of the tribe of Judah."

The Sign of the First Advent

> "Judah is a lion's whelp...he stooped down, he crouched as a lion, and as an old lion...The scepter shall not depart from Judah nor a lawgiver from between his feet until Shiloh come; and unto him shall the gathering of the people be. Binding his foal unto the vine, and his ass's colt unto the choice vine; he washed his garments in wine, and his clothes in the blood of grapes..." Genesis 49:9-12

Jacob gathered his 12 sons about his deathbed and pronounced a series of revelations concerning each one. Judah is earmarked as the Royal Tribe, from whom the kings would arise. He is therefore identified as a lion, the king of beasts. The sign of the lion, the constellation Leo, is the last of twelve starry symbols originally employed by the Creator to tell the story of redemption in the sky. It foretold Christ's arrival on a colt and the spilt blood of His sacrifice. "Jesus found a young donkey and sat upon it, as it is written, Do not be afraid O Daughter of Zion; see, your king is coming, seated on a donkey's colt." John 12:14-15. John quoted Zechariah 9:9. Isaiah 63 foretells Christ's sacrifice. "Who is this who comes from Bazrah with garments of crimson?... Why are your garments red as one who tread the winepress alone?" The answer comes: "It is I, mighty to save."

The Star of Bethlehem

Thus, Leo was the subject of close observation by astronomers of the ancient east, especially so as the prophecy of Daniel 9 neared the predicted time of its fulfillment. The "two and sixty-nine weeks," the 483 years were nearly expired depending on which decree to rebuild Jerusalem was accepted as the one to which Daniel spoke. It was, however, the words of Balaam that caught the Magi's attention. Although his prophecy in Numbers 24 was essentially a quoting of Genesis 49, his use of an explicit astronomical term was arresting.

"He couched, he lay down as a lion, and as a great lion: who shall stir him up?...

196 Prophesy Again! **Signs in the Heavens**

There shall come a *Star* out of Jacob, and a Scepter shall rise out of Israel, and shall smite the corners of Moab." Numbers 25:17.

Then it happened. A series of unusual astronomical events occurred over an 18-month period during the years of 3-2 B.C. In 1992, with the advent of advanced computers capable of calculating the precise positions of celestial objects, the American Philosophical Society published Brian Tuckerman's *Planetary, Lunar, and Solar Positions 601 BC to AD 1*. For the first time in modern history, ancient astronomical configurations became widely available for study and research. We can now reconstruct what the wise men saw.

The celestial performance began on May 19, 3 BC when two wandering "morning stars" appeared to come dangerously close to each other in the early morning hours just before sunrise. They rose in the eastern sky, separated only by a visual angle of less than one degree (40 minutes of arc). Saturn and Mercury had experienced an unusually close conjunction. The observers carefully made an entry in their logs.

As they continued watching over the next few weeks, Saturn slowly moved up and eastward to intercept the rapidly approaching Venus with a breathtaking conjunction that was separated by only 7.2 arc minutes on June 12.

Next, just weeks later, they watched as Jupiter, the King of planets, and Venus, Mother of planets, rendezvoused between the front feet of Leo, the King of constellations.

In the early morning hours of August 12, 3 BC, two bright lights in Leo fused into what appeared to be a single star. Actually, it was the planets Venus and Jupiter experiencing a major conjunction, lining up with an amazing separation of only 4.3 arc minutes — indistinguishable by the unaided eye.

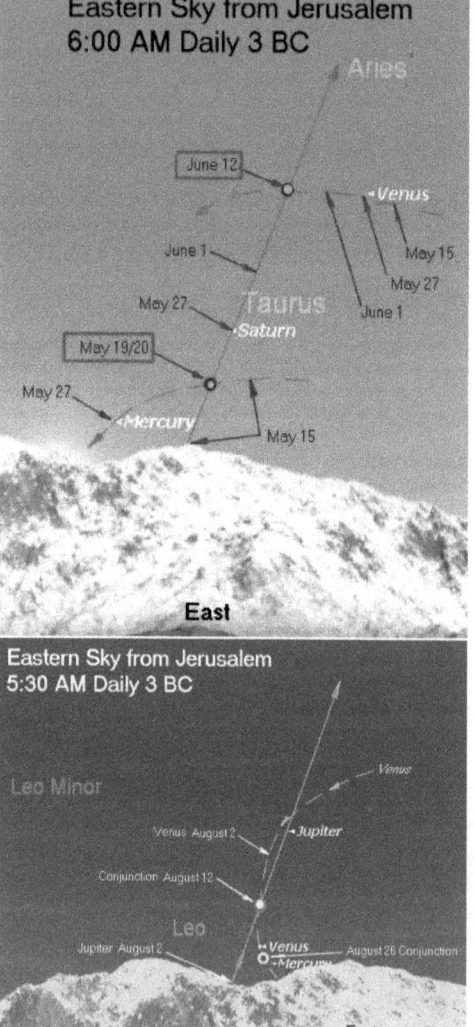

The lion had been visited, signaling a royal birth. Two weeks later Mercury visited Venus coming within 1/5 of a degree near midnight Babylonian time on August 26.

The Magi recognized this auspicious encounter as the Messenger (Mercury) informing the Mother (Venus) of the coming birth. So, they added another entry to the growing list of signs.

Now the first of three incredible events happened that consummated the matter. On September 11, Rosh Hoshana, the Jewish New Year and a new moon night, Jupiter approached Regulus, the prominent star in Leo's front feet. Its name is derived from *Regeleo* (regal leo, royal lion), the diminutive of the Latin Rex meaning "little king." The two reached a maximum conjunction of 22 arc minutes at 11:01 pm Babylonian time.

To the ancient stargazers, it appeared as though the King Planet Jupiter was circling over and around Regulus, the King Star, "homing in" on it and highlighting the significance of their meeting. This circular movement of Jupiter over Regulus signaled that a great king was soon destined to appear.

By February 15 Jupiter had reached Regulus again for a second conjunction reaching maximum at 6:13 pm, again separated by less than one degree (51 minutes of arc). Jupiter then continued on for another 40 days until it stopped again around April 1 and then resumed its normal forward motion heading back for a third pass over Regulus, the King star in Leo. On May 8 at 7:08pm the two converged with only 43.2 arc minutes of separation.

Jupiter, and other planets, demonstrate the phenomenon of apparent retrograde motion. This occurs because of the relative motion between earth (orbit ting fast and close to the sun) and Jupiter (orbiting slow and far from the sun). Jupiter moves across the sky, night after night, until the faster moving earth passes it up causing its forward motion to appear to stop and reverse directions. The diagram here demonstrates the change in relative position between Earth and Venus as the faster inner orbital overtakes the slower outer orbiting planet.

For Jupiter, as it hovered around Regulus, this occurred on December 1 and April 1. Then Jupiter began its reverse retrograde course back across the sky from where it came.

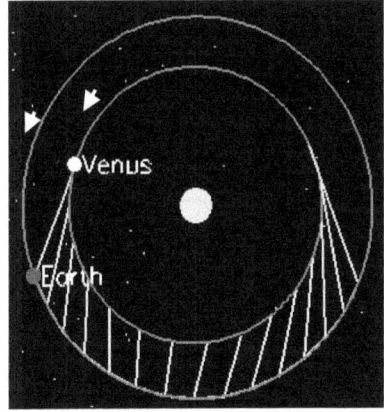

198 Prophesy Again! **Signs in the Heavens**

Finally, the climax came. Jupiter conjoined with Venus again in Leo. This time, it was a near perfect union of the two luminaries at 10:51pm on June 17 with an incredibly close separation that left the two appearing to perfectly fuse into a single very bright star.

Calculations vary between 3 arc minutes (Sinnott) and 0.1 arc minute (Carroll). The less the separation, the more rare the conjunction. The combination of a triple conjunction of Jupiter with Regulus followed immediately by an ultra-close conjunction of Jupiter with Venus in the same constellation is expected to occur between once every 38,000 years and once every 1,142,000 years. Truly, a once in a cosmic lifetime experience.

Summary of Astronomical Events in 3-2 BC

3 BC
May 19/20	Saturn and Mercury met
June 12	Saturn and Venus met
Aug 12	Jupiter and Venus met in the front feet of Leo. "Conception" 9 month clock begins
Aug 26-31	Mercury and Venus met
Sept 11-14	Jupiter approached Regulus for the first of three conjunctions. Rosh Hoshana
Dec 1	Jupiter stopped forward motion began retrograde

2 BC
Feb 17	second conjunction, the two were reunited. Continued retrograde another 40 days
April 1	stopped retrograde and resumed forward motion
May 8	third conjunction. Then, 9 months after the first Jupiter-Venus meeting…
June 17	Jupiter and Venus in Leo at Regulus "Birth of the new king" Magi begin journey.
July 17	Jupiter and Venus in the back feet of Leo
Aug 26	Jupiter and Mars (Venus, Mercury) "War" Magi arrive, Herod kills infants.
Aug 27	Jupiter and Venus, Mars and Mercury in Leo
Oct 14	Jupiter and Venus head of Virgo

References:
Carroll, Susan S. "The Star of Bethlehem: an Astronomical and Historical Perspective," 1998
Chester, Craig. "The Star of Bethlehem," *Imprimis* (December, 1993): 1-4.
Martin, Ernest L. *The Star That Astonished the World.* Portland, OR: ASK Publications, 1991.
Maunder, E. W. "Star of the Magi," *International Standard Bible Encyclopedia* (1939).
Sinnott, Roger. "Thoughts on the Star of Bethlehem," *Sky and Telescope* (December 1968): 384-386.
Tuckerman, Bryant. *Planetary, Lunar, and Solar Positions 601 B.C. to A.D. 1.* Philadelphia: American Philosophical Society, 1962.
Astronomical Plots performed on Starry Night software by Imaginova, Inc.

A second sign

Revelation 12:1 describes a "great portent" a "wonder in heaven:" a woman who is to give birth to a man child, stands on the moon and is clothed with the sun. Over Virgo's head is the constellation called "Coma." It is the "crown of twelve stars" mentioned in Revelation 12:1. Above her legs is located "Draco," the Dragon, ready to devour Virgo's child.

The moon passes through Virgo each month on different days. But in September 3 BC, the moon was in just the right position "under her feet" and the Sun was in just the right place so that she might be "clothed with the sun" on the 11th day of the month, Rosh Hoshana, just as Jupiter was approaching Regulus for the first of three conjunctions.

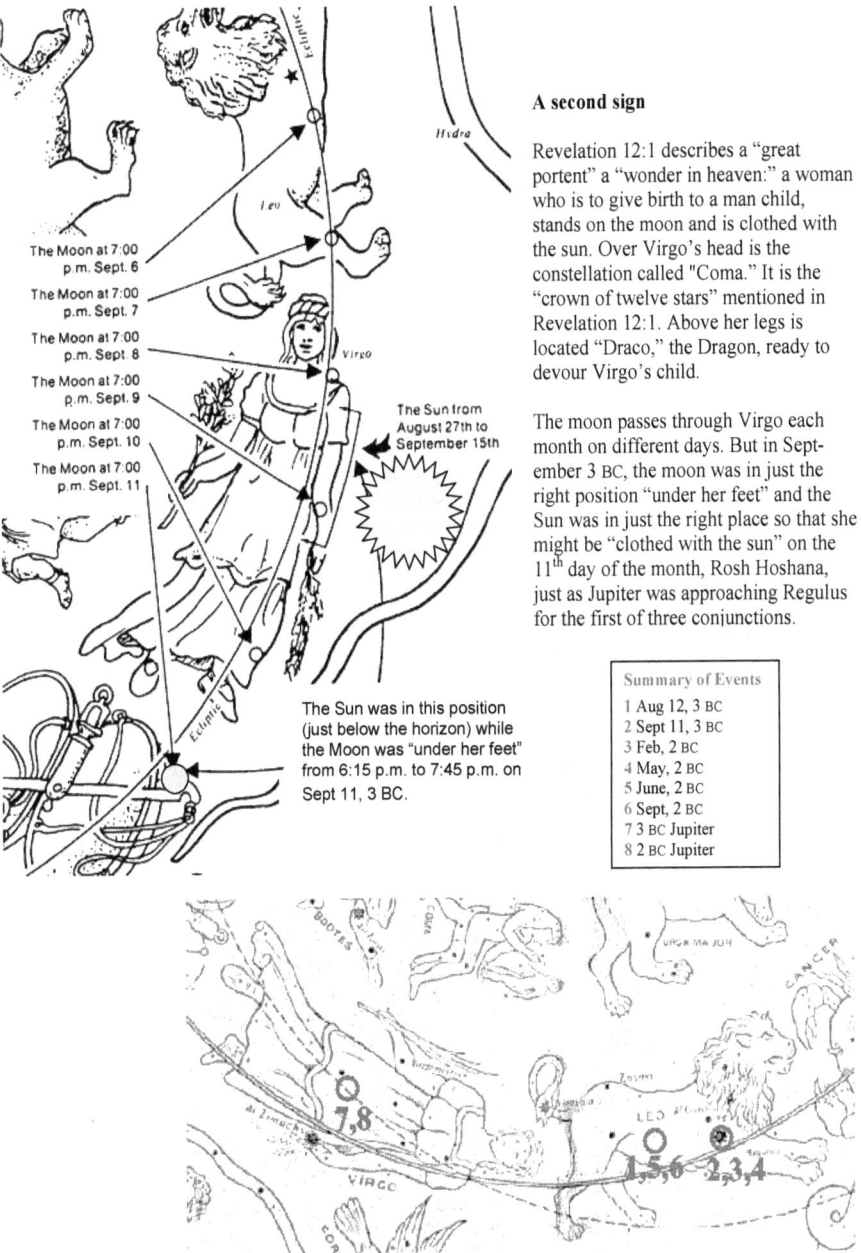

Summary of Events
1 Aug 12, 3 BC
2 Sept 11, 3 BC
3 Feb, 2 BC
4 May, 2 BC
5 June, 2 BC
6 Sept, 2 BC
7 3 BC Jupiter
8 2 BC Jupiter

200 Prophesy Again! Signs in the Heavens
Sign of the Second Advent

A repeat performance of the wandering stars took place again in the constellation Leo during 1991. In September, 1991 Leo was host to four planets: Mercury, Venus, Mars and Jupiter.

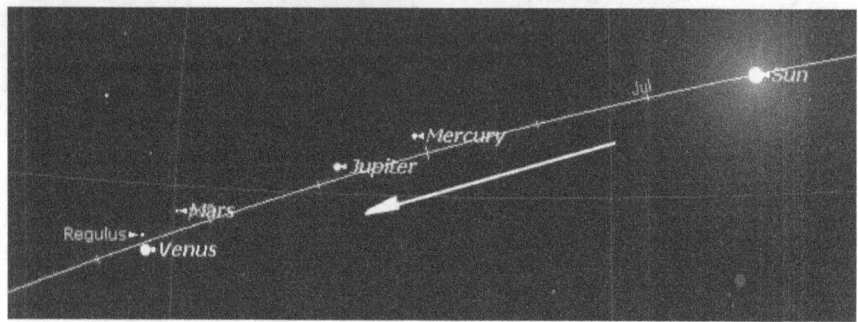

Mars was first to leave. Both Venus and Mercury had begun their retrograde motions in July of 1991.
By September Venus was moving between Leo and Hydra, the serpent lying under Leo's feet. Jupiter slowly moved eastward toward Regulus. With Venus still nearby, Mercury quickly overtook it during its retrograde cycle and met up with Jupiter exactly intersecting with a three-member conjugation at Regulus on September 10, 1991 with less than ½ degree of separation. Over the next few days, Jupiter moved slowly, but Mercury rapidly "departed from between" Leo's feet finally leaving them by September 23.

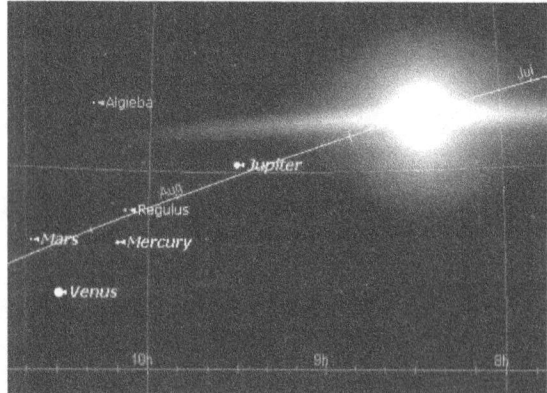

Jupiter, the King of planets, was the "scepter" that would not depart from Leo nor Mercury, the Messenger, "from between his feet" until Shiloh, Christ, the Messiah, would come. An indication of Mercury's status as the Messenger planet is the account in Acts 14:12 when Paul was called "Mercurius" by the people because he was the principle speaker while Barnabas was dubbed "Jupiter."

Yom Kippur, the Day of Atonement, occurred on September 19, during this interval of September 10 and 23, 1991.

As the same astronomic event occurred in 3-2 BC to signal the birth of the Messiah at His first coming, so this unusual sequence in 1991 marked the beginning of events leading to His second advent. In August, 3 BC Mercury met with Venus ending with the four-member grouping of Jupiter, Venus, Mercury and Mars in Leo exactly one year later on August, 2 BC. In 1991 the reverse occurred. The four-planet grouping happened first followed by the Jupiter-Venus conjunction on September 10, 1991 which was Tishri 1, the Feast of Trumpets.

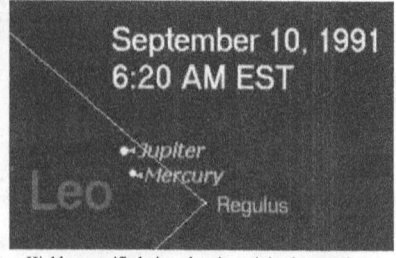

Highly magnified view showing minimal separation

Robert Scott Wadsworth, editor of Biblical Astronomy in Oregon City, OR, wrote in the June 1998 edition,

"I investigated all conjunctions of Jupiter and Mercury in the proximity of Regulus from 2000 B.C. (at least 250 years before Jacob's prophecy was given) to the present, and no other event comes close to the magnificence displayed by the conjunction of Jupiter, Mercury, and Regulus on September 10, 1991..." "At the closest conjunction of the three bodies. Jupiter and Mercury are the little bumps on top of Regulus. This occurred at 12:23 in the afternoon Israel Standard Time." "Mercury passed between Jupiter and Regulus between the early morning hours of September 10 and September 11. At the conjunction, Jupiter, the top planet, was about 1/3 of a degree from Regulus. The separation between Jupiter and Mercury was about 1/1,200th of a degree and they most likely appeared as one very bright object."

In addition to this phenomenal act, both Venus and Mercury performed triple conjunctions with Regulus during the same time period. Moreover, the constellation Virgo, the Virgin, gave "birth" to the moon every year from 1996 to 1999. The moon's ecliptic passed through the womb of Virgo each of these four years on the Jewish New Year (Rosh Hoshanah or the Feast of Trumpets), a very rare occurrence. By the year 2000, the moon's path had fallen beneath her legs so that she could truly be said to be standing on it. This positioning of Virgo and the moon on four consecutive Feast of Trumpets has never occurred before, and will never occur again for another 25,800 years, due to the precession of the equinoxes, the tiny wobble of earth as it circles the sun.

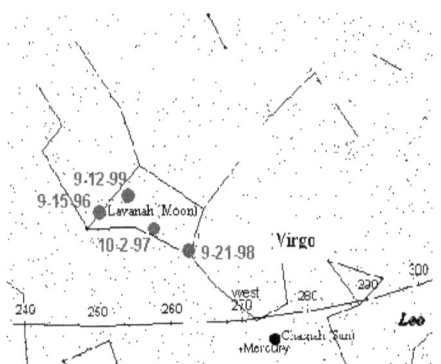 

These eclipses produced "blood red" moons. The first of these four years, 1996, began with:
A total lunar eclipse on the evening of **Passover**, Nisan 15 5757 AM, (April 3, 1996).
A second total lunar eclipse occurred on Tishri 14, (September 26, 1996), the Eve of the Feast of **Tabernacles**. A third near total lunar eclipse occurred on Shushan **Purim**, II Adar 15, (March 24, 1996).
Yet another total lunar eclipse occurred September 16, 1997 as the "Days of Teshuvah."
Another total lunar eclipse began the evening of Shevat 15, 5760 (1999).

The first and last of these four years (1996 and 1999) are special: the Feast of Trumpets fall on a Sabbath.

1991	1992	1993	1994	1995	**1996**	**1997**	**1998**	**1999**	2000	2001	2002	2003	2004
Leo					Virgo	Virgo	Virgo	Virgo		9-11			
Gulf War I					S		S						Gulf War II

Cosmic Signs and Wonders

Biblical prophecy is filled with references to various cosmic signs. The book of Revelation opens with a picture of Christ walking among the seven candlesticks in the heavenly sanctuary holding seven stars in His right hand. The lamps are identified as the pastors of the seven churches identified in chapters 2 and 3 as locations in what is today the nation of Turkey. Geographically these churches were situated in the foothills of the Taurus Mountains. Taurus is the bull constellation; the sacrifice of a bull or bullock was made for the high priest (Leviticus 3:6-14). Within the constellation of Taurus is the 7 star formation called the Pleiades (Job 9:9; 39:31).

Revelation 12 depicts the woman and child as a wonder in heaven, a picture of the constellation Virgo (the virgin). The prophetic vision continues with the appearance of a great red dragon who parallels the constellation Draco (dragon). The woman flees from the dragon, overcoming him by the blood of the Lamb (verse 11) who appears in the heavenly constellation Aries, the Ram.

Reoccurring "signs and wonders" are seen throughout scriptures:

Great signs in the heavens (Luke 21:25)
Darkened sun clothed in sackcloth (Joel 3:15; Matthew 24:29; Revelation 6:12)
Darkening of the constellations (Isaiah 13:10)
Moon turned to blood (Joel 2:31; Acts 2:20; Revelation 6:12)
Stars falling from heaven (Matthew 24:29)
Powers of heaven shaken (Luke 21:26)

Seven Eclipses

Jewish Rabbis believe that solar eclipses are a sign of trouble for the world; lunar eclipses are a bad omen for the nation of Israel. There is a theoretical limit of seven eclipses than can occur in any given year. Only two years in the 20th century had the full complement of eclipses: 1917 and 1973.
These were historically significant years.

In 1917 World War II ended and the Russian Revolution began, Israel was liberated from 400 years of Turkish control by General Allenby (a repeat of the 400 year subjection prophesied in Genesis 15) and became a British protectorate under the Belfour Declaration authorizing Jewish access to Palestine.

In 1973 the largest solar flare in recorded history was observed, the world was paralyzed as the Arab oil embargo crippled the industrialized nations, and the Yom Kippur War threatened the existence of Israel.

But it was the blood red lunar eclipses that began in 1996 which had the greatest significance. 1996 marked the 6000th anniversary of creation according to Bishop Ussher's chronology which placed the beginning of this world in 4004 BC. It was also the 3000th anniversary of the establishment of Jerusalem as the city of David when he conquered it from the Jebusites in 1004 BC. 1996 was the year in which a blood red moon appeared over Jerusalem on the first and last feast of Israel's liturgical year: Passover on April 3 and Tabernacles on September 26.

Ezekiel 32 contains a prophecy concerning Egypt which will be marked by a solar eclipse.
> "And when I shall put thee out, I will cover the heaven, and make the stars thereof dark: I will cover the sun with a cloud and the moon shall not give her light. The bright lights of heaven will I make dark over thee, and will set darkness upon the land saith the Lord God." Ezekiel 32:7,8.

Ezekiel 30:4-6 states that Ethiopia and Libya will be pulled into the conflict when a modern day Nebuchadnezzar conquers Egypt. Daniel 11:43 mentions that these same three nations will fall under the control of the king of the north at the end of time.

> "At Tehaphnehes also the day shall be darkened, when I shall break there the yokes of Egypt: and the pomp of her strength shall cease in her: as for her, a cloud shall cover her, and her daughters shall go into captivity" verse 18.

A total solar eclipse is scheduled for March 29, 2006 that will blanket a 114 mile wide swatch directly over Cairo, Egypt beginning 11.52 AM. March 29 happens to be the first of Nisan the date traditionally believed to have been the fall of the 9th plague on ancient Egypt: "the plague of darkness...even darkness which may be felt." (Exodus 10:21). The plague lasted for 3 days. Even as the cross was shrouded in darkness for 3 hours.

1994, the 40th jubilee from the end of the 70 weeks, was noted for a spectacular cosmic sign.
The Shoemaker-Levy comet collided with the planet Jupiter for seven straight days beginning July 16 (9th of Av) after breaking up into 21 fragments 16 of which bombarded the king star. July 16, 1994 is also noted for the Oslo Peace Treaty Talks between Israel and Egypt.

Let us remember that the signs are not only physical (literal) and spiritual (symbolic), they are also good and evil. The Prince of Darkness will produce signs to convince his followers as well:

> "Whose coming is after the working of Satan with all power and **signs and lying wonders**, and with all deceivableness of unrighteousness in them that perish; because they received not the love of the truth, that they might be saved. And for this cause God shall send them strong delusion, that they should believe a lie," 2 Thessalonians 2:9-11.

Today, we are inundated with news reports of weeping statues, bleeding wafers, apparitions, cinnamon rolls, fogged windows, mud splashes and snow drifts with the appearance of the virgin Mary. And that's just in the Roman Catholic world.

April 13, 2002
UZBEKISTAN: FERGANA MIRACLE
By Khalmuhammed Sabirov and Miassar Umarova in the Fergana valley

The birth of a lamb early this spring in the Ferghana with holy inscriptions emblazoned on its flanks, is being hailed as a miracle, attracting thousands of devout Muslims from the Central Asian nations that abut the fertile valley. The lamb, born in the village of Durmen in the Akhunbabaev region of Uzbekistan, has a black fleece with white spots, which look like the Arabic for Allah on one side and Mohammed on the other. Many believers consider this "holy" lamb to be a symbol sent by God, heralding the day of reckoning.

"I've seen the lamb. It's simply a miracle, a sign from above," said Imam Sultan Mohammedkhon Umarov.

References:
W. E. Bullinger, *Witness in the Stars*
Victor Paul Wierwille, *Jesus Christ, Our Promised Seed*
Ernest Martin, *The Star of Bethlehem: the Star that Astonished the World*

Daniel 11	Greek Era	Early Rome	Late Rome	Islam
20 Then shall stand up in his estate a raiser of taxes in the glory of the kingdom: but within few days he shall be destroyed, neither in anger, nor in battle.	Seleucus IV (king 187-175) taxed the poor heavily to maintain good relations with the Romans. Was finally poisoned, dying in his sleep, by his minister, Heliodrus.	**Caesar Augustus** decreed "that all the world should be taxed." Luke 2. **Paux Romana** was the Golden Age of Rome. Augustus died at age 76 peacefully in his sleep in 14 AD. The Caesar before and 7 after murdered.		
21 And in his estate shall stand up a vile person, to whom they shall not give the honor of the kingdom: but he shall come in peaceably, and obtain the kingdom by flatteries.	Antiochus IV Epiphanies (king 175-164) the brother of Seleucus IV, secured the throne of Syria, overriding both rightful heirs, through bribes after excaping from a Roman prison.	**Tiberius**, step-son of Augustus, was declared "too vile to wear the purple of Rome" by the emperor. Yet began to reign AD 12. Known for debauchery, intoxication, a ferocious despot, disgusting tyrant. Murdered in AD 37.	**Herod** also vile, obtained his office by corruptions.	Muhammed married an 9 year brde when he was 53 and ultimately had 14 legal wives. He began preaching peace but soon took up arms to conquer the world. He promised his followers "whosoever falls in battle, his sins are forgiven."
22 And with the arms of a flood shall they be overflown from before him, and shall be broken; yea, also the Prince of the covenant.	Antiochus made the office of high priest (prince of the covenant) a bartered position purchased through corruption to the highest bidder.	In the 15th year of Tiberius Caesar, John the Baptist appeared. Luke 3. This was AD 27. Four passovers later in **spring AD 31, Jesus was crucified.**		Early advances of Muslim empire building overtook Syria and Palestine, destroying Christian churches or converting them into mosques.
23 And after the league made with him shall work deceitfully: for he shall come up, and shall become strong with a small people.	He deceived his nephew (Ptolemy VI (181-145)) the king of Egypt, taking control of Egypt as his own possession.	The Jewish League was made with Rome in **161 BC** when it was a small minor nation. Julius Caesar deceives Egypt 48-47BC.	**Trajan** was the first emperor from the provinces. Caesers no longer enjoy hereditary rule. Politics now crucial to power.	Muhammed rises to power with a small people (40 converts) when he fled from Mecca.
24 He shall enter peaceably even upon the fattest places of the province; and he shall do that which his fathers have not done, nor his fathers' fathers; he shall scatter among them the prey, and spoil, and riches: yea, and he shall forecast his devices against the strong holds, even for a time.		Rome built its empire by negotiation, establishing local governors who managed the regional wealth, maintained law and order and collected Roman taxes. It emerged as the new superpower in AD 31 at the Battle of Actium and lasted "for a time" 360 years, **until 330 AD** when Constantine moved the capitol to Constantinople.		fat = oil Muslim OPEC nations control the world's oil reserves Rich sheiks share their wealth with the royal family

Daniel 11	Greek Era	Early Rome	Late Rome	Islam
25 And he shall stir up his power and his courage against the king of the south with a great army; and the king of the south shall be stirred up to battle with a very great and mighty army; but he shall not stand: for they shall forecast devices against him.	On his way back from Egypt, Antiochus terrorized Jerusalem.	The triumvirate of Antony, Augustus and Lepidus split when Antony aligned with Cleopatra in Egypt. Roman Civil War erupted threatening to divide the empire. Antony's greater number and larger ships conceded victory to Rome when Cleopatra fled from battle with her Egyptian fleet. This defining moment was Sept 2, 31 BC **Battle of Actium**.	Trajan was the first to conquer the Parthians and Arabia.	Battle of Tours 732 stopped the invasion of Moors into France, the German army routed them.
26 Yea, they that feed of the portion of his meat shall destroy him, and his army shall overflow: and many shall fall down slain.	8000 Jews were slain. Tried to burn the scroll of the law.	Antony's allies and troops deserted him, surrendering to Rome. He committed suicide in Egypt.		
27 And both of these kings' hearts shall be to do mischief, and they shall **speak lies at one table**; but it shall not prosper: for yet the end shall be at the time appointed.	Maccabean Revolt erupts.	**Antony and Augustus** were once united politically and through marriage of Antony to Olivia, sister of Augustus. But Antony's ambitions would not prosper. His end was appointed at the time of 31 BC.	Rome divided into Western and Eastern empires. Excessive riches lead to decadence, corruption, apathy. Rome in decline.	
28 Then shall he return into his land with great riches; and his heart shall be against the holy covenant; and he shall do exploits, and return to his own land.		Augustus returned to Rome with vast riches from Egypt. Vespasian invaded Judea in 66 AD, besieged Jerusalem for 3 ½ years, **destroying the city and the temple in 70** AD.	Constantine conquers Britain and returns to become emperor. He embraces Christianity and supports it.	Islam dreams of the day it will control Jerusalem again. After the Muslim empires wane they consolidate in Iraq/Iran and Middle East.
29 At the time appointed he shall return, and come toward the **south**; but it shall not be as the former, or as the latter.	Antiochus makes a second invasion of Egypt 167/167.		Constantine returned to the Holy Land and bought up holy sites and built monuments. After "a time" he returned to the south, (not as to Egypt or Judea for conquest and destruction) but this time moving the capitol from **Rome** to **Constantinople** in 330 AD.	Saddam Hussein invades Kuwait to open his southern borders and gain access to the Persian Gulf

Daniel 11	Greek Era	Late Rome	Papal Rome	Islam
30 For the ships of Chittim shall come against him: therefore he shall be grieved, and return, and have indignation against the holy covenant: so shall he do; he shall even return, and have intelligence with them that forsake the holy covenant.	Rome sent Popilius with Roman galleys from Italy at Egypt's call for help. Popilius ordered Antiochus to return home, but Antiochus asked for time to consider. Popilius drew a circle around him and said he must decide before stepping out of it. Antiochus then went to Jerusalem and took out his spite on the Jews.		Vandals from Carthage harrassed Rome annualy for 40 years. Pope Leo I begged help from the eastern empire. Justinian sent Belisarius to expel the Goths in 538. The Papacy blamed the Arian heresy on the availability of the Bible and removed it from the people by locking it in a dead language, finally making its reading a mortal sin.	But US Naval forces stream to the Gulf and Saudi Arabia, first as operation Desert Shield, and then Desert Storm Iraq lobs SKUD missiles at Israel. He plots with Al-Qaeda.
31 And arms shall stand on his part, and they shall pollute the sanctuary of strength, and shall take away the daily, and they shall place the abomination that maketh desolate.	Antiochus Epiphanes stopped temple services from 171-168 BC. Put an idol of Jupiter in the temple. Offered a pig on the altar. Maccabean revolt cleansed the temple Dec 25, 164. Romans destroy temple 70ad		Clovis in 508, Charlemagne in 776 dedicates the armies of France to defending the Papacy, forcing the powers of Europe to convert to Roman Christianity "taking away" their paganism, replacing it with the baptized paganism of the Papacy.	Attacks on WTC, Pentagon "pollute" Manhattan and Virginia and Pennsylvania Dow Jones daily stock market reports suspended
32 And such as do wickedly against the covenant shall he corrupt by flatteries: but the people that do know their God shall be strong, and do exploits.			Papacy grows in power, riches and corruption while the Waldenses, Albigenses, and Huguenots maintain the pure faith of Christ during the Dark Ages of the Little Horn. These are the "sanctuary and the host" in Dan 8:11	Suicide bombers are inspired by the promise of 72 virgins and instant entry to paradise.
33 And they that understand among the people shall instruct many: yet they shall fall by the sword, and by flame, by captivity, and by spoil, many days.		Constantine's Edict of Milan 313 AD gave the Church freedom and protection from persecution.	For 3 ½ time, 42 months, 1260 years the papal power persecuted the woman thru Crusade and Inquisition. Pope Pius VI was taken captive Feb 20, 1798	Reconstruction efforts are impaired by string of hostage taking, executions, many by beheading with swords, others burned in their vehicles, other held captive "many days"
34 Now when they shall fall, they shall be holpen with a little help: but many shall cleave to them with flatteries.			The earth "helped the woman" Rev 12. The Protestant Reformation gave the Bible to the people in their own language, protected by the European states. Reformed churches soon begin to accept civil support and from the state.	British and few other nations help the US, but many insurgents come from surrounding islamic countries.

Daniel 11	France	Soviet Empire	Papal Rome	Islam
35 And some of them of understanding shall fall, to try them, and to purge, and to make them white, even to the time of the end: because it is yet for a time appointed.	But persecution continued, eg. "Bloody Mary" Queen of Scotts in England. But at the "time of the end" 1798 the French Revolution would take away the Roman Church's power in Europe.			
36 And the king shall do according to his will; and he shall exalt himself, and magnify himself above every god, and shall speak marvellous things against the God of gods, and shall prosper till the indignation be accomplished: for that that is determined shall be done.	The French Revolution was born in anarchy, atheism and arrogance. The "reign of teror" began in 1793. The royalty were executed. France discarded the Bible, denied the existence of God. Churches were desecrated, bells cast into cannon, Bibles publicly burned. The week of seven days was changed to one of ten days.	Bolshevik Revolution 1917 was born in anarchy, atheism and arrogance. Lenin's "reign of terror" Civil War followed with the loss of 10 million. Czar Nicholas II and his royal family were executed in 1918. The largest empire yet spanning 11 time zones. Each empire increases in size.		Islam aspires to dominate the world, that Allah is the only god and denounce Jesus as blaspheming by claiming to be the son of God. Islam will continue to grow untill it causes an unforgiveable "indignation" against Christianity (bomb the Vatican?) Mosque with golden dome bombed Feb 2006
37 Neither shall he regard the God of his fathers, nor the desire of women, nor regard any god: for he shall magnify himself above all.	Divorce was legalized Sept 20, 1792. Family ties were dissolved, homes ceased to exist, children were abandoned, amorality flourished in Gay Paris. Napoleon was not Catholic or Protestant.	Godless, atheistic Communism embraced evolution and suppressed religion.	some would *"depart from the truth"* and *"forbid to marry"* **1Tim. 5:14.** Pope Leo XII Encyclical June 20, 1894 "We hold upon this earth the place of God Almighty." **2Thes 2:4.**	Moslems are children of Ishmael, the son of Abraham. But they do not regard the God of Abraham, Jehovah, rather a "strange god" Allah, nor Jesus the "desire of women" the desire of all nations. They also ignore the dignity of women.
38 But in his estate shall he honor the God of forces: and a god whom his fathers knew not shall he honor with gold, and silver, and with precious stones, and pleasant things.	1793 the **Goddess of Reason** was worshipped, Notre Dame cathedral was changed to the Temple of Reason. Paganism became the state religion. Napoleon put his trust in his armies.	Soviets wage arms race in global power struggle with West	Eucharist wafer is worshiped in the gold, silver and jeweled sunburst monstrance holder. Papacy elevates Mary to the Mother of God 431AD, a perpetual virgin 649AD, Immaculate Conception 1854, Assumption to heaven 1950, Co-Redemptrix 2003	Islam honors the god of force, it defends a violet theology of enforced conversion to Islam. Mosques are ornately decorated with gold domes, jewels and incense.
39 Thus shall he do in the most strong holds with a strange god, whom he shall acknowledge and increase with glory: and he shall cause them to rule over many, and shall divide the land for gain.	Napoleon is appointed consulate in 1799. **Estates** owned by nobility and the Church equalling 2/3 of the country are **confiscated** and parcels sold at auction for £700,000,000 sterling. He divided European control among his many relatives. Nepotism.	After WWI and WWII defeated European territories were repartitioned among the victors. After the fall of Communism the many states of the former Soviet Union became new markets for Beast and reclaimed membership for the Whore. Dioceses collect money.	Pope Roderigo Borgia published bull *Inter Cetera Divina*, dividing the New World between Spain and Portugal, in 1493	Allah is a strange god.

Daniel 11	France	Papacy	Ottoman Turks	Islam Today
40 And at the time of the end shall the king of the south push at him: and the king of the north shall come against him like a whirlwind, with chariots, and with horsemen, and with many ships; and he shall enter into the countries, and shall overflow and pass over.	March 5, 1798 Napoleon authorized to **invade** East, defeating Marmalukes at Battle of Pyramids July 21 and is now king of the South, **occupying Egypt**. Claims to free the peasants from tyranny. French soldiers rape Muslim Marmalike soldiers. Turkey declares war on France 9-11 and attacks with British-Russian-Austrian coalition.	French Revolution begins 1789 Feb, 1798 **Pope taken captive**, dies next year ending Papacy's millennium which started 800 AD Charlemagne gave the **Papal States**. Napoleon now **takes them back**. 1982 Reagan & John Paul II form Holy Alliance to topple atheistic communism in 1989. Vatican destroyed by terrorists.	South: Egypt, Saudi Arabia, Sudan, Libya, Ethiopia Islam sacked Rome, conquered Constantinople and renamed it Istanbul. Papacy responded by sending the Crusaders to capture Jerusalem.	**Islamic terrorists** launch first suicide bombing April 18, 1983 US embassy and Marine barracks in Lebenon. Muslim terrorist Mehmet Ali Agca shoots John Paul II May 13, 1981. Al-Qaeda terrorists attack **WTC and Pentagon Sept 11, 2001**. US with British-Turkish coalition invades Iraq, Afganistan 1991 and 2001, 2003. Western powers claim to be freeing people of Iraq from tyrany.
41 He shall enter also into the glorious land, and many countries shall be overthrown: but these shall escape out of his hand, even Edom, and Moab, and the chief of the children of Ammon.	Napoleon fights Syrians throughout **Palestine**. Loses 398 of his ships in the Battle of the Nile Aug 1, 1798 by British Admiral Lord Nelson. Jordan is not affected. He returns to France Oct 9, 1799.	Papal crusades launched.	Ottoman Turks never were able to subdue the nomadic territories of Jordan.	**US established bases** in Kazikstan, Uzbekistan, Turkey, Kuwait, Saudi Arabia, Qatar, Yemen, etc. Amman, Jordan attacked by Al Qaeda 11-9, 2005 triple suicide bombings killed 57.
42 He shall stretch forth his hand also upon the countries: and the land of Egypt shall not escape.	**Napoleon began in Egypt**, leaving his mark by blowing off the Sphinx's nose. Bible Societies flourish from 1803-1817.		Ottoman Emperoro Salem I conquered Egypt and carried many ship loads of wealth back to Istanbul.	Oct 7, 2004 Taba, Egypt truck bomb kills 31 July 22, 2005 Sharm El-Sheikh bomb kills 88, wound over 200.
43 But he shall have power over the treasures of gold and of silver, and over all the precious things of Egypt: and the Libyans and the Ethiopians shall be at his steps.	**Egyptian treasures** taken back to France including mummies, artifacts, gold, and the Rosetta Stone. He returned to France to be crowned emperor 1804 as Charlemagne's successor by the pope in Paris.		1550 the Turks placed Libya under their rule, then Ethiopia was levied a tribute tax.	Dec 19, 2003 Libya ends terrorism June 28, 2004 US resumes diplomatic relations after 24 years of isolation. Sept 20 US lifts all economic sanctions Oct 11 EU ends 11 years of sanctions
44 But tidings out of the east and out of the north shall trouble him: therefore he shall go forth with great fury to destroy, and utterly to make away many.	Napoleon fought virtually every power in Europe over a period of 11 years until 1812 when he was defeated in **Russia**.	Announcement that Christ is coming infuriates Satan who pretends to be christ!	Russia fought with Turkey beginning in the early 1700's finally ending in the Crimean War of 1853-1856	Pakistan, Syria, Iran denounce Israel and develop nuclear weapons. Feb 2005 **Syria-Iran** form alliance. US authorizes atomic weapon usage. Iran does the same.

Daniel 11	France	Papacy	Ottoman Turks	Islam Today
45 And he shall plant the tabernacles of his palace between the seas in the glorious holy mountain; yet he shall come to his end, and none shall help him.	Napoleon pitched his tents on **Mt Tabor** during his Palestine campaign. After Waterloo 1815 was exiled to St. Helena where he **died alone** in 1821.	Pope declares Jerusalem an international city under his jurisdiction and control. Jerusalem is located between seven seas: 1. Mediterranean 2. Sea of Galilee 3. Black Sea 4. Caspian Sea 5. Red Sea 6. Dead Sea 7. Persian Gulf	Ottoman Turks established their headquarters in Jerusalem during WWI at Mount Zion. After the war, the Ottoman empire collapsed.	America is broken and exhausted by Persian wars. Economic collapse follows unsustainable national debt.

Daniel 12

Abomination of Desolation	Little Time of Trouble Little Horn Rules 3 ½ years	Satan appears as Christ		Death Decree		
Church's Probation closes				**World's Probation closes**		
Passover		Pentecost	30 days	1290	45 days	Ingathering
Start	1260 days 2 witnesses prophecy	1260				1335
National Sunday Law Rev 13 Mark of the Beast now "sundaykeeping" *The Faith I Live By* p. 286	"wicked do wickedly" "many purified, made white" "wise understand" Dan 12:10 Dan 12:7 How Long? 3 ½ times: 1260 days	**Midnight Cry** Rev 18:1-4 "Come out!" **Latter Rain** "end of these wonders" "scatter power of holy people" Dan 12:6,7 "orders giving liberty… after a certain time (30 days) to put them to death" EW p. 282		**International Sunday Law** Satan sits down 2 Thess 2:4 **Michael stands up** Daniel 12:1 **Great Time of Trouble** **7 Last Plagues** 3rd plague: **Time of Jacob's Trouble** Four winds released (Christ's work done) EW p. 36 "abomination that makes desolate set up" Dan 12:11 **Death Decree**		**Lord utters His voice** Joel 2:11 GC 640 God declares Day & Hour "Blessed he who waits"
"daily taken away" Dan 12:11 "daily ministration…neglected" Acts 6:1						
Philistines capture the Law 1 Samuel 4, 5 The ark is among the Philistines 7 months		Sons of Eli slain, Eli dies, Phinehas' wife dies		She names her child Ichabod: the glory is departed Ark moved with plagues Ark placed in **Philistine temple**	"ark returns at wheat harvest"	
"The time is fulfilled" Mark 1:14 "**It is time** for thee, Lord, to work: for they have made void Thy law." Ps 119:126				Man of sin sits **in the temple** of God showing himself that he is God		
Flee to the country "our nation in the decree enforcing the papal sabbath will be a warning to…leave the large cities" *Maranatha* p.172				"**abomination of desolation** spoken of by Daniel" "stand in the holy place" Matt 24:15 "where it ought not" Mark 13:14		

Prophetic Timeline Chart

50 jubilees begin ... **2300 days begin...**
70 years begin... 80 years... 70 weeks begin...
50 jubilees end

586	536	457	27 31 34	70		1844
Temple Destroyed	Babylon Falls	Temple Rebuilt	Temple Destroyed	Temple Destroyed		Temple Restored

702 653 604 555 506 457 408 359 310 261 212 163 114 65 16 34 83
                                                                            9 10

BC | AD

5 Jubilees — **10 Jubilees**

70 Weeks 490 years Daniel 9

The 70th Week

4 BC — **27 AD** — **3½ years** — **31 AD** — **34 AD** — **Gospel to Gentiles**

Jerusalem delivered from Sennecharib
2 Kings 19, Isaiah 37

Jerusalem Decree to rebuild Ezra 7

Moriah
Malachi
Exodus 12:40
Genesis 15:13

Jerusalem Destroyed AD 70
Matt 23:38, Dan 9:27

Moses — **Messiah**

Desolations
Flood

---

4 BC
Decree unto all the world
Bethlehem Registration
Christ Born

27 AD
Baptism
Anointed
Tempted–Sealed
"The time is fulfilled"

3½ years
1260 days

31 AD
Crucifixion
Midst of week
Sacrifices Cease
"It is finished"
120 in upper room   Heb 2:3,4

"The time appointed"
Worship Law
Sealing

"It is done"
Latter Rain
"Midnight Cry"
Satan Appears

34 AD
Stephen Martyred
Jesus Standing
Close of Probation
Persecution Begins

Close of Probation
Michael Stands Up
Great Time of Trouble
Destruction of world   Rev 18:1
Flood of God's Glory
Flood after 120 years   Num 14:21
Earth filled   Hab 2:14

Solomon's temple dedicated 490 years after Exodus   1 Kings 6:1, 38
Dedication on Feast of Tabernacles   2 Chronicles 7:9
120,000 sheep sacrificed, 120 priests with trumpets   2 Chronicles 5:12

Mark 1:14, 15
Preaching the gospel
the time is fulfilled
kingdom is at hand
repent
believe the gospel

Revelation 14:6-12
Gospel to preach
the hour...is come
worship Him that made
keep the commandments
have the faith of Jesus

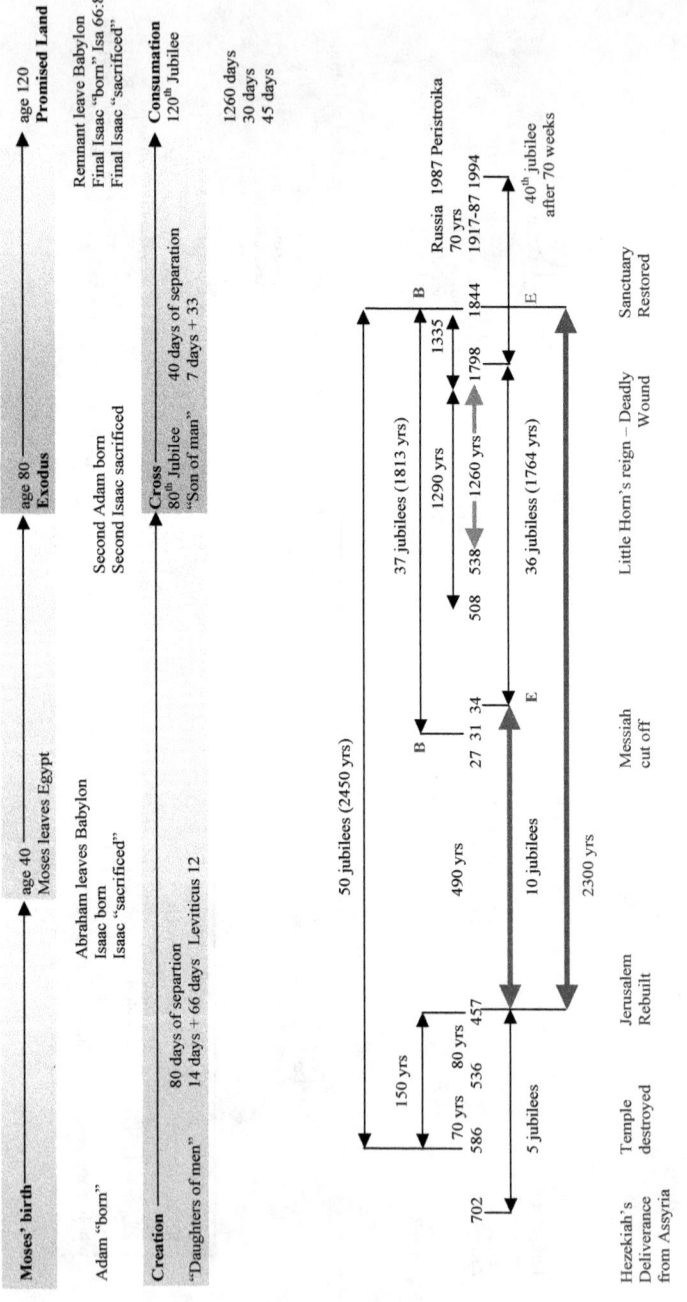

History Will Be Repeated

Christ

"He was loyal to God's commandments"
"Because of this He was hated and persecuted"
"He was accused as a Sabbathbreaker and blasphemer" COL p. 171
"We found this fellow perverting the nation" Luke 23:2

"He came unto his own and his own received him not" John 1:11
"The scenes of the betrayal, rejection, and crucifixion of Christ"...

Remnant

"History is repeated…those who are true to God's commandments"
"suffer reproach and persecution."
"His followers are accused and misrepresented" COL p. 171
"We shall be treated as traitors" 6 Testimonies p. 394

"This history…will be repeated again and again" Upward Look ch. 48
"will again be reenacted on an immense scale" 3 SM p. 415

Kings of the North and South in Ancient Times

"Much of the history…in the eleventh of Daniel…will be repeated"…
Verses 30-36 quoted
Greece-vs-Persia   Papacy-vs-Atheism

Kings of the North and South Today

"Scenes similar…will take place" Manuscript Releases V.13, p. 394

America-vs-Persia   Christianity-vs-Islam

Worship Commanded in Past

"False religion…the image of Babylon" was set up.
"All nations and tongues and peoples" were commanded to bow.
Daniel 3

Worship Commanded in Future

"History will be repeated….The first day of the week…will be set up"
"Decree enforcing the worship of this day is to go to all the world"
7BC 976 (1897)

Babylon	Persia	Greece	Rome			
Lion	Bear	Leopard	Papacy			
Image		12 years				

Daniel 7 sequence

Protestant Reformation	Rome	Germany	Russia	Britain-America
French Revolution	Papacy healed	Leopard	Bear	Lion
Deadly Wound		12 years		Image

1260 days   **Revelation 13 sequence**   42 months

Mirrored Dates of Prophetic Significance

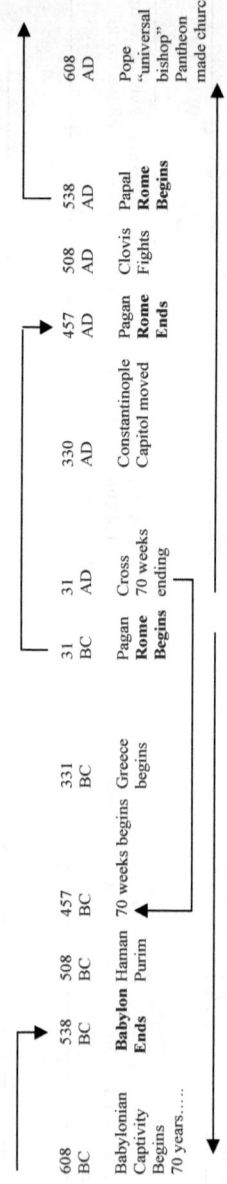

608 BC	538 BC	508 BC	457 BC	331 BC		31 BC	31 AD	330 AD	457 AD	508 AD	538 AD	608 AD
Babylonian Captivity Begins 70 years.....	**Babylon Ends**	Haman Purim	70 weeks begins	Greece begins		Pagan **Rome Begins**	Cross 70 weeks ending	Constantinople Capitol moved	Pagan **Rome Ends**	Clovis Fights	Papal **Rome Begins**	Pope "universal bishop" Pantheon made church

We'd love to have you download our catalog of
titles we publish at:

www.TEACHServices.com

or write or email us your thoughts,
reactions, or criticism about this
or any other book we publish at:

TEACH Services, Inc.
254 Donovan Road
Brushton, NY 12916

info@TEACHServices.com

or you may call us at:

518/358-3494

www.ingramcontent.com/pod-product-compliance
Lightning Source LLC
Chambersburg PA
CBHW070549160426
43199CB00014B/2436